BEYOND THE FRUSTRATED SELF

BEYOND THE FRUSTRATED SELF

Overcoming Avoidant Patterns and Opening to Life

Barbara Dowds

KARNAC

First published in 2014 by
Karnac Books Ltd
118 Finchley Road
London NW3 5HT

British Library Cataloguing in Publication Data

A C.I.P. for this book is available from the British Library

ISBN-13: 978-1-78220-052-9

Typeset by V Publishing Solutions Pvt Ltd., Chennai, India

Printed in Great Britain

www.karnacbooks.com

To Peter who is *sui generis*

CONTENTS

PART II: IMPINGEMENT AND LOSS OF SELF

PART III: THROWNNESS AND
LIMITATION: NAVIGATING THE SOCIAL WORLD

PART IV: BEYOND FRUSTRATION:
TOWARDS INTEGRATION AND WELL-BEING

ACKNOWLEDGEMENTS

My warm thanks go to the following friends, colleagues, and mentors for their encouragement and for reading parts of the manuscript: Dr. Gilbert Carr, Professor Gerald Corey, Siobhan Clifford, Professor Colin Feltham, Pauline Macey, Patrick Nolan, and Dr. Thecla Ryan. I am grateful to friends for putting up with my absences while writing. Most of all, I owe an enormous debt of gratitude to my partner Dr. Peter Labanyi for reading the entire manuscript (again and again) and for variously and lovingly inhabiting the roles of academic supervisor, stylistic editor, and therapist. He has discussed ideas, suggested quotes, located references, challenged foggy thinking, and listened and brought me back on track when I have fallen into despair. A few direct quotes of Peter's appear in the book and are attributed to him with his permission.

I acknowledge the following for permission to quote extracts of poetry or epigraphs:

"Harlem (2)" from *The Collected Poems of Langston Hughes* by Langston Hughes, edited by Arnold Rampersad with David Roessel, associate editor, copyright © 1994 by the Estate of Langston Hughes. Used by permission of Alfred A. Knopf, a division of Random House, Inc. Any third party use of this material, outside of this publication, is prohibited. Interested parties must apply directly to Random House, Inc. for permission.

"Sweet Darkness" from *The House of Belonging* by David Whyte (Many Rivers Press, 1996), copyright © Many Rivers Press, Langley, WA 98260, USA. Printed with permission of Many Rivers Press, www.davidwhyte.com.

The lines from "Advent" by Patrick Kavanagh are reprinted from *Collected Poems*, edited by Antoinette Quinn (Allen Lane, 2004), by kind permission of the Trustees of the Estate of the late Katherine B. Kavanagh, through the Jonathan Williams Literary Agency.

The extract from *Playing and Reality* by D. W. Winnicott (Routledge, 1991), used as an epigraph at the beginning of Chapter Three, is reprinted with the permission of Taylor & Francis.

Finally, I want to thank Rod Tweedy, my editor at Karnac Books, for his patience in the face of a lot of pesky questions from a novice at book publishing.

ABOUT THE AUTHOR

Barbara Dowds, BA, PhD, MIACP, MIAHIP, is a humanistic and integrative psychotherapist in the Dublin area. She teaches on the BSc in counselling and psychotherapy and is director of the MA in integrative psychotherapy in PCI College. For seven years she was editor of *Eisteach*, the journal of the IACP, and she has written extensively for it and for *Inside Out*, the journal of the IAHIP. Barbara was a senior lecturer in molecular genetics at the National University of Ireland, Maynooth, until 2002 when she changed careers and began practising as a psychotherapist.

INTRODUCTION

The focus of this book is existential: its themes are explored via a single individual, Brenda. While the issues presented are universal, the particular themes chosen may seem arbitrary. They are not. They have emerged organically from Brenda's particular struggles, and thus are particularly marked in her personality type and stage of development. However, it would be a mistake to think that these are just the issues of one neurotic individual. Brenda is a kind of every (wo)man, albeit one with a particular attachment style, which makes her more prone to inner conflict and frustration than are many others. However, we all—to varying degrees and in varying ways—struggle with existential issues. Brenda's avoidant/dismissing style is common, and arguably becoming more so as our globalised and alienating world both generates and rewards non-attachment—in an avoidant rather than Buddhist sense. This environment breeds the shallowavoidant contact, the meaninglessness, and spiritual emptiness that afflict Brenda.

Brenda has everything—and nothing. She has a supportive partner and a professional job; she lives in a beautiful place in a recession-bound but nevertheless—on a global scale—prosperous and peaceful country. But she is chewed up with existential angst and easily falls into a pit of anomie and self-hatred. She is embarrassed by this and writes it off when talking to others as her "being a depressive type". She may say things like: "This moaning about the meaning of life is all very well in Parisian intellectuals, but you are supposed to outgrow it. How boring is that, to be complaining about adolescent despair into midlife?" She wonders vaguely if her low mood could be attributed to a genetic predisposition, but has never researched this as a possibility. Her existential debates with her partner and friends are, paradoxically, too enjoyable and identity-affirming to risk their being undermined by a diagnosis of biochemical imbalance. While she appears in conversation not to take herself too seriously, there have been occasions—recently after being at the receiving end of a vicious emotional attack—when she verges on clinical depression. Then she is unable to face the world, becomes flooded with primal pain, shame, and panic, and fantasises about escape to a cave in the mountains where she will let fate take its course. Her suicide fantasies are passive—letting death take her— rather than active and/or violent. Apart from an earlier serious plunge into clinical depression (when her terror of the psychiatric services kept her from seeking help), Brenda stumbles along, lost but doing her best. It is the issues of this everyday, struggling Brenda, rather than the emergency depressive episodes, that are the focus of this book. The bouts of depression simply reveal her lack of resilience to social humiliation: the recent one triggered by an actual public attack, the earlier by an overwhelming career move that required her to face her terror of public speaking against a background of workaholic exhaustion. They are symptoms of her underlying self-structure, and I mention them to drive home Brenda's fragility, despite her offhand self-dismissal as one of the "worried well". I want to examine Brenda's self-structure under normal, non-threatening conditions, when she is driven by an unrelenting quest for meaning against a background despair that her life is running away from her as unstoppably as sand through an eggtimer.

She is marginally depressed, often anxious, and has difficulties with managing her energy. She is prone to boredom and out of touch with her creativity and imagination. She is conflicted about contact with others, and others are confused by her. To them, she seems somewhat armoured and uncaring, but underneath what she is willing to reveal lies quite a fragile self. She is easily overwhelmed by the pain and demands of others and as sensitive to the impingements of modern life as the princess to the pea under her dozen mattresses. The book includes two chapters on the personal meeting the political, where Brenda struggles with her alienation from a competitive culture and her double-bind around activism and ethical action. Overall then, Brenda has developed a moderately strong ego, but her self tends to be starved of nourishment. She looks back into the past with grief because she feels that she hasn't had a life, there being so little of it she can remember. Her stories emerge as disconnected episodes in which a population of different Brendas appear with little continuity of narrative. Worse than that, her memories are arid and superficial, without emotional suffusion. She has little sense of being an integrated person or of having lived a satisfying life.

Brenda veers between rage and despair, aggression and shyness; between anxiety and boredom, overstimulation, and exhaustion. She feels she has poor boundaries against impingement, but her friends and her partner experience her as unavailable. While her friends might imagine where they would go or what they would do if they only had a year left to live, Brenda knows that whether she has one year or forty years left; whether she is here or in paradise—whatever she is doing, it will still be the same old struggle with her inner demons. As Socrates remarked of the man not improved by travel: "I am sure he was not. He went with himself" (Montaigne, 1993, p. 268).

If there is a single word that describes Brenda, it is *frustration*. She knows her difficulties are not situational, and indeed she is practical and independent. Her inner life is another matter. She is aware she must take responsibility for her internal tangles, but she doesn't know how. For Brenda, as for those like her, the very process of selfing has been frustrated, and as a consequence her self—insofar as she has one—is, and feels, frustrated.

* * *

Is the self innate, and therefore something to be found within, or is it something we create? Most of the current evidence from the nature-nurture debate suggests that while we are born with certain temperaments and predispositions, the self is largely formed by the relationships and experiences we have and by the stories we tell ourselves and others. These processes will be examined in the book and illustrated by Brenda's life experiences.

If satisfaction is a completed gestalt, frustration is experienced when the gestalt is not completed. This dynamic is illustrated by one of Brenda's recurring dreams that recalls Scorsese's film *After Hours* based on comparable themes in Kafka. In this dream, Brenda is trying to get to an appointment but she is blocked at every turn. Geography changes so that she becomes lost; maps can't be read; attempts to make phone calls are thwarted because she loses the number or she finds it but can't read it, or it keeps changing; other people don't help, or disappear, or change the subject just as they are about to speak; she looks at her watch and she might just make the appointment a little late, but a second later she looks again and hours have passed. As the dream progresses she becomes more frantic: everything she tries is met with a further twist as reality shape-shifts and her goal, the completed gestalt, becomes even more unattainable. Finally, she wakes up exhausted and sweating with a scream locked inside her. It takes the morning for her to recover. Such dreams dramatise the impotence of the will: thinking harder and trying harder do not work.

This book is, overall, a theoretical account of a particular variant of self-formation illustrated by a portrait of Brenda. My perspective on her is that of the omniscient narrator who knows everything about her that she herself knows, and more than her therapist could ever know. She is presented, not so much as a psychotherapeutic case study than as a developmental and existential one; accordingly no therapeutic exchanges are shown. The book has been organised around the following themes: (I) energy regulation and its implications for boredom and creativity; (II) boundaries and their implications for impingement; (III) ego, power, and competitiveness; and (IV) the self, narrative, integration, and well-being. What we will see is how the phenomena of Brenda's inner terrain emerge out of her avoidant style of insecure attachment. This is a defensive pattern guaranteed to generate frustration and inner conflict. Each chapter deals with a different aspect of Brenda that is frustrated: Chapter One, energy release (excess charge battling overboundedness); Chapter Two, libido; Chapter Three, soul; Chapter Four, poor self-protection against the pain of the world; Chapter Five, losing herself in the face of impingements from the outside; Chapters Six and Seven, where her frustration is reinforced whenever the world drags her out of her deeper self back to an ego level to deal with competitiveness and power respectively; Chapter Eight, where she has no coherent sense of self, which manifests as poor memory and fragmented experience. Each chapter follows a trajectory in which we see Brenda's progress towards a solution. Many of them follow a similar arc from the egoic and personal to the transpersonal, indicating the pathway that Brenda is beginning to take, while the final two show what has been or would be involved in integrating her fragmented self and developing greater satisfaction, resilience, and cohesiveness.

The book brings together insights from psychotherapeutic theories of the development of the self (psychodynamic, humanistic, existential, body therapy, and transpersonal psychology), from affective neuroscience, as well as from philosophy and literature. Each topic, while discussed in general terms, is illustrated from Brenda's perspective, and occasionally from that of other psychotherapy clients. Some issues may be viewed as Brenda's failure to adapt to the social environment, but others may be attributed to a culture that itself frustrates some of our deepest needs. Our contemporary globalised, technologised, accelerated, and ceaselessly changing world is one that favours and helps generate avoidant relationships, so Brenda's particular difficulties increasingly coincide with and are intensified by the zeitgeist. They can therefore be seen as representative of many people who struggle with living in today's world.

At the same time, any resemblances between Brenda and the author of this book are inevitable. Indeed, it is, for me, axiomatic that the more subjective the discipline, the more the theory amounts to the psychic autobiography of the theorist—something Nietzsche preached and practised equally. Thus, whereas the physical sciences may be only marginally affected by the personal issues of the researchers, the human sciences, philosophy and psychotherapy are—though many in these fields would wish to deny it—overwhelmingly influenced by the personality and life experiences of the theorists. The therapist's own self is inextricably intertwined with both their client work and their theorising and writing and therefore, I have occasionally illustrated general points with my own personal experience. While some developmental theory is backed up by large-scale empirical research, much psychodynamic thinking is derived from the personal experience and awareness of the theorist, as well as from their observations of individual clients. I consider both of these ways of knowing to be valid. They are complementary: objective research provides breadth, while experiential awareness of self or other provides depth and grounding in reality. Both kinds of theory are utilised in the argument of this book. Empirical research on attachment styles inevitably draws generalised conclusions based on a group of subjects. One purpose of this book is to balance such population research with the study of an individual. This reminds us that within an attachment classification—as in any personality or self structure—there is individual variation stamped onto the general features of the syndrome. Thus, while Brenda may fall into the broad class of the avoidantly attached, she sometimes diverges from it because of other aspects of the facilitating environment that interacted with her parents' attachment style. This brings home the point that while we can, to a degree, argue backwards from behaviour or personality to cause, we should never argue forwards from upbringing to adult consequences. In developmental theorising, we must never lose sight of the fact that there are manifold influences on the self that interact in complex ways.

The texture of the book varies accordingly. Most chapters have a strong theoretical flavour, whereas Chapters Three and Five contain sections that are intended to evoke states of mind and therefore have a more "literary" feel. Parts of Chapters Five and Six switch into polemical mode, developing a moral and psychological argument against our culture's superficiality of experiencing (5) and against competitive individualism (6) where the pathology is seen as belonging to society, not to Brenda.

By focusing on the qualities that have been correlated with contentment or flourishing, self-help books typically offer a recipe that they claim will ensure happiness. There are a number of problems with this model. First, any one-size-fits-all approach ignores the developmental history and indeed the genetic and energetic make-up of the individual. Such an invitation to follow a universal path also blocks the individual from growing the self-awareness that is crucial to any self-development. Second, such models ignore the fact that we are embodied beings. Reading about something or even making a sincere attempt to follow the recipe cognitively will not work if we do not bodily and emotionally process our attempts at the prescribed behaviour, and this must include our resistance to it. Third, you cannot pursue happiness instrumentally. Flow is frequently cited as an experience associated with well-being. But that doesn't mean that flow can be *sought* in a goal-directed or will-driven manner. Flow is an *outcome*—of absorption in something cathected with meaning. It is this underlying meaning we must seek, not the flow itself. In *Beyond the Frustrated Self*, existential issues are examined but not foreclosed with premature, generalised, or instrumental advice. However, I hope that the reader, including the layperson, may resonate with these explorations and thereby be assisted towards some resolution of life's difficulties, which we all share.

PART I

THE FRUSTRATION OF ALIVENESS

CHAPTER ONE

How attachment styles are mirrored in energy regulation patterns

A t the beginning of a long period of therapy, Brenda's therapist experiences her as very polite, distant, self-analytical, and unemotional—apart from her eviscerating embarrassment about self-revelation and her crippling guilt about being in therapy at all when "there are so many people out there with real problems". She distrusts warmth or compassion—what she spittingly labels as pity but is exquisitely sensitive to a therapist's attunement and understanding. The slightest hint of not being heard or seen accurately or of unempathic analysis or rigidity sends her into retreat. Her presenting issue was lack of meaning in her life, and it was clear that she believed that she could analyse herself out of the problem if she—or her therapist— thought hard enough. The fact that she had been trying to figure out the point of life since her teens and still hadn't by the age of thirty-eight caused her despair. But it has never occurred to her that there was any other approach to the problem than through thinking. She worked in IT and was quite good at it but found it soul-destroying and didn't know how long she could continue to make herself do it; she wanted to return to college to study philosophy, anthropology, or English literature.

Brenda's most painful secret concerned a wound to her self-esteem that was so raw and bleeding it couldn't be touched. It was the central fact of her existence, but she couldn't speak about it directly, being far too proud and angry to acknowledge the extent to which she had been hurt by her father and brothers, and—most treacherously of all—by her mother. When she did—later—talk about it obliquely, it seemed that nothing was ever said out straight in the family. It was all a matter of presumption—that women were more stupid, more fearful, weaker, more vain, and clearly ("the evidence was there") had never contributed anything to civilisation. Therefore they should just accept their lot and get on with their menial duties to ease the lives of men. Most painfully, her mother never missed an opportunity to put down women or portray them as powerless victims who deserved no better. But Brenda felt equal or superior in intelligence, courage, and strength compared to her brothers with, in addition, an almighty will to succeed. Here, she had an inner stand-off. If she attacked the prejudice, this would reveal "their" victory in inflicting pain and hurt, and at the same time expose herself to the frustration and further humiliation when, inevitably, the charges would be denied. She was in a colossal energetic double-bind: damned if she defended herself; damned if she didn't. Her solution was to make them eat their own shit: she would achieve and gain renown. There was only one problem: she had no particular talents and was shy and introverted; she had nothing but a moderate intelligence and gigantic willpower. So, she was constantly harried by the knowledge that her chances of achieving fame or distinction were pretty meagre. At the same time, the drive to achieve was directly at odds with her longing to escape to her childhood bliss of blending into landscape and place or into the novels she read so voraciously. She was eternally caught in this battle between ego and soul: she believed one had to be sacrificed for the other, but at the same time she knew that she needed both.

Brenda remembers few specific incidents in her childhood, but has been told that because of a vomiting problem (that subsequently vanished of its own accord) she was in hospital for two weeks at the age of eighteen months. Here she was strapped to the bed, and by the time she was discharged she was no longer able to walk. Her parents were deeply wounded people, though possibly not exceptionally so for their time and place—Dublin in the 1970s. She describes her family of eight as seven planets (father, five sons, and one daughter) revolving round the burning out, almost extinct star that was the mother. At their most peaceful, they remained at a planetary distance from each other—as distant as Mercury and Venus or Mars and Jupiter. At other times, contact was of the harsh repulsing kind that arose out of frequent collisions in too small a space—a small soulless semi-detached suburban house—and in a family with few emotional resources. There was no tenderness, support, or intimacy—instead noise, crush, and ruthless competitiveness between the siblings, and sneering, shaming emotional brutality from the father. Unfortunately, this did not lead to the children becoming united against a common enemy and supporting each other. The doormat mother did not shield them but was another victim who protected herself by disappearing psychically. If you were to represent contact styles physically as a fist being met by a palm, the mother's palm is the one that evaporates as you approach so that you end up pushing into cloud. No meeting, no holding: immensely frustrating for the child seeking contact and relationship. In Brenda's adolescence, anxiety and self-loathing led to attacks of nausea and vomiting, which continued as a reflex long after her stomach was emptied. Her relationship with her parents deteriorated further with rage at her mother's betrayal and refusal to stand up for herself and an even greater loathing for her contemptuous, bullying father. At school, Brenda did well enough academically, but socially she was shy, lonely, and quite unable to connect with her classmates in the all-girls school. However, she had an iron-willed determination to succeed driven by her feminist-fuelled anger and her desperation to get out of a home where only boys were valued. She would never give up her independence to a man nor give over her power of self-determination to children. However emotionally ill-equipped she was, she would learn to fend for herself. In the meantime, she withdrew more and more and hid anything of importance from her parents and brothers.

Brenda's frustrating relational and energy patterns are superficially explained by the circumstances mentioned above, but understanding the deeper foundations requires attachment theory.

Attachment theory

Attachment theory originated with John Bowlby and was subsequently elaborated by Mary Ainsworth and Mary Main (Bowlby, 1971, 1973; Holmes, 1993, 2010; Gerhardt, 2004; Siegel, 2012). It was initially based on observation of animal and child behaviour, showing that the infant seeks proximity to the parent or other caregiver. Attachment kicks in at the same time as the child is becoming mobile around the age of six months, and is believed to function to keep the child safe from harm and separation from the group. Bowlby (1973) made it clear that the child sought, not just proximity, but emotional engagement with a responsive attachment figure, and Mary Ainsworth found that it was maternal sensitivity, rather than warmth *per se*, that was correlated with secure attachment (Siegel, 2012, p. 100). Secure attachment provides the individual with resilience to trauma or loss, whereas insecurity places the person at risk of emotional disturbance (Siegel, 2012, pp. 114–115). The attachment pattern in infancy is associated with characteristic processes of emotional regulation, social relatedness, access to biographical memory, and development of self-reflection and narrative (Siegel, 2012; Holmes, 2010). Schore (2003a), following Bowlby, argues that "attachment theory ... is fundamentally a regulatory theory. Attachment can thus be conceptualised as the interactive regulation of synchrony between psychobiologically attuned organisms" (p. 64). Secure attachment, then, facilitates the maximisation of pleasant feelings as well as modulating the intensity of affect. Thus, the over-excited child is calmed and the torpid child is stimulated (Gerhardt, 2004). "Separation stress, in essence, is a loss of maternal regulators of the infant's immature behavioural and physiological systems that results in the attachment patterns of protest, despair, and detachment" (Schore, 2003a, p. 65). Later in the chapter, I will elaborate this view of attachment by examining what is happening to the body and energy economy in insecure attachment.

In the Strange Situation test, devised by Mary Ainsworth, infants were assessed for their response to being in a strange environment: with mother; with mother plus a stranger; with the stranger only; then alone; and finally reunited with mother (Siegel, 2012, pp. 97–98). Children's responses to separation and reunion broke down into four classes: secure attachment with three kinds of insecure (anxious) attachment: avoidant, ambivalent (resistant), and disorganised. The secure child feels grief on mother's departure and runs to her for comfort on her return, after which he is able to resume play. The avoidant (now called deactivating) child ignores the comings and goings of mother, while the ambivalent (now called hyperactivating) clings to mother on her return but cannot be comforted (Holmes, 2010). The disorganised response displays a mixture of need and fear of the mother. Here I will contrast the avoidant—of which Brenda is a classic example—with the ambivalent, of which her partner is an example. The disorganised individual lacks a coherent defence, stemming from relational trauma, and will not be further mentioned here.

Attachment is most vividly experienced in its absence: when we are away from our loved ones we feel anxious, sad, or lonely. When we are with them we feel safe, good about ourselves, and comforted in times of stress: we are in a state of relaxed alertness and can begin to explore the world and pursue our interests and work. "All of us, from the cradle to the grave, are happiest when life is organised as a series of excursions, long or short, from the secure base provided by our attachment figures" (Bowlby, 1988, p. 62). In childhood and adulthood, "distress triggers attachment behaviours. Once activated, attachment overrides all other motivations—exploratory, playful, sexual, gustatory, etc." (Holmes, 2010, p. 31). But how may the insecurely attached adapt to their situation? They have learned that they cannot trust human relationships. The ambivalent cling and the avoidant ignore, but there is no secure attachment with the primary caregiver. However, if they have a loving grandparent, aunt, uncle, or neighbour, they may be able to attach to an alternative. On the other hand, children may not have a primary caregiver if they grow up in an institution with harsh, impersonal, or constantly changing staff, but even in this situation it may be possible for them to divert their attachment needs to the other children. But if there are no older children capable of forming such relationships, or if supportive relationships between the children are discouraged, then the individual is severely damaged emotionally. Parts of the brain that normally develop in the first year in the context of relationship simply do not develop, and if this continues up to the age of about three the individual may have a lifetime of being unable to feel empathy, regulate their emotions, relate to others, or manage stress, as found in Romanian orphans who experienced virtually no mothering (Gerhardt, 2004, pp. 38, 77, 127).

Insecure avoidant attachment

The avoidant child tries to minimise her needs to forestall rebuff by the caregiver; in this way she maintains some contact but at the price of both emotional expression and freedom of exploration (Holmes, 2010, p. 138). Both the neediness and the rejection remain out of awareness by a defence which Bowlby called defensive exclusion. This blocks processing of painful affect which leads to persistent feelings of hate and abandonment (Holmes, 1993, pp. 79–81). In Brenda's case, she won't allow herself to feel needy out of pride. If, in the interests of truth (which is important to her), she admits some needs to her therapist, it is without any affect—she wouldn't give *them* the satisfaction of having hurt her. Brenda's avowed hatred is focused on her parents' lack of respect for her. The rejection didn't seem directed at her as an individual since all the children received the same impersonal, indeed depersonalising treatment. But what did and does hurt her is the way she was singled out as the inferior one on account of her gender. This humiliation, rather than any generic parental distancing, is behind her hatred. Just as in society it is not poverty but inequality that generates social discord, in families it is not the nature of the relationships so much as an unfair difference in valuing that creates hatred and despair and crushes self-esteem.

Avoidant children tend to have neglectful or rejecting parents for whom power is more important than sensitivity (Holmes, 2010, p. 69) and who are emotionally unattuned and unresponsive. These children suffer from a lack of being seen, heard, understood, and mirrored. They do not react to mother's absence in the Strange Situation test because experience has told them that she doesn't meet their emotional needs. But their apparent insouciance is not matched by their physiology which shows increased heart rate and stress (Gerhardt, 2004, p. 26; Siegel, 2012, p. 120). In response to mother's failure to see the world from the infant's perspective, the child displays disappointment, self-soothing (like the rocking of Brenda and her siblings to get themselves to sleep in childhood), and gaze aversion. This last observation warrants some attention. The child has lost hope and given up seeking mirroring, understanding, or help in the face of an inept, non-empathic parent, or in the case of an actively hostile parent, they are avoiding the aggressive or annihilating gaze. During Brenda's first years in therapy, on her arrival at sessions, she was able to look her therapist in the eye and engage in normal, albeit very polite and shy social contact. However, once she got in touch with her own process, she could no more make eye contact than put her arm in the fire. At the end of sessions, the reassembly of her defences was palpable. When her therapist suggested that she might try to look her in the eye during a session, she confessed that if she forced herself to look, her hatred might kill the therapist. Brenda was caught in an agonised double-bind between a desperate need and an equal dread of being seen and heard. Her inner life was a raw wound into which she expected salt to be poured. As stated above, attachment theory is primarily a regulatory theory. For the avoidantly attached child, "the emotionally barren and non-cooperative nature of the patterns of communication lead to a non-responsive virtual (representational) parent and to excessive reliance on internal constraints to achieve self-regulation" (Siegel, 2012, p. 203). This, as Brenda illustrates, is an armoured substitute for the real thing, and we will see later some of the energetic consequences of this defensive structure. Siegel goes on to state that "reflective function is not developed well, in that the parent's mental state is not available to the child" (ibid., p. 203). In Brenda's case, her ability to reflect and mentalise was in fact quite advanced, a consequence, perhaps, of extensive reading of classic literature along with modelling by some exceptionally mature classmates in her teenage years. (See Holmes, 2010, Chapter Two for a detailed definition and justification of the term "mentalisation".)

Avoidant two-year-olds are hostile and distant with peers, and at age six are over-controlled; they are likely to be socially isolated as they grow up (Holmes, 1993, p. 115). By adulthood, insecurely attached people have learnt to have negative beliefs about themselves and others. Furthermore, according to Holmes (1993, p. 120), their distorted and restricted ability to generalise from events to basic beliefs about self and others leads to an inability to revise their working models in the light of love offered in adulthood. While Brenda certainly holds negative beliefs, she would disagree about the reasons. She claims that she doesn't actually want love. To her, love comes with far too many strings attached and she believes she would have to compromise something more precious—her authenticity. What she wants from others more than anything is respect. Her mother's masochistic insistence on women's inevitable inferiority and her father's sneering alongside her older brothers' wholesale swallowing of the family myth meant that she always felt under attack—it was like living in the trenches, but with the enemy on all sides and within the trench as well. Avoidant people remain on the emotional periphery of relationships—in Brenda's case often the third person in a triangle of women. While she can thereby have some contact without being overwhelmed by it, mainly this enables her to occupy her favourite position—that of fly on the wall observing others.

Avoidantly attached people exhibit a low tolerance for feelings. They repress feelings because, not having had emotional regulation, they don't know what to do with them. In families where feelings are denied, or even punished, "negative" feelings in the child such as anger, envy, or jealousy bring up discomfort in the parent who will push the feelings away—with anger or disapproval or a pretence that nothing is happening. Alternatively, all feelings, even the positive (joy, excitement, curiosity, etc.), may be rejected because the caregiver cannot tolerate the child's aliveness, as was the case for Brenda's exhausted mother. In effect, the child learns to protect the parent against her feelings by denying they exist or by blocking their expression. This blocking may be held in persistent body tensions, stress, and an unbalanced autonomic nervous system which sooner or later (e.g., in midlife) create pain or illness. One downstream effect of the inability to acknowledge or express feelings is suppression of the immune system leading to increased susceptibility to a variety of diseases (Gerhardt, 2004, pp. 96–97). The emotional and social outcomes of the negation or non-mirroring of feelings include the development of a false self, as well as lifelong difficulties with relationships. Of course, the details of the downstream effects of avoidant attachment depend on the totality and nuances of the family environment. Was the parental response hostile, punitive, or simply vague or absent? In Brenda's case, she had one of each: an emotionally absent, out-of-contact, doormat, powerless mother with a panicked, hand-wringing response to Brenda's "bilious attacks", combined with angry, contemptuous, bullying fathering. (The imbalance of adjectives reveals the respective weight of each parent in her psyche.)

Avoidant vs. ambivalent attachment

In contrast to the avoidant type, the ambivalent (resistant) class of insecure attachment is characterised by inconsistent parenting, which entails that the child has to focus closely on the parent's state of mind. The feelings of such children are very available and indeed exaggerated, creating a needy, hysterical, codependent pattern that can compromise the development of independence (Gerhardt, 2004, p. 26). While avoidants are terrified of contact, ambivalents are terrified of separation. They differ too in how they tell the stories of their lives; avoidants having a dismissive narrative style, whereas ambivalents have an enmeshed style (Holmes, 1993, p. 163) as discussed below and in Chapter Eight.

In comparing avoidant and ambivalent attachment issues, it seems clear that people do not always fall neatly into one type or another and that one can fear *both* abandonment and impingement; that one can be terrified of contact *and* of separation. This is because, underlying the avoidant's denial of their own neediness, the need for attachment is always there. The abandoned avoidant child may *appear* unconcerned, but in fact "their heart rate and autonomic arousal is rocketing" (Gerhardt, 2004, p. 26). Brenda knows the truth of this from the times when relationships with boyfriends have broken up. She remembers the experience of one of them (even more avoidant than she!) leaving her apartment and her resulting terror that she would go mad. But, as her pride was even stronger than her fear of insanity, she would not run after him and beg him to return. While he stood there uncertainly and guiltily, she lay on the couch moaning "just go, please go".

Adult attachment

The Adult Attachment Interview, developed by Mary Main and colleagues, showed that the parent's pattern of telling the story of her own early family life—her attitudes towards attachment—correlated with her child's attachment classification. The secure child equates with the autonomous adult; the avoidant child with the dismissing-detached adult; the ambivalent child is linked with the preoccupied-entangled adult; and the disorganised child with the unresolved adult (Holmes, 1993, p. 113; Siegel, 2012, pp. 99, 104). This correlation between parent and child attachment patterns suggests that childhood attachment tends to persist into adulthood (Siegel, 2012, p. 104), and it is thought that the internal model of attachment is the same in the child and adult equivalents (ibid., p. 122). Montaigne might have been writing a creed for the dismissing-detached adult when he said: "We should have wives, children, property and, above all, good health ... if we can: but we should not become so attached to them that our happiness depends on them" (Montaigne, 1993, p. 270).

Compared to secure children, insecurely attached ten-year-olds told less coherent lifestories, had more difficulty recalling memories (especially of pre-school years) and were less aware of their own thought processes (Holmes, 1993, p. 111)—incompetencies presumably deriving from deficits in attunement and mirroring. The avoidant/dismissing adult tends towards dry, logical thinking, and their autobiographical narrative lacks richness, depth, and meaning-making (Siegel, 2012, p. 121; Holmes, 2010, p. 49). This topic is returned to in Chapters

Eight and Nine where the connections between narrative style, adult attachment, self-formation, and integration are discussed.

Surprisingly, considering all the clichés about emotionally unavailable men, a large meta-study found no gender differences in attachment distribution (Howe, 2011, pp. 210–211). However, attachment classification can change over the lifespan, and the proportion of people in the avoidant/dismissing class increases with old age, perhaps because of a defence against the losses that characterise late life (Howe, 2011, pp. 122–123). As this implies, attachment styles and energy patterns are neither fixed nor static. Cozolino (2010, p. 335) summarises research on attachment plasticity to show that not only can attachment classification change during the lifespan, it can also change following relatively short periods of group or individual psychotherapy. Siegel (2012, p. 119) describes individuals as having "earned" secure status when emotional relationships with a close friend, romantic partner, or therapist has allowed them to move beyond childhood experiences that would be expected to have produced insecure attachment.

We should not think of attachment styles as rigidly adhered to; instead we have several working models of attachment, one of which is usually dominant. According to Pollard (2005, p. 206), "enmeshed attachment characteristically underlies avoidant attachment". This makes sense if we remember that the avoidant/dismissing style simply represents an externally-visible defensive pattern, not what is going on physiologically. The needy, dependent, and uncontained characteristics of the ambivalent/enmeshed type may sometimes be displayed briefly before being quickly suppressed.

The family systems therapist Thomas Fogarty (1979) writes about the commonly occurring relationship between the complementary types of detached and entangled adults—or what he more vividly refers to as "the distancer and the pursuer". Brenda is in exactly this kind of relationship with her partner; it goes without saying that she is the distancer and her partner, John, is the pursuer. Brenda's therapists (she has gone through several) tend to take Fogarty's advice: "never pursue a distance", but poor John has yet to learn this after more than a decade living with Brenda. She feels John sucking her into a suffocating and shameful babes-in-the-wood blancmange. He feels exhausted and resentful that he is the one who puts all the work into the relationship. He feels he gives his life to predicting her needs; she feels invaded, misunderstood, and raging with frustration and a need for space. When working with couples, Fogarty recommends working first with the pursuer who is, after all, available. John must be persuaded to pull back from the emotional chase, which leads him to encounter his inner emptiness. Brenda will feel relief, initially, but will then begin to miss John as she in turn encounters her emptiness. The distancer's inner life can be flat and somewhat depressed but, ironically, when she fears losing her partner she begins to come alive.

Libido and energy charge and discharge

As mentioned above, Schore (2003a) has argued that attachment theory is a theory of regulation. It should be apparent that Brenda's insecure attachment stance entails a constant negotiation of inner conflict and frustration, because her way of life is built on denial of the human needs for safety, love, and interdependence. Thus, she must appear cool when she feels most hurt or panic-stricken; what matters most must be hidden and she cannot let herself become dependent on anybody or attached to anything that could be taken away from her. Her basic attitude is one of distrust towards others and a consequent refusal to show her feelings combined with a fierce and proud independence. Her inner double-binds have outcomes for the way in which her body manifests and manages energy.

Basic lifeforce or libido depends on bodily excitement: arousal and discharge are in constant flow with each other in what Perls, Hefferline, and Goodman (1972) called the contact–withdrawal cycle. Freud believed that our drives were innate and independent of the object, but Gestalt theory and object relations argue that charge depends on *contact* with an object, whether external or a remembered internalised imago. We cathect "objects" (people, places, things, and experiences) that become associated, particularly in early life, with positive emotions. Individuals differ in the degree of charge and discharge, the relative time spent in each part of the cycle, and the flexibility of movement between them. The body psychotherapist Keleman (1981) defines two dimensions of excitement: charge, "the development of arousal"; and boundedness (containment), "how much of the charge is allowed to manifest in action" (Smith, 1985, p. 74). Charge levels can be inferred from breathing patterns and boundedness from muscle tone. An optimal level of muscle tone allows for a spontaneous build-up of charge until it is sufficient for action or interaction. At one end of the boundedness scale are those who are impulsive and unrestrained with poor boundaries, whereas the overbounded are constricted and rigid with muscular armouring. Degrees of aliveness may vary between the right and left sides or upper and lower segments of the body, affecting whatever functions are associated with these regions. In addition, excessive charge, particularly in an overbounded type, may burn out with age.

The different ways of managing energy are associated with different patterns of breathing (Boadella, 1987, pp. 78–79) and the degree of charge depends on the rate of breathing. The holding back and over-containment (overboundedness) of feelings is associated with thoracic breathing and incomplete exhalation. The opposite of this, the uncontained (underbound) hysterical type, correlates with complete exhalation that carries a scream or cry or other emotional expression, but there is a lack of conscious contact with the in-breath—as distinct from a panicky gulping of air. These individuals easily lose touch with their centre and need to contact the abdominal in-breath in body therapy.

Brenda went into therapy as an overcharged overbounded type. Her sympathetic nervous system was chronically aroused as she was caught between the double-bind of the repeated triggering of feelings of rage and anxiety countered by the prohibition against showing her feelings. At a body level she experienced immense frustration and the feeling of being blocked and trapped within her own body, as her breath fought against the chronically tight musculature of her chest and abdomen. She had recurrent dreams of trying to sprint but being held back by an invisible force even as her energy drove her forward. She used to experience this concretely in athletic events in school where she felt as if she were running with the brakes on. Being overcharged and overbounded, Brenda alternates between dashes of energy and burnout, and easily slumps into boredom or lassitude. A more extreme form of this energy pattern is manic depression.

Energy and attachment

How can we relate attachment, contact, and energy regulation to each other? The early facilitating environment plays a major role in how charge and boundaries develop. Excitement can be of the positive, libidinous, moving-towards-life type (equivalent to chemoattraction in lower organisms) or the negative, fearful, repelled fight-or-flight variety (equivalent to chemorepulsion). Perls, Hefferline, and Goodman (1972) maintained that anxiety is simply excitement with negative affect. In families where feelings—whether positive excitement or fear/anxiety/ anger—are unacceptable, there will be a strong prohibition towards displaying these feelings and they will be tightly contained (over-regulated and overbounded). This is the case for children in the avoidant class of insecure attachment. On the other hand, the inconsistent parenting of the ambivalently attached child causes the child to exaggerate their feelings, i.e., to be under-regulated and underbounded.

The greater the degree of unsafety experienced in these families, the greater is the negative arousal. Thus, families may punish expression of feelings by spanking, ridicule, humiliating (avoidants), or display particularly severe swings between invasive hostile attention and terrifying abandonment (ambivalents); this leads—in either case—to a high level of anxious arousal, i.e., overcharge. Conversely, the insecure attachment may arise from neglectful rather than abusive parenting. In these cases, the child is undercharged in both positive and negative ways.

The undercharged overbounded type is under-stimulated and has learned that one way of protecting a depressed, anxious, or unable-to-cope mother is to lower his available vitality. The undercharged underbounded type may have an attuned and capable but distracted mother, too preoccupied with other things to attend consistently to the child. Such children have no need to hold back their feelings, but they lack the contact that would stimulate the feelings in the first place.

In summary, I am linking boundedness with attachment type, and extremes of charge with abusive *vs.* neglectful parenting, as shown in the following table.

Relationship between attachment and energy management.

Attachment type Parenting type	Avoidant (Dismissing-detached)	Ambivalent (Preoccupied-entangled)
Hostile/Abusive	Overcharged Overbounded (engine racing, low gear)	Overcharged Underbounded (engine racing, high gear)
Neglectful/Absent	Undercharged Overbounded (engine idling, low gear)	Undercharged Underbounded (engine idling, high gear)

The point I want to make is that attachment patterns in childhood lay the foundation for charge and boundedness in adulthood (see table for summary). These patterns determine how we manage excitement and engage with the mirror-image pair of cathexis and boredom. Smith (1985) uses the analogy of the car engine to define each energy type: the charge is equivalent to the engine speed, and the boundedness to the gear ratio that contains and transmits the energy. The overcharged overbound thus have the engine racing but are in low gear; they don't cover much ground before running out of fuel. The undercharged (engine idling) underbounded (high gear) will stall easily and lack the power to climb a steep hill. A client who falls into this category has great difficulty carrying any major projects through;he never manages to go on holiday because his leave expires while he is still researching where to go, but his calm—even equanimity—suggests somebody who has done years of meditation though in fact he hasn't. Another client who is again undercharged but overbound also has problems with completion of practical matters. However, she is conflicted, closed, and constipated in speaking: the inner censor comes to the fore as she struggles to clear a path for her energy against the prohibitions of a punitive superego. Her opposite type, the overcharged underbound, will appear manic and flog herself until she drops.

When the style of parenting differs between mother and father, the more charged of the two will predominate. Thus, Brenda is an overcharged overbounded type because of her father's emotionally abusive parenting. We can speculate that in his absence, with her mother's unattuned but not overtly hostile parenting, she would probably have been an undercharged overbounded type.

Interrelationships between holding, containment, boundedness, and armouring

Boundedness and muscular armouring seem similar concepts, but boundedness is more likely to be used to suggest an optimum level of muscle tone with its associated availability of energy, while armouring implies an excessive muscular tension and high levels of repression. There is a link between Winnicott's concept of holding and the early relationships that lay down different degrees of muscular armouring or boundedness in the developing child. Holding creates psychic structure and integration in the infant; in its absence, we experience un-integration.

Reich argued that muscular armouring was a consequence of our anxiety about unleashing the uncontrolled energy and chaos of the id. Nowadays, we would probably extend that anxiety to encompass not just a fear of the madness of the unrestrained id, but also of the relational consequences if we spontaneously unleash our desires, whether for rage in the boardroom or sex with a stranger. In either case, feelings are experienced as unsafe, and muscular armouring gradually inhibits not just their expression but their experiencing as well. Such overbound individuals repress their feelings to avoid parental censure, while the underbound exaggerate them to the edge of hysteria in order to get the parent's attention.

It is initially the parents' responsibility to regulate the infant's feelings and energy because babies do not yet possess the brain structures that would allow them to do this for themselves (Gerhardt, 2004). Some parents over-regulate (characteristic of avoidant attachment) while others under-regulate (ambivalent attachment) leading to the overbound and underbound pathologies respectively. Good-enough, optimallyholding parents regulate *appropriately*; they soothe the over-aroused child and stimulate the under-aroused. This creates a contained, flexible, responsive child, balanced between extremes. Under- and over-containment is equivalent to under- and over-boundedness.

Carroll (2005a, pp. 24–26) elaborates the neuroscience of the three states of: repression (overbound), hysteria (underbound), and balance (contained). The self is constructed from internalisation of preverbal interactions with others, which creates muscular and motor patterns and patterns of regulation of physiological (e.g., visceral) states via the autonomic nervous system. The function of the right hemisphere of the brain (which correlates with the unconscious) is to "maintain a coherent, continuous, and unified sense of self" (ibid., p. 25), both anchored in and emerging from bodily regulatory patterns. When the child has not had their feelings consistently regulated by mother (ambivalent attachment), in the event of stress the sympathetic nervous system easily overwhelms regulation by the right brain leading to hysteria or dissociation. In the case of emotional repression (avoidant attachment), the left brain controls the right, which in turn controls the sympathetic nervous system. There is consequently no bottom-up bodily information being received by the brain. In this case, the left brain constructs narratives which cover up or distort the underlying bodily information about feelings (ibid., p. 25). In the integrated child—"held" in the Winnicottian sense and securely attached—there is two-way communication between the brain and the body. The individual is embodied, thinking and feeling are balanced, and he/she can exist in a state of relaxed alertness, capable of both arousal and relaxation as appropriate to the demands of the environment.

Dynamics of energy management

Attachment schemas can be relatively stable throughout the lifespan (Cozolino, 2010, p. 209), though there is wide variation in the research data (ibid., p. 335). But what about body and energy types? What is the trajectory for someone like Brenda with respect to her charge and containment? It is common for the overcharged and overbounded type to burn out so that the charge diminishes (Smith, 1985). How did Brenda fare in this respect? In her early thirties, she had a breakdown that seems to have directly stemmed from an escalation in her already high level of anxiety combined with her having worked herself into a state of exhaustion. She got a promotion at work that required her to speak in public. At the same time, she and her boyfriend bought a house together, despite her doubts about him and their life together and despite her claustrophobic anxiety about commitment. She found herself having panic attacks before public speaking, and in the bank while arranging a mortgage. Suddenly her terror was spilling out beyond her control. However, her ferocious willpower and superego did not allow for withdrawing from commitments once she had made them, so she went ahead with the relationship, the house, and the promotion. A dark period of increasing anxiety, depression, and depersonalisation followed which was only broken by the drama of a sexual affair, the break-up with her boyfriend, and the sale of the house. Her container had been shattered.

As she slowly accustomed herself to public speaking and as other causes of stress were removed, Brenda discovered and embraced the co-counselling movement like a born-again religion. She learned less inhibition in expressing feelings as she responded to the let-it-all-hang-out culture and grew to trust that she was accepted as she was. (This was something that one-to-one therapy could not have given her.) Thus, she became less bounded for a time: she acquired lovers and a precious female friend and learned to express her love, longing, and playfulness. Even more challenging, she found her voice and learned to scream out her rage and frustration in a shift that wasn't always moderate or pretty. She took baby steps in becoming more assertive, despite the acute anxiety this provoked in her. She discovered some creativity and with it began to imagine that it might be possible for her to become empowered in the presence of others. She even began to facilitate workshops. Unfortunately, a row and subsequent schism in the local co-counselling community caused Brenda to leave, and in the absence of this influence she returned to more severe regulation of her feelings, albeit not as ruthlessly and tightly controlled as before. For many years she mourned co-counselling: she remembers this period as the golden years of her life, like a protracted honeymoon of love, spontaneity, creativity, and sensuality.

With time in therapy and perhaps aided by the calmness (or tiredness?) of getting older, Brenda's charge has diminished. She has become less angry and more accepting of herself. This was greatly helped by her cutting herself off from her family and working hard on establishing a set of values that were true to her rather than undigested family introjects. She followed her enthusiasm, did a degree in English literature and now has a job teaching adult students. But she has built up her intellect at the expense of her feelings, and alongside a lowering in anxiety and anger, positive excitation and enthusiasm have diminished for Brenda. She is aware of flinching away from excitement because it feels too close to anxiety. Her current outlook is stable but grey, and though only in her fifties and in good health, she is preoccupied by death and the need to achieve something before she dies.

One possible way forward for Brenda now is heart-centred meditation. The teachings of Judith Blackstone, for example, go further than the sensory awareness of the front of the body that can be obtained from body scans like Gendlin's focusing. Rather, Blackstone's practice is aimed at deep embodiment: you inhabit your body rather than merely observing it and become aware of the space you occupy. Furthermore, her embodiment practice entails sensing—and connecting—the breath from the core of different chakras, including the head, the heart, and the power chakra. Brenda's imbalance derives from her unoccupied heart chakra, without which life is dry and unnourished.

Attachment, nomadism, and Buddhism

There is a joke about a child on a journey who keeps asking excitedly: "Daddy, Daddy, when will we get there?" to which father replies, "You're a nomad, son". Brenda may have the same misconception.

As a young adult, she joined the ambitious youth of her country and emigrated—and returned, but she expected that this exploration and conquest would be accompanied by accumulation—by getting there. It was—for a while—but every time she became comfortable in a house, job, career; comfortable with a partner and with friends, she had to move on. This demand came from within: claustrophobic panic, dissatisfaction, boredom, or excitement about another path drove her on—and she always moved on without looking back. Is Brenda's imperative to keep on the move about more than avoidant attachment? In our evolutionary past, we have only 10,000 years of settled history but millions of years of roaming as hunter-gatherers before that. As a nomad, before the era of settled agriculture and the overpopulation of the planet, there was no need to choose between freedom and attachment (to the land). Chatwin (1988) and Berman (2000) have proposed that religion is a response to anxiety and that the movement of nomadic people across the landscape is such a vivid and immediate experience, as well as a form of physical catharsis, that the need for religion is obviated (Dowds, 2010). The relationship to nature provides all spiritual needs. It is not surprising that aboriginal tribes have fared so badly in 'civilisation'; their hearts broken over the loss or destruction of their territory.

Twenty-first-century globalised youth are the new nomads, wanderers, flâneurs of life. This is understandable if the imperative is exploring, not root forming. Brenda has fought an internal battle between rooting and moving on all her life, a battle that has a particular twist in Ireland where emigration away from this small island has always been the solution for the impoverished, the ambitious, or the culturally stifled. But Brenda has been fighting the battle with anguish, with a vague but unconceptualised awareness that something is desperately wrong. The difference between modern nomads and our 10,000 year old ancestors is that, today, we are divorced from nature—*this* is the source of our alienation. The separation that has generated this gaping absence could be understood as part of the chain of separations—from nature, community, family, parents that has gone into the making of the twenty-first-century isolated, individual ego. The new field of ecopsychology seeks to re-envisage the self as part of, not separate from, nature; the ego boundary extending to encompass a larger identity (Abram, 1997; Fisher, 2002). Our longing is for the soul: the soul in nature, but also the soul in our homes, the soul in old made things. Without what Thomas Moore (1992) called the care of the soul, we are rendered homeless, with nothing to care for and nowhere to rest. We will return to this topic in Chapters Two and Three.

Psychotherapy claims that attachment is one of our most fundamental needs; Buddhism claims that attachment is the root of suffering. Which is right? There is little doubt that children need security and that they get security from attachment. Bowlby believed that we continued with this need throughout our lives, taking longer or shorter excursions from our attachment figures. However, the theory may need to be rewritten for later life, as we approach the inevitable detachment of death. In India, once their children are launched in life, some older people relinquish home and family to go on a spiritual quest as a bridge to death and the next life. Perhaps attachment theory applies to early life, and non-attachment theory (Buddhism) to later life, at least for the more introverted and spiritually-inclined. Sara Maitland (2008) describes a Western version of this in *A Book of Silence* where, once her children have grown, she departs to live alone amid unpeopled mountains, moorland, and desert. There is a tension between our need to attach and cathect, and our growing experience and understanding of loss as we get closer to old age and death. Buddhist practice that opens the heart helps us to resolve this by broadening our focus from the personal to the transpersonal: as we let go of narrow possessive attachments we move towards a less personal and non-possessive connection to the cosmos. For Brenda, now, her rooting imperative is becoming more generalised—perhaps as a consequence of age. A safe, if non-cathected, home, and an attachment to nature in general—rather than one specific piece of it—seem adequate for now. It's the best compromise she can manage in current circumstances. The longing for something more is met with occasional nomadic weeks in nature. Dissatisfaction, desire, boredom, and alienation all fade away on walking holidays with a different destination each day as in hiking the GR10 in the Pyrenees. "There is a joy and satisfaction beyond words in the moods of the ever-changing landscape and weather, the soothing physical exercise, the genuine hunger at the end of the day and the holding provided by the need to reach the destination with its attendant food and shelter" (Dowds, 2010). The landscape encountered in this way is experienced as sacred, and indeed we might speculate that the pilgrimages of Christianity and other religions are based on earlier nomadic movement through an ever-changing landscape (see Berman, 2000 for more on this topic). In any case, this temporary immersion in nature may be the best that most of modern mankind can hope for in our urbanised, overpopulated, and intensivelyfarmed world.

Psychotherapy maintains that a major cause of suffering is failure in attachment, while Buddhism claims that the cause of suffering is attachment itself. According to Tara Brach (2003), however, Buddhists are referring, not to attachment *per se*, but rather to the extremes of grasping, greed, and aversion. Nevertheless, ascetic Buddhism is contraindicated for those with avoidant attachment. For such individuals, non-attachment is all too easy, and leads to a sterile void which can be mistaken for the emptiness of no self. "The mark of true emptiness is joy" (Kornfield, 1994, p. 205)—not the depression, inner poverty, meaninglessness, deadness, or inauthenticity that some practitioners of Buddhism may mistake for self-lessness and the path to enlightenment. Insecure attachment and other disorders of the self must be healed—whether through psychotherapy or a psychologically sophisticated meditation teaching—before authentic spiritual development can take place.

Boorstein (1997, p. 17) agrees that psychological development is "a necessary precursor of genuine spiritual development". As Kornfield (1994, p. 198) says: "There are two parallel tasks in spiritual life. One is to discover selflessness, the other is to develop a healthy sense of self. Both sides of that apparent paradox must be fulfilled for us to awaken". While Boorstein (1997, p. 17) maintains that meditation increases ego strength by increasing one's capacity to be aware of changing mind states, it is acknowledged elsewhere in a book he edited that the Buddhist ego is not the same as Freud's ego, but rather a collective term for the different selves such as "I", "me" and "the observer" (Deatherage, 1996, p. 215). The Buddhist ego that must be transcended appears to be the individualist, egotistical self, which in psychotherapeutic terms is frequently a rather weak, immature self, and it remains the case that a great many people bypass or cement their pathologies in a misunderstanding of the true nature of Buddhist principles. In the absence of a strong sense of self, meditation practices aimed at a state of "No Boundary" will not only fail to bring spiritual awakening, they may endanger the self and deepen the pathology. Meditation aimed at a sense of union with the universe is accompanied by a loss of boundaries that could be very dangerous for those who have never had strong boundaries in the first place (see Maitland, 2008, pp. 62–72 for a discussion of this issue). Such participative consciousness is our initial state of being in early childhood. It is important not to fall into what Wilber (2000) calls the pre/trans fallacy: the prepersonal and the transpersonal are not the same thing. For those who have failed to develop a strong sense of self, apparent transcendence of ego may well be a regression into a pre-self rather than a progression towards a trans-self.

* * *

Brenda fits into the avoidant/dismissing class of attachment along with an associated overcharged overbounded form of energy management, and it has become clear that these consequences of her early development are fundamental to her self-frustrating emotional and energy patterns. Here is Brenda now coming towards the end of years of therapy. She loves nature, fiction, theatre, and old houses—including the isolated country cottage she has renovated. She actively dislikes and avoids her family, and indeed finds all family life quite repellent. She has friends but needs to control their access to her, and her phone is off to incoming calls. She doesn't know why or for how long people will put up with her. She is still with John who is highly supportive and dependent, and as long as he doesn't become too demanding, she can relax about her fears of abandonment. Close and warm relationships with women friends are a dangerous double-bind to her: on the one hand she risks loss of freedom and engulfment, on the other she risks abandonment and isolation. The core of her attachment style has not changed in a stable way, though she has healed many of the symptoms of avoidant attachment as will become clear in Chapters Nine and Ten. She was temporarily less bounded and more available for contact during her halcyon days in co-counselling, and she has succeeded in reducing her negative charge. She has moved away from abusive "friendships" and is, she realises, indeed surrounded by a loving partner and friends. This for her carries its own problems of dealing with invasion. The main issues she is left with concern her boundaries with others, her lack of solid or accumulating achievement, and the fact that time is running out. She still has episodes of boredom sliding into depression and meaninglessness. I would argue that this, more than relationship difficulties *per se*, is what brings the avoidant individual into therapy. As long as he has a pursuing partner, the avoidant is happy in his distancing, while any difficulties in relationship can be blamed on the pursuer. What does, however, cause suffering for the avoidant type is his experience of the world as an empty and meaningless place, which of course is the result of his difficulty with cathecting, whether a person or the world. This type of bored depression will be the subject of the next chapter.

Summary

Attachment theory is linked to body energy regulation. Brenda fits into the avoidant/dismissing class of insecure attachment along with an associated overcharged, overbounded form of energy management. It becomes clear that these consequences of her early development underlie her self-frustrating emotional and energy patterns. Some spiritual aspects of attachment are teased out, including our bond with the earth. The Buddhist idea of attachment as the major source of suffering is reconciled with psychology's view of attachment as essential for a healthy psyche.

CHAPTER TWO

The roots of boredom and addiction

In the last chapter, we saw how the hostility and humiliation Brenda experienced in her family, particularly in her teenage years, led to her being highly charged with anxiety, anger, and shame. But the distant and unattuned parenting she received in childhood ensured that the energy remained—however strongly felt—unexpressed and trapped within. Nevertheless, Brenda was also exposed to beauty and soul in nature, old houses, and literature, and she does know what it is to love the world around her. What effect did her energy regulation have on the expression of her loving feelings? Was she again blocked and frustrated in self-expression? And how does expression of charge affect the feelings themselves? Was her love for the non-human world just a compensation for the inadequacies of her human relationships? This chapter will explore the theme of cathexis.

Cathexis and transitional objects

What enables us to charge objects and experiences with excitation and value? Infants in their first or second year bond to an inanimate object which they can control. These transitional objects—as Winnicott called them—are magically charged, and on them depends our early safety;

they are the equivalent of fetish objects for primitive peoples who have not yet had superstition cut through by scientific thinking. Bowlby (1971) regarded transitional objects simply as alternative attachment figures for use when mother was unavailable. Winnicott, on the other hand, proposed that transitional phenomena represent "the infant's transition from a state of being merged with the mother to a state of being in relation to the mother as something outside and separate" (1991, pp. 14–15). To the infant with the illusion of omnipotence, mother is within his control, whereas the older child begins to realise that mother is separate and has her own agenda in life and that she frequently does not do what he wants. The transitional object supports the intra-psychic process involved in the shocking loss of omnipotence. Here, control is regained and softens the anxiety and frustration of mother moving away from primary maternal preoccupation. This object is non-self, but also self—in the sense that it can be infused with any quality the child wants to project onto it; the teddy or the blankie will not refuse the projection. In this way it bridges the gap between the mother-who-was-self and the mother-who-is-becoming-not-self. Winnicott (1991) believed that use of transitional objects was the beginning of symbolism for the child and thereby formed the basis of adult creativity.

Winnicott observed that transitional objects become gradually decathected and meaningless in the face of prolonged separation from mother (1991, p. 15). Bowlby found that the relationship to transitional objects reflected the relationship to the carer (1971, pp. 369–371). Most of the children who had a special cuddly object also enjoyed being cuddled by mother. At the other end of the scale, amongst children who spent their first year in a depriving institution, none of them became attached to a cuddly object. Thus, we expect that the ambivalent child will cling as tightly to teddy as to mother and that the avoidant child will be somewhat depressed and will not cathect a transitional object, since he denies he has any relational needs at all. An ambivalent (or to use the adult term preoccupied-entangled) adult may then go on to endow adult toys like cars or motorbikes with a significance so great that he is inconsolable in their absence.

Brenda, as one might expect, cannot remember having a transitional object, and indeed has no time for inanimate objects unless they have a specific use. She loathes clutter and her greatest happiness is taking bags of *stuff* to the Oxfam shop or the recycling centre. Nothing is exempt— nothing is so charged with emotional significance that it cannot end up in the throw-out box. One of the conflicts in her relationship is that her partner John cathects objects and therefore loves to accumulate, while she needs to discard. She feels impinged upon by objects, but any crude assumption that her mother was impinging turns out to be incorrect; indeed she was the polar opposite. For a time, Brenda couldn't understand her aversion to *things*, but it became clear that the problem was that her mother did not *protect* her against the world's impingements, whether by inanimate objects, social embarrassment or her father's aggression. As a result, Brenda is stressed by sorting—Psyche's first task—and indeed by any unstructured mess. Every morning is fraught as she struggles to decide what to wear, for she regards clothes, not as a form of self-expression, but as camouflage—thus she is choosing from the perspective of another, not from her own view. Brenda's world then is not one of precious objects highly charged with significance, but rather one of unwanted objects threatening stress and chaos and having symbolic significance for others they do not have for herself. Sometimes her defences turn against her—as defences are wont to do. Her rejection of the material world can give her life the quality of a blasted heath. In trying to control over-stimulus, she can be left empty, flat, and despairing; her life stripped of meaning.

Desire and its shadow—boredom

The world humans engage with is framed for us in facts and our subjective responses to them, i.e., stories. Tallis (2008) distinguishes between *appetites*, which may be satisfied, and *desire*, which is intrinsically insatiable. He maintains that it is our stories that "mark the point at which our appetites become desires" (p. 81). We may imagine desiring a Mediterranean holiday, but there will always be a gap between the desire and the capacity of any particular experience to match our expectation. This gap is a function not just of the facts—the place, the weather, our interaction with our fellow tourists—but also of our ability to be present to them. Tallis's view of desire is like that of Lacan—both conceive of it as an absence which is insatiable. The Buddhist solution to man's suffering is to give up on expectation—which is really the same as giving up on desire—and accept what comes. This need not be as bleak as it sounds, if by following a practice of mindfulness we can begin to be more open and present to the world as it is, so that we experience what is much more fully.

Not knowing what you want is, according to Smith (1985, p. 35), the cause of boredom. Accurate mirroring helps us to know *what* we want, and young children often ask for such help quite explicitly: "would I like those chocolates, Mummy?" I want to argue that it is only one cause in a complex phenomenon, as I will outline below. As Kohut has pointed out, the requirement for mirroring extends beyond childhood (Lessem, 2005). Our need to be told who we are, how we are valued and what we want is fundamentally distorted in our instrumentalising and consumerist society, where we are shown what we are good *for*, or what advertisers want us to buy. (We then become the person projected onto us and begin to instrumentalise ourselves.)

We cannot value what we don't cathect and we cannot cathect what we don't value. The character of Kevin, in Lionel Shriver's *We Need to Talk About Kevin*, cannot be punished because he cares about and values nobody and nothing. As a teenager, he goes on to commit mass murder in a completely gratuitous attack, apparently motivated by nothing more than boredom. Kevin symbolises the exhaustion of desire in the capitalist West, particularly the USA. He is an example of the postmodernist schizo-subject outlined by Deleuze and Guattari who were fascinated by transgression and the smashing of rules and boundaries (Elliott, 2002, p. 159). Where there is no desire and no valuing, there is a destructive hatred of the world, an affectless lassitude that edges on depression.

Kevin lives in freedom and comfort with infinite riches accessible to him. In Emma Donoghue's novel *Room*, five-year-old Jack was born and lives as a prisoner, along with his mother, in a locked room twelve foot square in a severely impoverished physical, social, and cultural environment. Yet, Jack proclaims with exuberance that he and his mother have thousands of things to do each morning (2011, p. 10). Kevin feels boredom and contempt for the world; Jack an innocent immersion and love. There are two key differences in the circumstances of these two characters. Jack's mother (or 'Ma') adores him and depends on him; now that she has a purpose in life—her child—she puts sustained energy into stimulating him and dividing the days into maintaining the environment, getting exercise, creating games, and planning their escape. Whatever the task, it becomes another enjoyable game and reassuring ritual for Jack. Kevin's mother, on the other hand, *tries* hard but is ambivalent about motherhood from the beginning, while his father is truth-denying, non-limit-setting, full of phoney camaraderie, and one of the most dishonest, irresponsible, and treacherous (towards the mother) characters I have ever had the pleasure of hating in fiction. The studies of Hartner and colleagues suggest that the more adolescents experience their lives as inauthentic, the more turmoil they feel (cited in Siegel, 2012, p. 354). It is impossible for Kevin to value a world in which the founding people in his life refuse to recognise and mirror who he is. He is not valued, so he cannot care about anyone or anything.

The second difference between Kevin's and Jack's circumstances concerns the material and social surroundings. It is possible that what we think of as a poor environment is as much as most people can cope with. In the "civilised" world, we are constantly battered with impinging stimuli—exemplified by what Tallis calls the "Paraquat of bass beat" (2008, p. 40)—and are forced to defend ourselves against them. (And indeed, when Ma and Jack *do* escape, he finds it very difficult to adapt to the onslaught of the outside world.) In protecting ourselves against the excessive, offensive overwhelm, we may also shut out what is nourishing and adapted to our needs. We are particularly sensitive to impingement if mother was insufficiently attuned to our needs to present the world to us in manageable doses. Good enough object presentation is about letting the baby *find* the object rather than forcing it upon them (Winnicott, 1990). In response to such invasive mothering, we may defend ourselves against stimulus. Our sensitivity towards the world is blunted and we become bored: not because of impoverished surroundings, but because we are over-defended against the environment. Kafka's hunger artist (Kafka, 1978), who starves himself to death because the world didn't provide him with the food he wanted, is a retroflective variant of Kevin. Both reject a world that fails to meet their needs, but Kevin punishes the world, whereas the hunger artist withdraws from it and slowly self-immolates.

Mihaly Csikszentmihalyi has studied the experience of creatively losing oneself in an activity, which he calls "flow". He suggests that flow involves movement between the boredom of rigidity and order and the anxiety of randomness and chaos (Siegel, 2012, p. 363). This view of boredom implies that it is a defence against its opposite extreme of anxiety. This is probably the most fundamental cause of boredom and therefore suggests a way out of it—by learning to tolerate moderate levels of anxiety rather than automatically flinching away from it. In Brenda's case, her anxiety derived from the stress of a contemptuous and bullying father and the ever-present danger of annihilating humiliation.

Boredom represents a lack of imagination: "as things become dulled and inauthentic, they become conceptualised rather than experienced" (McGilchrist, 1990, p. 154). The right brain, which is stimulated by the fresh or the new, is under-engaged, and the left hemisphere, which is triggered by the practice of familiar skills or information, is over-used (ibid., p. 40). The attention of the left brain is sticky and inflexible (pp. 45, 87): it is Hamlet's excessive use of his analytic left hemisphere that led him to experience his life as being "weary, stale, flat, and unprofitable". Kavanagh knew we had to retrieve the child's eye to find this fresh perspective in "the newness that was in every stale thing/ When we looked at it as children" ("Advent", 1996).

Boredom can result from seeing the world through eyes dulled by habit as well as through the irrational belief that nothing will ever change. Since it is the consequence of a failure of imagination, it can be cured by harnessing the imagination. Plutarch—perhaps one of the first cognitive behavioural therapists—conjured up cognitive tricks to cope with all sorts of emotional ills from bereavement to depression (Bakewell, 2010, p. 111). In the case of feeling tired of everything, you might imagine losing the person, place, or uneventful time that bores you; in the face of loss, you realise the value of what you have. Alternatively, many writers and philosophers de-familiarise the familiar by seeing things from the perspective of another (Bakewell, 2010, p. 182) such as an animal or Martian, a Stone-Age warrior or a Neanderthal. When Brenda tried this trick, she imagined Amazonian tribesmen coming to visit her childhood home. But, instead of the Indians bringing a fresh perspective, they themselves became coated in boredom: in her imagination, her family treated them with the same stifling propriety, denial, and fear that was meted out to all visitors. It is crucial to tailor the fantasy to the exact thing that needs to be challenged. In Brenda's case, only a clown who could mock the inane and petty pretensions would combat the patriarchal rigidity and anxiety hardening the lungs of her family. Here, a fresh view alone is not sufficient; rather, for her situation, a sharply critical deconstruction is needed.

It seems that boredom can result from a breakdown in a variety of processes including: being helped to know what we want through accurate mirroring; the capacity to value through being valued; being exposed to the optimum level of stimulus along with the related capacity to be open to experience. Too much stimulation or chaos leads to defensive shutting down; too little of the new leads to habitual left-brain sticky thinking and a loss of imagination. We can avoid sinking into the slough of boredom if we know ourselves, value the world, and are fully open to deep experiencing. These depend on our early object relations, including adequate experiences of mirroring, object presenting, and holding (Winnicott, 1990). The importance of the first two are discussed above, while the topic of holding was introduced in Chapter One and is further examined below.

Holding and boredom

We saw in the last chapter how energy management is a function of both charge and boundedness. Thus, it is not surprising that boredom results from an absence of *containment* as well as cathexis. An interest, like a lit bonfire, flickers and dies unless given sufficient oxygen to feed the flames and, conversely, unless protected against excessive extinguishing winds: it needs shelter for the charge to build beyond a threshold where the fire has "caught". This shelter is the screen or wall which contains. Sit in a void and think about your interests: chances are they will flicker and die. Contain them with a deadline backed up with a convincing motivation and they may take off. This is containment by time and social pressure, but you can contain yourself in other ways. You can meditate with CDs, where the voice holds you like a parent figure. You can turn the individual pursuit into a group one where it is the group pressures that hold. *Intend* to put shape on flickers and the boredom ceases. Shape into a story or picture, focus on the complex mix of thoughts, feelings, and the technology of getting these into words, a picture, a piece of music, a garden, a cake, some DIY, a community group, a book club, or any group that surrounds you with people on a similar quest.

But, this crushes the original idea; it is left with no oxygen. The dream feels like it can be consummated only with the equivalent of Erica Jong's "zipless fuck" (*Fear of Flying*, 1973). By the time you have dealt with the other person, their needs, beliefs, values, personality, the other people in their heads, their words or clothes or buttons or zips or transport to a private place, your desire will have well and truly evaporated, leaving a cold miasma of boredom behind. This metaphor helps us to get behind the issue of boredom. Getting past the zipless fuck problem is not about delaying gratification by earning it with some deferral first. A lifetime of this makes the deferral its own reward and the individual incapable of enjoying sex, or anything else. As Langston Hughes ("Dream Deferred", 1994) asks: "What happens to a dream deferred?/Does it dry up/Like a raisin in the sun?" No, deferral is not the answer for the bored and depressed. They are probably bored and depressed because they have waited too long for their needs to be met and they have despaired that they ever will come home to themselves. No, there is something here about enjoying the moment, taking in all aspects of the zip and the body behind it. Don't be in such a hurry to get to the fucking end. Be in the moment, be present. Live in the present, not the future. Relish the brush strokes on the canvas. Experience the easy enjoyment of the detail—but while also holding the bigger picture of what you are trying to achieve. The achievement may be internal or external, an inner state or an outer goal, some more immediate than others: the sexual consummation, the picture painted, the exam passed, the group formed, the political action carried through. Whatever the goal, reaching it involves a contradiction that is inherent in meditation. We must allow what comes, while at the same time holding an intention to move towards a particular outcome (e.g., to a place of self-forgiveness or loving kindness).

While empathic mirroring helps us know *what* we want, the ability to *hold* and *maintain* interest rests on containment, and the capacity for that containment is also laid down in the early relationship between mother and infant. Good enough holding leads to integration of the infant self, to "going-on-being": what Stern later referred to as a line of continuity (Holmes, p. 139). The infant is then able to cope with temporary separations from mother, who empathically understands what degree of object constancy the child has attained. An attuned mother facilitates the illusion of omnipotence in the child so that he develops basic trust that the world will meet his needs. The sensitively held child is able to relax, free of annihilating impingements. "Relaxation for an infant means not feeling a need to integrate, the mother's ego-supportive function being taken for granted" (Winnicott, 1990, p. 61). Boredom is the beginning of the sense of annihilation at not-being-held: you lose a sense of who you are and what you want. You lose energy, interest, and orientation and fall into a featureless void. Holding provides not just secure attachment but the feeling of existing. When there is nowhere to attach my libido, I cease to feel I exist. The reason why music, literature, or drama can safeguard us from boredom and the void it intimates is that we surrender ourselves into the hands of the holding other. Thus, we are able to disengage the will and are fully and wholeheartedly present to experience.

Those who have not internalised a mother's holding have a constant addictive need for the holding provided by others. However, this is combined with distrust and anxiety about others, which leaves the individual in a constant state of stress, alternating between the dread of the void and the fear of impingement. One longer-term consequence of this non-holding is depression.

Boredom and relating to the frustrating object

The absence of secure attachment does not necessarily mean that the parents are not loved by the child. Fairbairn, in a theory that combines concepts from both Freud (repression) and Klein (splitting), constructed a detailed model for how we manage early neglect or abuse psychodynamically. We repress, not just our own badness but also the badness of the other. We relate consciously to the world with a central ego (the self as we like to believe we are) connecting to the ideal object (others the way we would like them to be). Consigned to the unconscious are two further aspects of the ego: the anti-libidinal ego bound to the rejecting object and the libidinal (needy) ego bonded to the exciting object. The needy libidinal ego is further rejected and disowned by the angry anti-libidinal ego. As Gomez says (1997, p. 65): "By taking the burden of badness within, we can continue to see the needed external person as good enough, and can therefore continue trusting them and relating to them." Fairbairn suggests that we consolidate the ideal object by internalising good experiences.

What happens to our available libido in that moment when the charged object is less than ideal, when we have not been heard or mirrored and we experience disappointment, frustration, or rejection? Initially, we may react with angry protest, but later we may defend ourselves against the pain and confusion by withdrawing our energy. We then become caught in the deadening swamp of boredom, feeling lacking and agitated. Libido is withdrawn to protect it against the insult of not being met, just as we may lose sexual interest in the absence of response from the other. Frustration leads to withdrawal (like the loss of an erection) in the face of an indifferent or hostile response. Arousal needs to be met to be maintained. But we are not yet in the state of long-term deadness that is one kind of depression. We still have the chance to recover, to have some reparative contact with the other. We can consign this experience to the bin managed by the anti-libidinal ego and go back to semi-hopeful business as usual with the idealised object.

Boredom and depression

If, however, we reach a threshold where we no longer experience any hope, we give up attempting to make contact with the world and fall into a state of depression. This might be accompanied by some awareness of our idealisation and repressed feelings, and we may discover our inner insecurity, conflict, and persecution. Our ideals have been punctured and our inner world seems false, grim, and without resource.

There are many kinds of psychopathology referred to by the common term "depression". These include: excessive unresolved grief, mixed anxiety and depression disorder, manic depression, existential despair (melancholia), and lack of affect. Some of these conditions are associated with an excess of affect (such as grief or anxiety) and others with an absence of affect. They have different psychogenic aetiologies and a great variety of theories explaining them, from Freud's model of depression as repressed anger to theories focusing on the central role of relationships, existential meaning or maladaptive cognitive structures in generating depression (Coyne, 1985; Leader, 2009; Yalom, 1980).

A client Tom talks about the summer holidays when he was a student. He did nothing and saw nobody; he was in a state of overwhelming, bored inertia without impulse or charge, but otherwise he lacked affect. This is where boredom veers into a longer term affectless depression. He can now recognise the mixture of repressed feelings that underlie the stasis: helplessness at the loss of containment, the anxiety about experiencing anything new, and the lack of expectation that the world would meet him. All are associated with insecure attachment. He couldn't leave what had never been provided: a secure base. The lack of attunement to his needs that he unconsciously expected to encounter in the world was the very thing that had created the insecurity in the first place. (This might be partly attributed to his parents' experience of the Second World War and then communism in Eastern Europe, followed by emigration when Tom was three.) The holding his parents hadn't provided was ordinarily supplied by the external routine of college, but in the holidays there was no inner structure ready to take the place of the external scaffolding. This kind of depression is a sort of long-term boredom, where you have lost the hope to try again with the world: it's scary out there; you believe the world will not meet your needs; and you can't contain any weak positive charge of curiosity or face-saving pride.

This kind of listless but restless and dissatisfied torpor was called accidie by early Christian ascetics who regarded it as a sin "that lays waste at noonday" (quoted in Maitland, 2008, p. 112). This demon was to be fought through discipline and hard work. Maitland names accidie as one of the negative effects of prolonged silence and she attributes it to the shadow side of "givenness" that is one of the gifts of silence. "If everything is a gift from outside one's own ego, then one may well experience an unnerving sense of passivity—that no action or decision is worth taking for oneself" (ibid., p. 111). In other cases, like Tom's, the passivity arises out of a more negative powerlessness, where one's own communications with the world have not been received or mirrored. You thus enter a state of what Seligman called "learned helplessness" (Coyne, 1985). The depression of indifference or apathy is associated with right-hemisphere damage to the brain, whereas anxious disturbed depression correlates with left-brain lesions (McGilchrist, 2009, p. 64). The reason for this will become clear in Chapter Three when we look at the different functional characteristics of the two hemispheres.

When Brenda is asked to slow down, a wave of boredom washes over her, like the breath of nausea. She knows intellectually that it is she and not the world that is boring her. This boredom is really despair at the external blocking of her energy (e.g., being asked to wait), which is already so blocked from within. She craves stimuli and new ideas, but doesn't want the bother of chewing over them properly and integrating them into a structured form. She is in thrall to addiction, where the end product is the only reward and the process is simply a series of obstacles between her and the end. She is trying to run faster than the pain that is pursuing her—the pain of not being good enough. She has defended herself against the pain of not being loved and so has to fight her own armouring in every encounter with the world. To use Smith's metaphor (Chapter One), she is permanently in low gear and has to compensate by jamming down the accelerator to get any movement at all. She is dimly aware that to be present in the moment and to be mindful allows the possibility of nourishment—but, equally, of pain.

The contact–withdrawal cycle and addiction

The contact–withdrawal cycle (Perls, Hefferline, & Goodman, 1972; Smith, 1985) is one of expansion and contraction, mediated respectively by the sympathetic and parasympathetic branches of the autonomic nervous system. When a need or a want arises, we become physiologically mobilised into a state of arousal that is experienced subjectively as an emotion. The emotion calls for action in the body, which in turn leads to interaction with the environment and, finally, satisfaction of the need. We then retreat into relaxed withdrawal and contraction. As long as the contact–withdrawal cycles emerge and recede smoothly, we are in a state of psychobiological health and, in principle, we can move towards self-actualisation. However, the environment may lack some things we need (or want), or we may block ourselves in the rhythmic flow of the cycle. The latter self-interruption can occur at any stage of the cycle: (1) not knowing what you want; (2) being unaware of your physiological arousal; (3) not fully realising exactly what you are feeling (you may label excitation as tension, for example); (4) blocking movement from the awareness half of the contact episode to the expression half; (5) not allowing the action to become an interaction with the target; (6) not allowing satisfaction; (7) satisfaction turning to disgust if contact is not withdrawn in time.

Psychopathology can be envisaged as an interruption in the flow of the contact–withdrawal cycle at any of the stages outlined. In our over-stimulating, impinging, noisy, overcrowded urban world, we are in a crisis of receptivity that makes it difficult to start, deepen, or complete the contact–withdrawal cycle. We can avoid full satisfaction of impulses and completely block or partially inhibit the flow by (a) quieting our arousal through insufficient breathing; (b) clouding our awareness; (c) not acting mediated by body armouring; and (d) not interacting by retroflecting the action—i.e., doing to yourself what you would like to do to another or another to do to you. Perls considered self-control, self-hate, and self-love (narcissism) to be the three most important retroflections (Smith, 1985, p. 41). As Reich noted, the inhibition of a primary impulse produces a secondary impulse and anxiety (ibid., p. 45), which ultimately leads to addiction. In summary then, failure to identify or satisfy our needs leads to frustration in its many guises: boredom, depression, addiction, disembodiment, shame, and narcissism; some of the most prevalent psychological dysfunctions in the Western world.

Not meeting our needs or desires generates boredom in the short term or low-affect depression in the long term as argued above. Even when meeting our desire, the satisfaction of sensory experiences declines because "the neural response to a stimulus fades when the stimulus is sustained or repeated" (Tallis, 2008, p. 41). Rather than heeding the way the sense of novelty is blunted, we are often driven to consume more and more food, alcohol, or drugs to try to recapture that first moment of intensity, or indeed to pursue the anticipated experience that eluded us even in the first mouthful: we are now moving into the realm of addiction.

Furthermore, when a failed primary impulse is replaced by a secondary alternative, the alternative can never meet the real need, and therefore inevitably becomes addictive. No amount of alcohol, shopping or success at work can compensate for a need to be loved or a need for unboundaried connection with the cosmos, or the desire to regress to the oceanic bliss of the baby at the breast in a state of union with mother. One central early object relations need is that for holding or containment. We create our own containers in later life in timetables and self-imposed discipline. We cathect surrogate objects when the real solution—that is the containing (m)other—is not available. In the past, parents' containment in childhood was supplemented and replaced by society's containment: its beliefs, values, conventions, rules, expectations, rhythms and cycles, religious rituals, demands, and prohibitions. We are now living in a time of unparalleled freedom and the price of that freedom is taking on the burden of self-holding: this is why Sartre (1948, p. 34) could write: "Man is *condemned* to be free" (my italics). We have become the victims of our culture's "success" and excess. "Throughout history, crushing necessity has been the usual problem, but the contemporary self is being driven mad by infinite possibility" (Foley, 2011, p. 46).

Containing ourselves in the face of infinite possibility demands a lot of energy, and our belief in the surrogate (for the holding other) is shaky: it is hard to knuckle down to a self-imposed timetable or the latest invented project. Sometimes we want a holiday from self-holding and the id goes on a spree. We have a treat: a cream cake or a pint or any self-soothing substitute. We are really driven by the need just to *be* and to rest from the exhausting labour of self-holding. Winnicott (1990) claims that our ability to enjoy solitude as adults originates in our experience of being alone in the presence of the mother in a state of unimpinging, impulse-free peace and silence. Guntrip (1992, p. 254) maintains:

> The experience of doing in the absence of a secure sense of being degenerates into a meaningless succession of mere activities (as in

the obsessional's meaningless repetition of the same thought, word
or act), not performed for their own proper purpose but as a futile
effort to "keep oneself in being", to manufacture a sense of "being"
one does not possess.

Just like Beckett's Molloy who sequentially sucks his sixteen stones, but
obsessively redistributes them between his four pockets so that he can
be certain that he does not pick the same stone as the last time when
he next feels the desire to suck (Beckett, 1979, p. 64). Obsessive activity is just one way of expressing addiction. Whatever form of addiction chooses us, we cathect the substitute holding when the real is not
available. But the surrogate container is a shoddy, leaking version of
the real thing. Constant feeding is required to attempt to fill the container but because it continues to leak, there is never true satisfaction.
Addiction is not just about holding, but—as a focusing of libido—also
about meaning. Through his obsessively repeated sequence, Molloy is
making a rudimentary attempt to create not just order, but—via the act
of willed mastery over randomness—meaning.

   Brian Dillon regards addiction as "a way of structuring time" (2005,
p. 173). I live this out in a particularly literal way: I find a project to
obsess me, in which the driver is public disgrace if I don't apply myself.
Thus, I put weeks of work into preparing public lectures which hold
and contain me so long as they last, and then I lose all interest and
charge. Like Schopenhauer in his perpetual oscillation between suffering and boredom, we long for the exams to be over, but fall into
the pit of anticlimax once they are. Tallis calls it "a kind of toothless
hunger—a hunger for hunger—in which it is life, rather than the stomach, that feels empty" (2008, p. 61). Pascal noticed how much time,
energy, and passion we give to our diversions, hunting being the sport
of choice for his reflections (the equivalent of soccer today). The chase
was, for Pascal, not the means to an end but the end itself. However, it
is crucial that the participants are not aware of this or else the activity
becomes an empty charade—as football is for me or as hunting was for
Oscar Wilde: "the unspeakable in pursuit of the inedible". It doesn't
matter that Victorian explorers gave over their lives and, in some cases,
ended them in great suffering, to locate the source of the Nile—only to
discover that it was roughly where Ptolemy had placed it! Without our
divertissements, we would have no civilisation, no culture, no exploration. Perhaps that is the meaning of the ending of Camus' version of the

myth of Sisyphus: "Each atom of that stone, each mineral flake of that night-filled mountain, in itself forms a world. *The struggle itself* towards the heights is enough to fill a man's heart. One must imagine Sisyphus happy" (1975, p. 111; my italics).

Tallis, in referring to the ways in which our habits shape the limits of our freedom, notes that the addict is permanently obsessed with the next fix, so that his world "may be almost as shrunken as that of someone who is starving" (2008, p. 56). On the other hand, "the cultivation of habits that support long-term goals that we ourselves desire 'wholeheartedly' or 'wholeselvedly' is one way in which we provide favourable conditions for the exercise of our freedom" (ibid., p. 56). Diets or addiction programmes maintain the obsession with the prohibited substance. Getting in touch with the real need and creating a way of either meeting the need or transforming it into a larger project is the only way to move beyond addiction. The novels of Anita Brookner all seem, to me, to circle round the pain and emptiness of not belonging. The author doesn't resolve the problem for her protagonists, but she has redemptively transformed the need into *form*: works of art that help the reader cope with their own pain of non-belonging. The form mediates the dialogue between writer and reader. As ordered experience, fictional stories provide *mirroring* (of emotional content), *holding* (in the experience of reading the novel), and *meaning* (in making contact with characters and author and knowing you are not alone in your pain).

It is partly our lack of societal holding in the West, the shadow side of our freedom, that has led to such a chronic sense of dis-ease; we drown, instead, in addiction, depression, shame, and narcissism. When you consider the connection of these individual dysfunctions to corporate greed and exploitation, destructive competitiveness, crime, cultural collapse and the despoiling of the natural environment, it becomes urgent to try to heal the problem. What we unconsciously long for, I would argue, is embodiment, beauty, expansion, and moments of impulse-free beingness.

Boredom and contact

Reflecting on the tedium of his childhood in his anti-memoir, Brian Dillon grasps that: "this boredom has to do with the intolerable weight of things" (2005, p. 205). He had a sense that at the heart of all the spiritual lessons of the church was "just the meaningless persistence of matter".

Brenda was a similarly puncturing child, stripping away the meanings that adults claimed to attach to their routines and rituals, intuitively sensing the hollowness of their assertions. She was bored beyond breath, forever whining to her mother and receiving utterly ineffectual "solutions". In thrall to her chore-addiction, her mother never engaged with her to help her find the real problem. Such *contact* would itself have been the solution and saved Brenda years of searching for existential meaning—for the point of existence—that all along really resided in human relationship. Hegel asserted that the root of all desires was the longing to be acknowledged by the other—we are *because* the other sees us (Tallis, 2008, p. 87). Sartre too grasped that we are constituted by the gaze of the other: we are *how* the other sees us. Winnicott (1990, 1991) has shown how faulty mirroring in childhood leads to the child developing a false self, one who matches the *parent's* expectations, not his own core being. Hegel, Sartre, and Winnicott are, in their various ways, describing the constituting of the self. I would go a step further in regard to Brenda and her mother and say that human relatedness doesn't just confirm the self but confers spiritual fulfilment on the self. When I am truly met by the other, which I experience as being loved by the other, this recognition provides meaning in my world.

Cathexis of the natural world

Spare clarity and diffuse mystery are counterpointed in "The Moon and the Yew Tree", one of Sylvia Plath's later poems (Plath, 1965). We are transported into the moonlit graveyard, the yew trees stark amongst the "fumey, spirituous mists", the author as God padding barefoot and silent through the wet grasses—I imagine her like the figure of Christ carrying a lantern in Holman Hunt's painting *The Light of the World*. The reader holds their breath to protect the sanctity of the stillness and silence. The figures of the mind are black trees silhouetted against a moon-blue cosmic space. The mind is clear and cold in a bald and wild world; there is no tenderness, however longed for. There is the mind that writes this poem, but there is no answering voice. The poet has "fallen a long way". She is alone in planetary space, outside both the mess and the compassion and potential fulfilment of human relations. The message is stark, cold—and beautiful, the beauty of the extra-human, the extramundane. Not long afterwards, Plath took her own life.

of the collective unconscious as an evolutionary theory. Just as all life forms from bacteria through plants, animals, and humans share common cell structures, genes, and biochemical pathways, it is reasonable to assume that we share archetypes, not just with our human ancestors, but also our evolutionary antecedents. Roszak hints that it is through these shared archetypes that we experience ourselves as part of nature. Our urbanisation and education have divorced us from this expanded sense of identity, and this "estrangement from Gaia" leaves an underlying neurosis (Roszak, 1993, p. 304).

Anita Barrows and other ecopsychologists have pointed out the reductionism and anthropocentrism of psychology. A key process in infant development is viewed as the separation of child away from mother to form an independent and isolated ego. Barrows (1995) proposes a developmental theory that encompasses more than a single aspect of growth. She suggests a shift in emphasis, so that instead of seeing the toddler as simply separating from mother, we give equal weight to what he is moving towards: exploration of the world. She is critical of Frances Tustin who sees the awareness of body separateness as a tragedy, whereas Barrows views this sense of separateness as an illusion. Rather, what we move towards is a widened sense of oneness. She says that psychoanalytic theory fails to do justice to the reality of the broadening of our identification when, with its pathologising of merger, "it envisions health as a narrowing and drawing-in of the experiences constituting the self". She posits that a new ecologically based developmental theory will take account of *both* of two opposing tendencies: the movement towards shape/coherence and the tendency to yield/dissolve. Allowing ourselves such merger is what will heal our loneliness, boredom, and addiction. This is what will give our lives meaning and make it impossible for us to continue to view the world as separate and objectified, ours to use and abuse. If we do not heal this split, neither human beings nor the earth can thrive or, arguably, survive.

Contact vs. merger

I have suggested in the last two sections that true contact with a loved one or merger with nature can cure us of many of the ills of Western living. But what is the difference between contact and merger, and why do I recommend one for human relations and the other as an expression of our biophilia? Contact can be defined as a boundaried interaction between individuals. Fusion or merger is a state that describes the mother in primary maternal preoccupation with her young baby or two people at the in-love stage of their relationship. Richard Wagner described this beautifully in a letter to his lover: "When I look into your eyes there is nothing more to say … It is there that the distinction between the object and the subject ceases. There all is one and all at one, profound, infinite harmony! Oh, there is peace, and in that peace perfect realization of life!" (quoted in Sabor, 1989, p. 114). Such confluence is all very well as a transient state when you are in love, but would be a profoundly regressive and infantile way of living permanently as an adult. We wouldn't care about anybody or anything else so long as we were in this state of bliss. We would be unable to see others or distinguish ourselves from them or meet anybody's needs. We would expect the other to never behave in a way that implies that we are different. Indeed, psychoanalysis and Gestalt therapy take a very dim view of regressive merger with the other into what Freud called oceanic bliss.

But it is a lonely, bleak, and alienated existence when we maintain rigid boundaries against the world all the time, and in this stance we are likely to treat others—and the natural world—with cold detachment at best or objectified cruelty at worst. Perls, Hefferline, and Goodman (1972) believed that true contact (across boundaries) was sufficient satisfaction, but Perls' kind of contact was strongly ego-based, of a tough, sparring variety. I believe, like Anita Barrows, that sometimes we do need to enter a state of merger: this is the only place where we truly rest and find meaning—it is where we go in love, sex, or sleep to find restoration. Merger is only a problem when it is imposed by another or when we are unable to reinstate boundaries: "Losing boundaries needs to be voluntary, rather than being overwhelmed, flooded, seduced" (Totton, 2005, p. 173).

In many spiritual traditions and in transpersonal psychotherapy, meditation and prayer are aimed at a state of mystical experience where we have a no-boundary union with God. This is particularly true of the non-dual Eastern traditions. By contrast, the Judeo-Christian Western philosophy espouses a *relationship* with God. The transpersonal theorist Michael Washburn has devised a developmental pathway that implicitly recognises the place of merger, not only in infancy, but in old age as well. In childhood, the ego gradually emerges from what he calls the "dynamic ground" (roughly equivalent to Jung's collective unconscious), and after midlife it begins to return to this place as it de-cathects the world. Cortright (1997) has identified two schools of transpersonal development. Ken Wilber's scheme, following Eastern thought, rests on a belief in continuous upward development where we ultimately dissolve self into identity with Buddha-nature. In drawing attention to what he calls the "pre/trans" fallacy in psychology, Wilber contrasts the prepersonal states of infants and psychotics with the only superficially similar transpersonal states of realised beings. The former haven't yet developed the ego, whereas the latter have transcended it—the transpersonal individual is "self-reflexive but not ego bound" (p. 65). By contrast, Washburn following in Jung's Western tradition claims that spiritual development entails "regression in the service of transcendence" (quoted p. 85). The ego returns to its early origins in the unconscious in order to integrate the two. Washburn believes that transcendence does not eliminate the self, but transforms it into a higher unity with its source in the dynamic ground.

If Washburn is right—and my own experience suggests to me that he is—then we don't need to worry about episodes of regression whether to childhood states of merger with nature (participative consciousness) or to painful replays of childhood psychodynamics. We will emerge again, but with a freshly nourished and enlightened perspective on what matters in life. Indeed, ecopsychotherapy should be regarded as a branch of transpersonal therapy and can assist clients with temporary melting of boundaries against the natural world. These are the most profound and precious states we can access. If we are fortunate enough to have experienced such moments, they are times we will never forget, and we may go through life ever after trying to recapture or recreate them. It is often suggested that this is the real drive behind addictions to mind-altering drugs and alcohol. Addiction is really a spiritual quest which has been derailed. It is our distrust and blocking of such moments of union that drives despairing people into the arms of alcohol and drugs. Of course there are some people who have never differentiated and separated away from the other, who have not yet developed a boundaried ego; they already experience too much merger with the world and their path involves putting more shape on the self. But in our urban, industrialised societies most people—and certainly the avoidantly attached—veer far too much in the direction of separation and have almost no experience of dissolving their boundaries. For this majority, dissolution of boundaries is a necessary counterbalance to an excessively isolated and armoured ego and the frustration, emptiness, and alienation this generates.

Summary

One of Brenda's self-frustrating patterns is her tendency to react with boredom to situations others find stimulating or interesting. What is it that governs our ability to charge objects and experiences with value and excitement? We see how the young child cathects transitional objects as a substitute for the temporary loss of mother's attention. The nature of desire and its shadow, boredom, is teased out with the help of philosophy, fiction, neuroscience, body psychotherapy, and Gestalt therapy. We learn that it is the completion of a contact–withdrawal cycle—a gestalt—that generates satisfaction. Incomplete gestalts lead to boredom or addiction, or in the long term to a kind of depression. Developing the capacity for satisfaction depends on the capacity of a child's early object relations to provide mirroring (knowing what we want), object presentation (exposure to an optimal level of stimulus) and the holding or containing of our response to stimulus. The solution to both boredom and addiction is *contact*. This may involve relationship with other people, but ecopsychology argues that contact with the natural world also plays an important role in our identity and well-being. For Brenda who is avoidant and/or ambivalent about human relationships, nature occupies a central place in her heart and spirit.

CHAPTER THREE

Attention and the soul: the scientist versus the poet

Who can calculate the orbit of his own soul?

—Oscar Wilde, 1905, *De Profundis*

If you bring forth what is within you, what you bring forth will save you. If you do not bring forth what is within you, what you do not bring forth will destroy you.

—The Gospel according to Thomas

It is creative apperception more than anything else that makes the individual feel that life is worth living.

—Winnicott, 1991, p. 65

Once she was a child and never imagined that the magic could end. But, the science project began aged fifteen as a bull-like effort of will, forcing herself to engage with the rebarbative, abstract, impersonal detail of chemistry, physics, and maths. Brenda was slapping herself awake out of the misty gaze of childhood, the romantic dreamer in a treetop, in ecstatic merger with the natural environment.

47

The struggle to make herself eat the repellent diet of science textbooks and technical manuals gradually became easier. Eventually she could read research papers with something approaching ease and pleasure. She was like a horse that had finally been broken in. Brenda had some-how limped into adulthood and independence, she had a modicum of self-respect, a good-enough career, and existential questions were kept in abeyance with busy-ness and her determined climbing of the career ladder. The strategist had triumphed, but to what end? Two parts of her struggled: one, the computer scientist was practical, logical, dis-ciplined, focused, and faced the truth, however hard. The other, the dreamer, held on to childhood enchantment and sought envelopment by nature, literature, and drama. This side was feeling, romantic and mystical and understood by merger, identification, and empathy. The scientist had no desire to kill off the mystical dreamer, but it knew that to live an independent life, the dreamer would have to be limited to a spare time luxury. Thus, Brenda walked with a foot on each path: on the outside she looked rational, ambitious, and reliable, but the hidden child mystic was always there demanding a "life".

Decades later, Brenda believed that returning to her first love, read-ing novels, might provide a more meaningful and nourishing way of life. She left her high-paying job in IT, did a second degree in English literature and, eventually, moved into teaching contemporary fiction to adults in night classes. This turned out to be, like the proverbial curate's egg, good in parts. But the pay was bad, the environment ugly, the bureaucracy unending, and there was pressure from her relentlessly trendy boss to coldly deconstruct the novels that were so precious to her. As a result, she still found herself pervaded by unnourished and cerebral states of being, and even the literature itself now became con-taminated by its new associations and context. The imagination, feeling, and the spirit were once again swept into second place in her life and work. Once again, she was frustrated—this time in her quest for soul.

Science has two sides: the project of enlightenment and its shadow, disenchantment. I want to examine the scientist and poet-mystic, not as professional types, but as complementary archetypes. Both are seek-ers; both explore the world around them, the scientist with an objec-tive and generalising eye, the poet with a subjective and specific voice. The scientist uses his curiosity to understand, whereas the poet trans-forms the world through his imagination. I want to focus in particular on the scientist or other scholar who has burned out with over-focus, overanalysis, excessive attention to the outside world at the expense of his feelings, his inner world and a particular kind of poetic imagination. This is the dominant archetype of our times and you do not need to be a professional scientist to have an overtrained left brain and a right brain starved of stimulation.

The epigraph from Thomas's gospel warns that "what you do not bring forth will destroy you". In what way is the science-minded person ignoring his own needs; what shadow or inferior function has he not brought forth? I suggest that it is the capacity to live with disorder, uncertainty, and partial sight: we need to relearn how to "see through a glass darkly" (1 Corinthians 13:11–12). Soul may be discovered when we view the world in a sepia photograph or through its reflection in an antique mirror. It's not so much that there is more room for imagination as the sensation of being held in a place of shadows where discovery does not have to be satisfied. There is no relentless striving either towards understanding or towards creating a product of the imagination. It is enough that it is and I am. Thomas Moore warns of the danger of living in a society "devoted to light" (1992, p. 137) and of believing that we have everything figured out: "Often our personal philosophies and our values seem to be all too neatly wrapped, leaving little room for mystery. Depression comes along then and opens up a hole" (1992, p. 143). "Mystery provides meaning", says Mark Vernon, because "the meaning human understanding can provide is inevitably limited" (2008, p. 79). Here I want to explore attention and soulful living. To what do we attend; from where within us does that attention spring; what is the quality of our attention and what do we do with it? First of all, let us examine the desire that lies behind scholarly exploration: what we might term curiosity or seeking.

Curiosity

Jaak Panksepp (2006) has argued that there are at least seven basic emotional systems which are situated in the same brain regions in all mammals. By stimulating specific regions of the brain, he can elicit behaviours that indicate feelings of fear, rage, lust, care (attachment), panic, playfulness, and seeking. While psychotherapy has paid great attention to six of these systems, the last, that of seeking, is not generally recognised as an emotion or as of particular interest to therapy. Panksepp emphasises that seeking is not the same as the behaviourist concept of reinforcement, but refers to animals' love of self-activation, which reveals a positive expectation that the world contains much to meet our interest and satisfy our desires. It is thought to underpin foraging behaviour as well as safety-seeking in animals and libidinous, goal-directed behaviours in humans. It interacts with higher cognitive functions and helps maintain fluidity in learning and other behaviours. It is the drive behind all forms of learning and exploration.

A neurobiologically based theory names novelty-seeking as one of the four components of personality, alongside harm avoidance, reward dependence, and persistence. A novelty-seeking gene has been identified which codes for a dopamine receptor and accounts for about four per cent of the variance in novelty seeking. One allele of this gene is associated with impulsive, excitable, exploratory behaviour, and it has been hypothesised that these individuals are dopamine deficient and seek novelty to increase release of this neurotransmitter (Plomin, DeFries, McClearn, & McGuffin, 2008, pp. 260–261).

Thus, both genetics and neurobiology reveal that curiosity is innate and linked with positive excitement about the world around us. But, here is our dilemma: we are curious beings, we are drawn to mystery; but in exploring the mystery we can all too easily use it up and destroy it, leaving ourselves bereft. We then become like Beckett's tramps, trapped in the hell of a closed circle of obsessive, repetitive thinking in a dead world. This, it turns out, is a characteristic of the left hemisphere of the brain, what Iain McGilchrist (2009, pp. 45, 87) calls the "stickiness" of its attention. Most biological systems are maintained in a homeostatic state through negative feedback loops which self-correct like a thermostat. However, the left hemisphere tends towards positive feedback and can become stuck in inflexible obsessive, or addictive, patterns. The problem arises when we bring the wrong kind of attention to mystery: too much of the will-driven alienated, atomistic, analytic left brain thinking, not enough of the holistic, embodied, and emotionally-suffused right brain variety. The right brain is present to life as it is lived whereas the left re-presents experience in abstract, categorised, dead fragments. Reiterated *re-presentation* by the left brain empties life of meaning, whereas ever deeper engagement through holistic receptiveness and affect-laden exploration, seeing the familiar in unfamiliar ways via the right hemisphere, enriches our experience (ibid., p. 173).

The barriers to attention

One reason for this left-brain dominance lies in what is valued and therefore encouraged or discouraged in our society. This impacts on what and how we may think, imagine, and speak: what is *not* spoken then reinforces the empty space uninhabited by the unmirrored. This is what happens in a world that has become blind, or that tramples and scoffs, or is contemptuous and impatient with what it resents because it has denied such things for itself. We then block our own paths to sensitivity, openness, imagination, soul, and spirit. The paths to the centre that we most need to keep open are the very ones we close off, like a war-time invasion defence scheme where the roads from the vulnerable coastline to the capital and other large cities in the interior are blocked. The most necessary routes are also the paths where we are vulnerable. However, we have to realise that, for most of us, we are still sheltering from a childhood bombardment that is in the past and we are living mean and diminished lives as a result, like the apocryphal Japanese soldiers who remained at their posts on tiny islands in the South Pacific for decades, not realising that World War Two was long over.

Winnicott (1991, p. 65) views creative living as an approach to external reality that is the opposite of compliance. Part of living creatively requires having a vision of other possibilities. When we give up on that—as in totalitarian regimes out of fear, or in monocultures such as late capitalism, because of brainwashing—we no longer view our lives creatively. This has catastrophic consequences for the project of self-creation for "it is only in being creative that the individual discovers the self" (ibid., p. 54).

Imagination and re-enchantment

How can we open up the roads to the interior and begin to explore or build on them—indeed which do we need to do? Is the self there ready and waiting to be explored, as Winnicott (1990) implies, or is the interior a wasteland that needs sensitive gardening to create a nourishing space? Do we find or create the self? John O'Donohue (2003, p. 153) says that creativity "endeavours to bring some of our hidden life to expression in order that we might come to see who we are". Our moment-by-moment being emerges from our contact with the environment. The inner space must be gardened, but it is not something we do alone;

it emerges from our interaction with the world of nature or of other people or of art or beauty in any form. Thus, there is something within to be found, but this can only develop through the tending that arises from how we interact with the world. It is not so much the locus of attention that matters as the *manner* in which we explore. The left hemisphere just sees what it expects to see (i.e., its own constructs), whereas the right is open to the new (McGilchrist, 2010, p. 163). We may walk the same route, but see it for the first time—with the poet's eye. This is not the same as the novelty generated by a will-driven recombination of known elements into bizarre, new, shocking combinations, which is a left-brain activity. It is rather a gentler, more receptive *being* with something until we see it anew, evoking perhaps awe or amazement or the stirring of the heart. This is the creative new of the right hemisphere, an unfolding of what is already there to which we have hitherto been blind (ibid., p. 173).

O'Donohue writes of the imagination as being like a lantern that illuminates our inner landscapes (2003, p. 155). Peering into a dark subterranean cavern we can make out in one corner cathedral spires of stalactites and stalagmites, in another an adjoining passage or a still pond emerges. A gurgling sound tells us of an underground stream flowing over a jumble of rocks. What was empty space has become populated with riches. Now the lantern reveals here an animal skeleton, there a smoke-blackened rock face or, miraculously, a cave painting whereby the rich mineral world becomes inhabited with animal and human life. By shining the light of open and flexible attention our inner world too becomes populated. It is most important to let go of the will, of contraction and analysis, to cease the relentless why-and-how questioning and simply receive with wonder.

It is no accident that the word "imagination" incorporates the visual. There is a visual element in most of our art forms, even those which spring predominantly from the other senses; even the nonrepresentational medium of music may generate pictures within the listener. Haute cuisine is designed to appeal to our taste and smell, but increasingly its appearance is given equal status—think of all those television cookery programmes and the food porn of lusciously illustrated cook books. The art forms of fashion and gardening are primarily about the visual image, though the sensual pleasure of touch or smell may also be satisfied by the smooth slinkiness of satin, the crunch of taffeta, the sinking softness of velvet or, in the case of gardening, the swooning suffocation of the scent of jasmine or daphne. As Proust knew, the senses of smell and taste most stimulate our implicit (unconscious) memory, but our explicit voluntary memory tends to be visual (Cozolino, 2010, p. 78). Our imagination, our ability to create and to populate the inner landscape, is based largely on the visual image, though some may also be able to call up music/sounds or other sensory stimuli. In all creative psychotherapy, an important element of the work involves engaging with imagery. Even in body psychotherapy, which attempts to voyage beneath the verbal layer to the unconscious and the preverbal, the proprioceptive sensations are often accompanied by images, as worked with quite explicitly in focusing-oriented psychotherapy and process-oriented psychology. In therapy then, the attention can move back and forth between imagery and body sensations, each of them enriching and deepening the experience and understanding of the other.

So how might the non-creative amongst us find and clear the path to imagination and creativity, central sources of both nourishment and wisdom? This takes courage and faith because we are moving into the unknown or the barely remembered, and we have no certainty that we are taking the right turning. David Whyte ("Sweet Darkness", 1996) writes:

> When your vision has gone
> no part of the world can find you.
>
> Time to go into the dark
> where the night has eyes
> to recognise its own.

At the end of the poem, he tells us what we are seeking in the "sweet darkness". We must:

> Give up all the other worlds
> except the one to which you belong.
>
> ...
>
> Anything or anyone
> that does not bring you alive
> is too small for you.

So, we will know if we are on the right track when we feel our excitement and vitality. We can nourish the imagination by attending to what fascinates, what triggers a deep desire to explore: a place, thing, person or process that calls to our soul. On Brenda's perambulations round the nineteenth-century core of the seaside town where she lives, she walks between old beech trees and a towering hedge in which she notices a narrow garden gate. On the other side lies a winding overgrown dirt path leading to a house barely glimpsed—like Sleeping Beauty's castle—through a jungle of trees and shrubs. The house—Arts and Crafts with a turret and Rapunzel window and a veranda opening on to the garden—has some broken window panes and a few slates missing from the roof. She had thought it was abandoned until one evening she noticed a light on in the hall, its bare hanging bulb visible through the fanlight above the hall door. She then saw a bunch of wild flowers in a vase on the window sill. For a year or more, the only signs of life were the freshly picked flowers and the hall light. Now there are no flowers or light, more windows are broken and part of the roof is beginning to cave in. Here is beauty, mystery, loss—and the call of the soul.

Another exploration: an old Mass path raised above a stream in woodland which opens into a field with a mysterious raised stone structure, like a humpbacked bridge. A turnstile at the far side leads to a narrow floodable path between a stream on the right and a ten foot high stone wall on the left. After fifty yards the path takes a sharp left following the wall and then a right turn moving away from the walled garden. It now skirts a hedged field through which a manor house is visible behind. The land ahead opens up to views of the sea and the blue rolling hills. The landscape holds clues and mysteries which call for exploration—as does the human psyche. I have been privileged to participate in psychodrama groups where through the enchantment of investing belief, a young woman becomes an old man, a hulking man becomes a child, a few tables and chairs become a distant land. We take our time and sit with stuck relationships; we try out experiments—bring in another figure, say something new, do something different—and rigid patterns become mobile.

If we follow the impulse, we will find ourselves; if we lose attention for what calls us, we sink.

Quality of attention

Finding the magic is not difficult. But what then? How to make sure that we don't simply rush past and fail to absorb it or, alternately, kill it with a jaded projection of familiarity through too much of a certain kind of contracted and penetrating attention? Do we research the history and write a monograph that removes all mystery? Do we invent a fiction about the house, a painting of the Mass path, a poem of the shape-shifting of psychodrama? What happens at the interface between me and the other, me and the environment? My hitherto unconscious belief was that the world belongs to itself, not to me, and that I intrude and exploit when I attempt to create (though this hasn't stopped me gardening, one of the most flagrant kinds of improvement on nature!). Do I stop myself delving or intruding, invading what is sacrosanct? May I integrate it into myself, or must I respect its separateness and inviolable right to privacy? This self-prohibition and limitation is challenged by O'Donohue's vision of the divine creation as unfinished: thus it invites the human imagination to carry the work a step further (2003, p. 152): "We are neither strangers nor foreign bodies in a closed-off world. We are the ultimate participants here—the more we give ourselves to experience and strive for expression, the deeper it opens before us" (ibid., p. 151). As Rilke says: "… all this/that's here, so fleeting, seems to require us …" ("The Ninth Elegy", 1964). A similar belief in co-creation—this time of their own work—is found in artists who deliberately leave their paintings unfinished (e.g., Duchamp's "The Large Glass") to provide the viewer with the job of completing the work in their imaginations (Leader, 2002, p. 121). Indeed creativity is inevitable. We do not just receive the world in some objective form. In reality we both receive and generate in our relationship with the world (McGilchrist, 2010, p. 196). We see with a particular kind of eye, we filter, we respond, and even the most passive, avoidant stance is a statement: "Mind not only beholds but shapes all" (Skolimowski, 1994, p. xiii).

Brenda feels nauseous as she tries to possess the world with too tight a grip. The problem is how to internalise lightly without fixing and destroying. As she photographs scenes on holiday, she blocks her experience of place in her anxious focus on the shot and her grasping insistence on not missing anything. This is a problem of engaging with the world through her ego and without the full-bodied, relaxed, attentive slowness that is required for her to be open or to give herself to the world. As this suggests, it is the quality of our attention as much as the level of the self from which it emanates, that determines what we experience. Proust wrote of "a past made arid by the intellect" and the will reducing fragments of reality "by preserving of them only what is suitable for the utilitarian, narrowly human purpose for which it intends them" (Proust, 1996, p. 224).

According to Gestalt psychology, we perceive figures arising out of the ground of our attention. But the philosopher David Michael Levin criticises Perls, Hefferline, and Goodman (1972) for their blindness in viewing the ground of vision as mere emptiness. Levin argues that:

> the ground is not an object; it cannot be experienced as it is in its presencing by a gaze whose intentionality, or attentiveness, is focused according to the metaphysical values of rationalism and instrumentalism. Their experience of the figure-ground differentiation is governed by a gaze which is not yet prepared to receive, and be responsive to, the presencing of ground as ground. (Levin, 1988, p. 208)

Levin views this blindness to ground as symptomatic of a nihilistic ideology of subject-object dualism. The quality of our attention—the instrumentalising look—is linked to our dualistic belief that we are separate from the world.

Neuropsychology defines attention along two axes: selectivity and intensity. Selectivity may be *focused* or *divided*, while intensity has the three elements of: *alertness, sustained attention* and *vigilance*. Without alertness, we lack sustained attention, and vigilance is needed for attending to new stimuli. While focused attention is most associated with the left hemisphere, the remaining four kinds of attention are primarily reliant on the right half of the brain (McGilchrist, 2010, pp. 38–40). If my attention is too narrow, tight, and focused, I lose the potential to see the rich, juicy essence of the world. It is significant that the left hemisphere attends to the man-made and non-living, while the right brain engages with the living, the embodied, the emotional and relational. Too much left brain attention is sticky, over-focused, and objectifying. The internalised object is stripped of life, leaving the viewer experiencing the world as inanimate. The objectifying gaze also kills the target through depersonalising the other in relationship, or through the literal taking of the life of a living being, such as animals used in research. It is clear that we need right-brain empathy, embodiment and emotional intelligence to facilitate relationship with other humans and sentient beings. But this is also true of the inanimate world. If we view a mountain or the ocean as mere matter we will very quickly exploit and destroy them. However if we can appreciate the sheer quiddity of the mountain as a thing or being in its own right, if we can regard it as a gift whose beauty we are privileged to enjoy, we may live off its bounty; but we will give back as we remove, we will take only what we need, and we will leave as light a footprint as possible. It is the distinction between exploitation and reverence. The difference in attitude and outcome is as great as that between rape and consensual relationship.

Musil beautifully evokes the difference between left and right brain attention:

> During this time and from the moment she had stayed behind alone, Agathe had been living in a state of utter release from all ties to the world, in a sweetly wistful suspension of will; a condition that was like a great height, where only the wide blue sky is to be seen. (1995, p. 924)

But he goes on to identify its preconditions: "At no time did her mind deliberately take hold of it with that motion of inner grasping which gives to every act of cold understanding a certain violence as well as a certain futility, for it drives away the joy that is in things" (ibid., p. 925). Musil understands that the grasping will—even if only grasping for "understanding"—is the enemy of openness and presence. In such a state of receptivity, the boundaries against the world melt and we are at one. (This melting of boundaries is explored in Chapter Four.)

The theologian Jacob Needleman writes that "the quality of man's attention is the key to the meaning of our lives and the possible growth of our being" (2009, p. 204). This is because "*I am my attention.* Everything else is given, is not *mine*" (ibid., p. 205). He found that his practice of self-observation did much more than provide him with information about himself. It *changed* him, bringing more sensitivity, presence, and being, as well as an experience of his own inner helplessness. Needleman had an experience as a young man that he never forgot. In an encounter with the great Zen teacher Suzuki, he found that "I—that is, my mental attention—had for a fleeting moment, and to a certain extent, withdrawn from my thoughts and fears and had descended into the whole of my body" (ibid., p. 21). Decades later, he asks: "To what extent is humanity's entire concept of how God is supposed to act in the world of man a greatly imagined projection of how the higher attention acts within the human body?" (ibid., p. 217). God is indeed in our attention—in how we attend, from where within us we attend, and in what we attend to.

Science and scientism

While technology and industry regard the world as plunder for mankind to possess, exploit, and fight over, what about pure science, which simply seeks to explore and understand? We may explore the environment through artistic transformation or scholarly understanding. The Lacanian analyst Darian Leader views art and science as different ways of sublimating our bodily drives. Science, he maintains, is a more complete sublimation process in which, at the abstract end point "of formalization, the world is empty rather than full of body" (2002, p. 104). Art, on the other hand, in that it creates an object, is a less complete form of sublimation. Where art engages with the world in an embodied way through creating, science engages by destroying in order to understand: as Wordsworth observed, "we murder to dissect" ("The Tables Turned", www.poetryfoundation.org). Art illuminates context, science decontextualises. Scientific research—like academic scholarship in general—approaches the material with a penetrating and dissecting eye that disenchants and shuts down. It emerges from the disembodied intellect and is tightly circumscribed: the scientist investigates the questions for which he is capable of designing experiments and for which he can get funding, rather than the questions that might most interest or nourish us. Science can provide mechanisms for processes such as photosynthesis or the neuroscience of vision. It is superbly useful in laying the foundations for the applied sciences of medicine, engineering, or IT. Which of us would choose a post-apocalyptic world without painkillers or anaesthesia, or without electricity, sewers, or mechanised food production and distribution in an urbanised world?

On the other hand, science cannot help us with existential issues: to know ourselves, to understand others, to define or live a good life, to experience love or beauty, face death, reduce conflict or to find any but the most trivial truth. Indeed, science frequently adds to our problems inadvertently or indirectly. Don't misunderstand me: I have no desire to decry science or scientists, or to underestimate how they have enhanced our material well-being and overcome our sense of helplessness and terrified superstition. But *scientism* must be put in its place: what Peter Hacker described as "the illicit extension of the methods and categories of science beyond their legitimate domain" (quoted in McGilchrist, 2010, p. 157). The problem is that scientific knowledge, rather than being regarded as a useful model for practical purposes, is viewed by many in positions of influence as not just the truth, but the only truth, the complete truth, or at the very least as the most important truth.

The analytic and objectifying view of the world found in scientific research is no longer the exclusive realm of professional scientists but extends to our Western worldview in general. The aims and objectives of applied science and technology carry this objectifying relationship further into exploiting the natural and social world for its own ends. In science, the researcher often destroys in quite a literal sense. The cell or molecular biologist or biochemist kills the mouse and throws the liver—or brain—into a homogeniser to extract enzymes or nucleic acids. Even the ecologist or ethologist intrudes in the ecosystem in order to study it and impacts on the social relationships between the animals studied or between them and mankind. The chimpanzees at Gombe became violent and murderous in competing for the bananas the observers provided for them. In order to conduct controlled experiments, the chemist, physicist, or biologist must extract or isolate away from the whole. He therefore understands the components in isolation, but not the whole system. So we have destruction here at many levels: physical or social destruction of organisms or ecosystems and destruction of wholeness in our own minds and understanding. This then leads to us treating parts as if they were wholes. A patient visits a medical consultant who examines his gastrointestinal tract because that, after all, is his speciality. He finds nothing wrong and dismisses the patient who dies a few months later from a heart attack. The other major—and largely unacknowledged—destruction wrought by science is the way it disenchants the world. By following through with our seeking impulse with left-brain analytic curiosity, we destroy the very mystery that triggered our impulse. The scientist or scholar wants to get to the bottom of things, but once understood, the harshness of the searchlights blights beauty, mystery, and even wholeness. The implicit has become explicit and explicitness changes the nature of what is being observed. McGilchrist notes that too much awareness destroys the living quality of things and turns them into lifeless mechanisms (2010, pp. 180, 209).

We must revive a respect and sensitivity for the shadowy unknown, for the absence rather than the presence. We must become aware that where we have clarity we have only a superficial truth. This is practically useful, but must be balanced by the depth of unknowing and the wisdom of the holistic. The project of science dismisses the unknown that cannot readily be explored because of limitations in our thinking or technology. It will never understand what consciousness feels like, though it may well describe the biological correlates of religious experience, death, or dying. However, scientists often reduce the vastly complex to the simplistic (e.g., in consciousness research), or confuse the subjective with the objective or what makes the left brain uneasy with what does not exist. The latter topics then become unmentionable, or rubbished through a category error—arguing that God doesn't exist on the basis of a lack of material evidence rather than investigating the subjective meaning of religious or spiritual practice as perhaps an attitude of veneration towards the world. A quick way of losing your standing in the scientific community, along with your funding and acceptance of your work by refereed journals, would be to propose a systematic study of paranormal phenomena. While I think such naked prejudice is blind, reprehensible, and completely anti-scientific, my concern here is not to argue for the acceptability of research into the paranormal or the religious impulse. My point is that, as a culture, we imagine we know almost everything with just a few details to be filled in as John Maddox has announced with such hubris through his book title, *What Remains to Be Discovered*. In fact, our thinking has simply narrowed so that we are completely unaware of the vast mysteries around us. We are stuck in the mechanisms of the left brain, which has a tendency to confabulate, to draw conclusions based on the limited available evidence, as if this was the whole picture (McGilchrist, 2010, p. 81). Based on experiments with patients whose corpus callosum has been severed, thus isolating the two halves of the brain, it is apparent that the left hemisphere draws conclusions only from the information available to it and never considers that there may be a great deal of other relevant information out there of which it knows nothing.

Science is so materialist, reductionist, and non-holistic that all we see are the isolated things and laws of the physical world. A stark example of science's view of humans as monads is the approach taken by doctors to try to combat the high mortality rate of children in orphanages in the early twentieth century. Thinking that infectious diseases were the cause, they isolated the children from each other and handled them even less. Not surprisingly, given what we now know about attachment, the death rate continued unabated until consistently available staff cuddled and played with the children (study cited in Cozolino, 2010, p. 178).

Some of our greatest mysteries lie in the human heart and the field of connectedness that holds us in the environmental matrix. I have no idea who I am, much less who you are and how you experience the world. I don't know if there is a world soul that experiences joy and pain. I have some tiny inkling of the extraordinary mysteries of group synchronicity, telepathy, dream-invasion, and vicarious trauma; the inhabiting of another's experience and how it evokes something in us that feels like a memory but is not one in any literal sense. Rupert Sheldrake (1995) has named some extraordinary powers, such as pets knowing when their owners are returning or people sensing when they are being stared at, that all point to an extended mind. Anyone who has worked with groups will be aware of this phenomenon of a mental field and yet this may only be whispered in respectable scientific circles.

Sheldrake suggests some experiments that could be done to further investigate these phenomena, but I am deeply ambivalent about knowing more. Of course, I *want* to know more—but then the unknown will feel known. In reality, we will just know whatever left-brain science has been able to uncover, which is not usually the most interesting or important feature of anything. Nevertheless, we will believe we understand it and thereby shut down our openness to the gradual curtain-opening revelation that can accompany deep attention. The real enemy is the false clarity of scientific thinking, which Wittgenstein viewed as a way of sending us to sleep and cutting us off from the religious impulse to wonder (McGilchrist, 2010, p. 157). Heidegger similarly argued that to see things distinctly is to block them "presencing" to us (ibid., pp. 151–152). This is what McGilchrist calls "left hemisphere *re*-presentation" (p. 152), in which our blind and arrogant left brain defines the ineffable and believes it has arrived at the truth. This is the confabulation of the left hemisphere (p. 81). What I want is for us to attend to the unknown with our right brains and simply rejoice in the vast mysteries of the universe without always having to domesticate and defile them with left-brain "understanding". I am asking for the re-enchantment of the world through open, relaxed right-brain presence; for restraint of the contracting, life-squeezing left brain: in other words, for a curiosity of being, not doing.

Re-enchantment

To re-enchant then, we must meditate with deep attention to go through what O'Donohue calls the "adventure of revelation" (2003, p. 158). It is crucial that we do this with the shadowy eye of the poet, not the searchlights of the scientific enterprise. His "Advent-darkened room" taught Patrick Kavanagh: "through a chink too wide there comes in no wonder" ("Advent", 1996). We need to learn to see the world through narrow chinks, new perspectives, dim light, appropriate distance, blurred focus, minimum input. Clarity is the enemy of the imagination and the soul; clarity is an illusion of understanding.

Excess is another enemy. Kavanagh's "dry black bread and the sugarless tea of penance" and Proust's madeleine (a very plain sponge cake) both "charm back the luxury of a child's soul", that capacity for presence to unfolding wonder. One of the problems of adulthood is the multitasking that comes with responsibility. Our attention becomes too divided and time always seems in short supply. When we suddenly have time—as on holidays—it can take most of the vacation for us to adjust our speediness and split attention and to learn to sit in simplicity, to give ourselves to the grainy texture of the sand or the ripples of the waves. Over-stimulus in the Western world (a topic that is covered in Chapter Five) shuts us down into space-out or speeds us up into very short attention spans. We must endure the impinging noise of traffic, hyped-up conversations like the screeching of a tropical bird enclosure, "music" that literally deafens, the beeping demands of the mobile phone, and the visual overkill of advertising hoardings, shop fronts, newspaper headlines, magazine covers, flickering TVs, computer screens, and body-contracting text messages. We go into either sympathetic nervous system over-arousal or parasympathetic shutdown, or we alternate between the two. Neither is conducive to the still small voice of the dung beetle rolling his Sisyphean boulder uphill. Of course, climate and nature are vicious and violent as well as calm and cooperative, so we are adapted to extremes of stimulus. But we are not adapted to such unrelenting and rapidly-changing inputs and to living so completely outside of nature.

As Proust and Kavanagh both knew, the major cause of disenchantment is the loss of the child's unconscious soul. To live with joy is to participate in life, not to reflect upon it or analyse it, as Wittgenstein was aware. According to McGilchrist: consciousness threatens to disrupt "our active, embodied engagement with the world" (2009, p. 223). Brenda too knows this, but cannot voluntarily return to the unconsciousness of childhood, though she may very occasionally be surprised by an epiphany. As Ken Wilber warns us, in spiritual development the way forward is not back but a synthesis and transcendence of all the stages to the present. The way forward is the integration of child right-brain with adult left-brain consciousness.

Proust's protagonist Marcel was surprised by joy when he broke with habit and took tea and a madeleine. But he had to work to locate the association and fill out the momentary pleasure with the full depths of embodied memory. Leading up to the culminating epiphany of Combray regained, we see him as an explorer or researcher of his own consciousness. To draw the memory up from the depths, he had to eliminate current distractions, then recuperate by thinking of something else, then "create an empty space" (Proust, 2003, p. 48), and try again. "Seek? Not only that: create … Ten times I must begin again, lean down towards it" (Proust, pp. 48–49). And suddenly, in the midst of all this effort, the memory of childhood came flooding back—his aunt in her bedroom in Combray, the house, the garden, the village, the very marrow of his childhood. On another occasion, on seeing the spires of Martinville, he again had to create as much as receive to reach the full depth of the impact. Having described the scene in writing, "I was so happy, I felt I had so perfectly relieved myself of those steeples and what they had hiding behind them, that, as if I myself were a hen and had just laid an egg, I began to sing at the top of my voice" (ibid., p. 182). Re-enchantment depends on the optimal balance between conscious intent and unconscious receptivity. Proust teaches us how, through immersive attention and a balance between receptivity and active seeking, we can live creatively.

Memory and imagination

Memory and imagination are intertwined: memory feeds imagination; imagination embellishes memory. To take the latter point first, memory is malleable, subject to suggestion and distortion. False "memories" can be implanted experimentally so that the subject becomes convinced that they are real (Cozolino, 2010, p. 89). In therapy, the outcomes can be negative (e.g., false memory syndrome) or positive (e.g., use of visualisation, psychodrama, etc. to create a consciously more positive view of the past) depending on the awareness of the therapist.

More important for the argument here is the fact that imagination depends on memory. If imagination is the ability to cognitively manipulate internalised images and other sensory experiences, it is dependent on having internalised and retained these experiences in the first place. People with amnesia because of damage to the hippocampus were found to have difficulty envisaging scenarios they might expect to encounter in the future (Miller, 2007). The imagination is really a way of selecting and integrating past experiences and projecting this knowledge into a future that bears some similarity to the past but is not identical. This gives us flexibility in adapting to constant change. In Chapter Eight we will see that narrative, like memory, never simply describes, but creates, projects, edits, and assembles new possibilities. Consequently, narrative is therapeutic, because it is creative.

Humans have two forms of memory: implicit or unconscious and explicit or conscious. Implicit memory includes the procedural (acquired skills that become automatic such as walking, talking, and riding a bike) and the emotional. The latter develops in the womb and includes unconscious body and emotional memories: for example, we are born recognising the sound of our mother's voice. Implicit memory depends on the parts of the brain that develop early, notably the amygdala, which is central to appraising and processing fear and also plays a role in bonding and attachment. Importantly, "these implicit memory encodings are more than simple recollections; they shape the growing child's architecture of the self" (Siegel, 2012, p. 55). Another way of putting this is that implicit or body memory is as much about *structure* as about content: early implicit memories shape our patterned reactions to subsequent stimuli, relationships, and events. Explicit memory starts about the age of three and associates visual memories with time and place, which ensures that the memory can be retrieved into consciousness. The hippocampus lays these explicit memories down in the cortex in the location where the experience was originally received, a process that can take up to two years (Wilkinson, 2006). Explicit memory allows us to tag sensory information with words and is organised by language into episodes and narratives. The hippocampus develops after speech has been acquired and continues to develop into early adulthood.

The crucial point for our purposes here is the interaction between amygdala- and hippocampus-based memories. Sensory input can reach the amygdala directly from the thalamus or can go there via the cortex and hippocampus. The first route is an emergency rapid response route, whereas the second slower route facilitates cognitive appraisal. The amygdala jumps to instant conclusions while the hippocampus reflects (Cozolino, 2010, p. 85). The amygdala causes us to jump and prepare for flight at the sound of the fire alarm, but the hippocampus intervenes with some reality-testing by reminding us that this is just a drill or that someone has been smoking in the toilets again. Traumatised or depressed people may be controlled by the amygdala because early abuse or neglect impairs the development of the hippocampus.

The amygdala is key to emotional and somatic organisation of experience, whereas the hippocampus is central to conscious, logical, and cooperative social functioning. The amygdala heightens our attention to specific aspects of the environment, while the hippocampus inhibits attention due to habituation. Young children depend on caretakers to modulate amygdala responses, but the absence of a mature, reflective hippocampus also facilitates the fascinated attention to the miniscule. God is in the detail. Everything seems fresh and new, whereas as we get older we become jaded by habituation to a world that can seem stale and boring. Hippocampus discrimination is a two edged sword. Early impulsivity is replaced by a calmer thoughtfulness where we learn to distinguish between safety and danger, but our heightened sensitivity to the environment is blunted and spontaneity is muted. The novel and the habituated are processed by different sides of the brain, the right side absorbing new gestalts and learning new skills and information, whereas the left hemisphere takes over once something becomes known and familiar (McGilchrist, 2010, p. 40). While gaining familiarity with a wide range of skills is an essential part of our development, as Fritz Perls declared: "only the novel is nourishing" (Perls, Hefferline, & Goodman, 1972, p. 230).

Yet, this is not the complete picture: for Proust "the true paradises are the paradises we have lost" (1996, p. 222). We all have moments when a smell, for example, transports us back to our early years and we reconnect with the beingness, the egolessness, the pure presence of childhood. When Brenda sniffs a musty scent she travels back in time to her grandmother's farmhouse, or the smell of sacks of flour, sugar, and other dry goods returns her to the shady pantry with the blind permanently pulled down. Even the more recent adult past has a patina of perfection that the experience did not have at the time. Wordsworth spoke of poetry originating in "emotion recollected in tranquillity" (preface to *Lyrical Ballads*, www.thevalve.org) and it is the *present* tranquillity that irons the wrinkles out of the past crumpled experience. Brenda thinks back over a holiday taken when she was quite seriously depressed. She unrelentingly craved food for comfort and sleep for oblivion. But she pictures a particular landscape through which she and John walked— she dragging herself along, exhausted with depression—and now imagines moments of paradise. It is important to emphasise this: she does not *remember* those moments (she is pretty sure they didn't exist); rather, she *project*s her current equanimity onto a beautiful landscape that is a true memory and thereby generates a composite that is a work of the imagination. There were also a few excited moments on that holiday where she recovered some libido and curiosity, but they occurred within the town and not in the particular spot onto which she later projected epiphany. The question arises, why does she not spontaneously return to the town scene at this moment? It is, I think, because the open landscape with the distant mountains, big sky, and hot sun matches her current mood which is one of tranquillity more than excitement. She is attracted to the roaming possibilities of the open countryside and it is in that place she finds the mirror of her current mood, despite her depressed state when she actually visited that landscape.

So if every thought encompasses multiple time zones and is a mixture of past memory edited by and cut with current feelings and imagination, and perhaps future hopes or expectations, how do we transform a depressed self into a joyful one? The self is experienced in the moment but influenced by the past and continuously co-created out of our interaction with the environment. The self is inherently a process: creative, dynamic, and relational. But for many of us like Brenda, it feels like a thing: stuck, grim, and isolated. While we are clearly not defined by our memories, we can be trapped within depressive and uncreative neural circuits. Most people are capable of visualising to introduce energy into depressive thought patterns or safety into terrifying memories. We may worry that we will lose sight of reality or betray ourselves or others by changing the past. But we would just be doing what creative children do with their present circumstances or what we all do with our pasts anyway, but doing so in a more directed and positive manner. Brenda looks back at a fog without distinct figures or episodes. Somewhere in the depths of the fog is her self, hiding from the sneers and contempt, undeveloped because it has never been brought forth by positive mirroring of its primitive movements and reaching out. But she can visualise a family that *would* feel safe and affirming. Being true to her own experience and authenticity does not mean having to remain stuck in self-defeating imaginal patterns. A client who has been abandoned can, in her imagination, find a fairy godmother to rescue her; another who has lived in fear can fly out of the situation in his magic toy airplane and move to a place he experienced as safe. Moreno worked through the medium of psychodrama to help the individual grow into the parts of self (the "roles") that had hitherto not been brought forth, such as a schizophrenic boy who believed he was turning into a girl and chose to play roles of aggressive masculinity on the psychodrama stage (Moreno, 1987, p. 78).

Mindfulness and containing chaos

O'Donohue's vision that we are participants in the unfinished creation of the world requires us to be open to that world. We cannot engage if we space out or hide ourselves away (some of which can take place in full view, as in narcissistic acting out). But it is essential that engagement takes place from the authentic self and not merely the ego for it to be meaningful. The popularity of mindfulness meditation suggests a growing awareness of our propensity to space out and an emerging dissatisfaction with our failure to live our lives. So if being present is so great, why do we avoid it so much?

The interlocking problems of time and holding raise their heads. Time that when I was busy seemed so scarce, now seems very long indeed. How will I fill these hours? How will I contain myself? I will be bored just looking at an orange, or even smelling it as well. But if I stop a moment and look—really look—at the keyboard, for example, I discover all sorts of surprising things I had never noticed before. There is a crescent moon on the escape key, a half-blacked-out sun on F5 similar to the sign on plants indicating that they thrive in conditions of semi-shade. Having first prudently saved everything, I risk pressing this key. I expected a screen-saving dimming of the light, but what actually happened was the appearance of a "find and replace" box. I'll now take a bigger risk and press the F12 key with a padlock on it. Will there be any way back from this move except for a Houdini-like escape artist? No problem, it was just a "save as" shortcut. The cocktail glass on F9 and the winged runner (Hermes?) on F8 did nothing. The American-style mailbox with the cross was another shortcut that revealed a mistake in my previous sentence, and pressing the battery key achieved nothing. I play around with some other keys and feel pleasantly excited by my new-found knowledge and confidence, but what now—that just took five minutes. I could have a cup of tea, but that would be an avoidance. Of what? I feel a bit speedy with all this mindfulness. I sniff the keyboard and it smells like a radiator when first turned on after a summer of disuse. There are other mysteries too, especially on the built-in mouse which I never use. A risky move there produced two pages side-by-side on the screen, but by some miracle—because the move seems so imprecise—I actually managed to return to a single page. Better not push my luck with other finger movements. What now? I'm sure that mindfulness is about more than fiddling with a keyboard—which doesn't seem to have done anything for my spiritual receptiveness. Perhaps this is too stimulating for the logic and anxiety circuits. Surely mindfulness is about slowing down to take in the world. That's the problem: I have been speeding up to get through this exercise. The background hum of the laptop is calming. I am in danger of falling asleep, but then the fan switching on woke me and no doubt perked up the machine. Perhaps I will take a break.

One problem with the above short exercise was that my sympathetic nervous system experienced more arousal than it is used to and that felt like anxiety, though as Gestalt therapists know there is a thin line between anxiety and excitement. Polster, E. and Polster, M. note in their Gestalt classic (1974) that we are phobic about chaos. But, if we have the courage to stay with our experiences, it is inevitable that we will encounter novelty (p. 48). The "movement from chaos to clarity is inherent in creativity" (p. 41) and it is important to recognise the moment of completion and not try to squeeze more out of an experience that is finished. My anxiety seemed to stem from lack of containment—my attention was bouncing round in too random a fashion. Where does this end? Oh no, it doesn't end until death. How can I hold and shape all of this input? I am on the edge between chaos and order, arousal and inhibition. I constantly fear overwhelm by the sympathetic nervous system and don't trust the parasympathetic to calm things down in time. Perhaps there is a very good reason why so many of us drowse through life on the snooze button or resort to unquestioning routine or mindless TV to deal with the whole issue of being held. Guntrip (1992) and Winnicott (1990) maintained that holding by a non-impinging mother generates a capacity for being-ness (see Chapter Two), but I know of almost nobody who can do this, and one who may be able to has no awareness of how to get there. In the absence of an adequate holding cultural environment in adulthood, it seems unlikely that having had good-enough mothering as a child is sufficient for receptivity—to what Heidegger called "the presencing of Being" (Levin, 1988, p. 272). Many anthropologists and explorers have written about the relaxed alertness of indigenous tribal people in their natural setting that comes from belonging in their world and the corresponding disintegration of their psyches into addiction when they are dislocated into urban life. In their natural environment, they are held by the jungle itself, as well as by community, tradition, material necessity and lack of excessive choice. These containers break down in an urban and atomised environment where "anything goes" and there is no longer an immediate relationship between work and survival (see for example Benedict Allen, 1992 and his subsequent works).

The presence and the absence

There is nothing as enticing to the imagination as an absence, an incompletion, a sense of possibility, as Proust recognised:

> So often, in the course of my life, reality had disappointed me because at the instant when my senses perceived it my imagination, which was the only organ that I possessed for the enjoyment of beauty, could not apply itself to it, in virtue of that ineluctable law which ordains that we can only imagine what is absent. (1996, p. 223)

Writing about Henry James, Hermione Lee observes: "'Moments of refusal, events that don't happen', gaps in time, things not said, are what fire his imagination" (Lee, 2012). Anita Desai when interviewed by her daughter, fellow novelist Kiran Desai (Desai & Desai, 2011), speaks of lost landscapes and languages which populate the fringes of her work. The half-known or half-remembered loss, the incomplete creation, the atmosphere of age, twilight or mystery, our outsider status, the hole in ourselves that demands mirroring or nourishment—all signify an absence that we are impelled to fill. For Darian Leader (2002), art is a way of entering the unknown spaces of early pre-verbal childhood (pp. 59–60); or more generally, creation is driven by lack or loss, the gap in the network of signs (p. 65). The tentative, gentle stimulus, the whispering voice that invites but does not insist, that entices like Yeats' fairy kingdom: "Come away, O human child! / To the waters and the wild / With a faery, hand in hand" ("The Stolen Child", 1974)—this befriends and elicits imagination.

The enemies of soul and imagination are the weight of actuality, completion, clarity, logic, busyness, incessant input and demands, excessive impinging stimuli that lead to shutdown, or equally the opposite—a poverty of stimulus. Also we may cling for safety onto one narrow view and never look up to see some of the other possibilities. Under any of these conditions there is no space within the subject or gap in the object to facilitate the imagination. Alternatively, we may suffer from insider-blindness—the problem of habituated attention where we are brainwashed into one broad view and have lost touch with the micro-vision that would facilitate an alternative broad view. This veil of blindness can be lifted by the innocent outsider, the newcomer into a culture who hasn't yet learned the "correct" ways, or the non-expert in a discipline who asks a child's questions and suggests a different interpretation of the state of the emperor's clothing.

How did it all work out so badly?

McGilchrist (2009) argues that the two hemispheres of the brain are less concerned with different functions than with different ways of processing information and experience. The right is holistic while the left processes pieces of information in isolation, so that in the case of birds, for example, the right avoids predators and the left distinguishes between food such as seeds and the surrounding grit. Both halves contribute, though often in different ways, to most processes. Both sides are essential for communication, with the left hemisphere producing language, while the right detects tone of voice and facial expression and is responsible for empathy and emotional intelligence as well as many aspects of art and religion. Allan Schore (2010) proposes that the right brain represents Freud's pre-conscious, the left the conscious mind. He shows that the left brain does not have direct contact with the body's emotional signals, but only via the right hemisphere which interacts with the autonomic nervous system via the limbic system. Schore argues that it is therefore the right brain that should be targeted in psychotherapy because it is the seat of our unconscious, our embodiment and emotional regulation; it predominates in coping with novel situations and comes up with a range of alternative solutions to problems in a manner that is holistic and connected to lived reality.

The world we experience depends on which hemisphere comes to dominate in individuals or whole cultures. Harmony between the two hemispheres facilitated the cultural flowering of Ancient Greece, the Renaissance and Romanticism. By contrast, McGilchrist (2009) believes that the Roman Empire, the Reformation, the Enlightenment, and the Industrial Revolution as well as the modern world are characterised by left-hemisphere dominance. The harmonising, integrated cultures centre on the idea of embodied soul in the world, while the separated cultures emphasise rational control (power) and disenchantment of the world. McGilchrist writes of the right brain as the "master" and the left as the "emissary", who should be in service to the master. However, he claims, in the twenty-first-century West the emissary has got above himself, usurped the master and instituted a reign of tyranny. The right brain, with its holistic view, is where vision and wisdom reside; the left is a mere bureaucrat whose gifts are in administration, not in formulating policy or grasping the values on which a good life is built. However in practice, at the level of the individual, the institution, or the state, it is the strategist that now rules, whereas the values or vision on which strategy must rest are in darkness. The bureaucrat rules to enhance the bureaucracy while the master lies forgotten in his prison cell. We live in a world of what Freud called secondary process (rational understanding), and the primary processes of instinct, intuition, and the unconscious are denied and out of awareness.

McGilchrist proposes that even small differences in potential between the hemispheres or an accumulation of small effects might lead to a considerable bias in the ways in which the individual or society views the world (2010, pp. 10–11). (See Chapter Nine below for the non-linear dynamics of complex systems.) This effect can then be magnified because the left hemisphere has an inbuilt advantage as it looks out only for itself, unlike the more encompassing right brain (ibid., p. 218). Brenda began, like everyone, on the right brain route, but strategic considerations that were ultimately about protecting the right-hemisphere vision ironically led to the hegemony of the left. The question is, having gone down the left logical pathway, can she along with other left-afflicted individuals and our world in general retrieve their right minds? We must find a way of bridging polarities: not throwing out the left brain (as if we could), but reasserting the role of the right as master.

Reintegration

McGilchrist argues—by analogy to the Hegelian triad of thesis, antithesis, and synthesis—that complete and rich processing of experience requires a sequence of transfers between the hemispheres in the following order: right, left, and then right again. This entails: holistic experiencing by the right brain; logical examination and categorisation by the left; and then a return to the right for a final synthesis of the original gestalt with the abstract analysis, so as to generate an integrated and transformed whole that is more than the sum of its parts. For example, our first holistic impression of a painting may be followed by focused analysis, and then stepping back to gain a new understanding. The difference between our first impression and the new synthesis is similar to the difference between the prepersonal and transpersonal in spiritual development. Poetry may be seen as the supreme example of this synthesis, where language—a left-brain function—and processing of experience is assembled into a new whole that is a reflection of, but greater than, the original experience. Nature, art, religion, human relationships, and the body are all beyond the power or comprehension of the left brain. The right brain—which mediates the implicit and intuitive—can appreciate them, but the incorporation of left-brain language, intense focus and analysis can transform raw experience into something that transcends the products of either hemisphere acting in isolation. Without the self-consciousness of the left hemisphere, we may experience life in its richness; however we will not be creative—in life or in art— without the dynamic interaction of the two sides of the brain. Leonardo da Vinci can be seen undergoing this process over the course of his lifetime. After a childhood spent absorbed in the Tuscan countryside, his early adulthood was occupied with mastering the craft of painting and, subsequently, his experiments and observations in science and engineering. His later paintings, particularly the newly discovered *Salvator Mundi*, have a numinous quality that combines the technical expertise made possible by his left brain with a new depth of vision that emerges from the right brain's capacity for a wide overview.

Wallace Stevens is a poet who both exemplifies and theorises the transcendence of left-right brain duality in his dialectic between reality and the imagination (Critchley, 1997; Bate, 2001). His poem "The Idea of Order at Key West" (Stevens, 2006) contrasts right-brain Dionysian wildness of content (the sea) with the left brain Apollonian "idea of order". We hear the reality/imagination duality played out between nature—the sea, and culture—the singer striding along the shore. The poet makes it clear that while her song reflects the sea, "it was she and not the sea that we heard". Art mimics reality and reality becomes enchanted through art. The song in the poem—like the poem itself—transcends both the right-brain experience of the spirit of the sea and the left-brain creation of order through language.

This discussion begs the question that has been hanging over this entire chapter: is the world itself already enchanted, or is it just inert matter that our right-brain vision enchants? The posing of this question in the first place is dualistic: it depends on the separation of humans from our environment. But if we are part of the "environment", then it is ourselves we depersonalise if we disenchant the natural world. So there is no difference between sacralising ourselves or the earth. A second line of argument concerns the unique energy quality or presence of particular places, which seems not to depend on the individual who is perceiving them. Benedict Allen (1992) writes about Amazonian Indians who can tell which parts of the jungle contain spirits and which have been abandoned by spirit. Even in the over-rationalised Western world, many people will acknowledge that some places—often those where ancient ritual sites were built—have a palpable, but unnameable, sacred quality.

Critchley maintains that "the form of our questions about the meaning and value of human life is still religious, but that we find the claims of religion increasingly incredible" (1997, p. 236). It is this that gives our existence in modernity a tragic quality. We look for help in places that are not equipped to supply an answer. The answer—to the extent that there is one—lies in right-brain experiences such as accessing the body's flow through dance or sport, or immersion in nature, art or religion. The answer for Stevens was nature and poetry: "a sanctifying of experience that renders the real holy without turning us away from this world to another" (ibid., p. 235). Jonathan Bate (2001) argues that poetry can save the earth as well as rescuing mankind by opening our eyes and hearts to nature and thereby returning us home. The answer for others is a new spirituality without the institutional control, superstitious beliefs or dogma that characterise many religions. This involves a particular attitude towards the world, ourselves, other people, other species, and the founding world of inorganic rocks, water, and minerals: one of awe and wonder, love, respect, care, and worship. It is crucial that whatever consolation we choose, whether art or nature-spirituality or something else, we realise that we cannot do it alone. This would be like sand-bagging your home while the rest of the community removes the flood water defences. Shared and regular ritual and the support of a community of like-minded worshippers are necessary. Any answer, as much for the individual as for the world, must incorporate both the individual and the collective.

Summary

Brenda's life followed a trajectory from childhood immersion in nature to disciplined, focused, and objective scientist, and then an attempt to regain some nourishment in her life through a career change. However, the mental patterns she brought with her have frustrated her longing for re-enchantment. Different kinds of attention are associated with the archetypes of scientist and poet, dominated by the left and right hemispheres of the brain respectively. The former way of perceiving and thinking is analytic, logical, arid and not grounded in reality, with a sticky, focused, and objectifying kind of attention; the latter is holistic, contextual, immersive, and grounded in the body and emotions. Mystery, immersion, implicit memory, and imagination all play roles in soulful living, and to live mindfully, we must be willing to tolerate transitory chaos. It is through harmonious interaction between the left and right hemispheres of the brain, but with the right hemisphere firmly in charge, that we can move towards rich and meaningful processing of experience as well as creativity in art and life.

PART II

IMPINGEMENT AND LOSS OF SELF

CHAPTER FOUR

Boundaries and contact: outer and inner distortions

> *So far as the anxieties of the outer life penetrate into it, and the inconsistently-minded, unknown, unloved or hostile society is allowed ... to cross the threshold, it ceases to be home; it is then only a part of that outer world which you have roofed over and lighted fire in.*
>
> —John Ruskin, *Sesame and Lilies*, 1865

In Seville, Brenda sees behind the student tapas bars and tourist sites the fires of the Inquisition. Looking at Italian Renaissance art, she cannot avoid the blood, terror, and torture amid which it was painted. She is in confluence with suffering. Mary Oliver, like many poets, has thin boundaries against the world. She describes giving to a child beggar in Jakarta: the look of cunning she received back she carries "like a bead of acid"—in my mind, the acid used in etching to carve lines into metal ("Acid", 1992). In another shocking poem ("Rage", 1992), she evokes the sex abuser at the moment when, in his dreams, his armouring against empathy collapses. Even he, Oliver imagines, is tormented by what he has done to the child who, stunted, "will never come to leaf". In these examples, we see how open boundaries permit us to feel the pain of

77

the surrounding world, though not always in a way, or at a time, that is useful to us or to others.

When she began therapy, Brenda had thin, ineffective boundaries, despite being overbound in terms of energy regulation. Her dreams were crowded with people: she could not keep others out. We can make sense of this by distinguishing between what she let out and what she took in. Her favourite position was that of the fly on the wall. She revealed nothing of herself, but when in a position of safety against exposure, she automatically went into observation mode, absorbing the emotional life that was otherwise unavailable to her. She watched others in the same way as she immersed herself in novels or watched emotionally-absorbing drama. Her engagement was entirely empathic and she never exploited what she saw, though she did fear that she might be an emotional vampire. However her absorptive and empathising capacities had two downsides. One lay in her skinless exposure to the world's horrors which were so multifarious that she was paralysed from actually doing anything about them. The second downside lay in the way she sided with the other—whether the real or the imagined other—against herself. In Brenda's early years in therapy, she used to describe her uncentred sense of self with the image of a fence between her and the other. There was nothing but a cardboard cut-out on "her" side of the fence: *she* was on the other person's side. Over there, "she" was "objectively", so she claimed, evaluating her thoughts, feelings, and behaviour, judging, insisting, expecting—from (her projection of) the other person's viewpoint. This monstrous, projected, shaming, and demanding superego governed and strangled her life. Every time she assembled a modicum of self—and self-worth—she passed it through the mincer of this objectifying, punitive eye.

An introjected, fear-driven, overscrupulous superego censored every statement, so that it was impossible to speak anything but the most choked and neutralised utterances, which in turn created an equal counterweight of fury and frustration. To survive she must be unimpeachable in argument and action, not show emotion, weakness, uncertainty, irrationality or dishonesty. At the same time, she must never expose the other to the kind of humiliation that she herself dreaded, so she was always fighting her corner with her weapons locked up. Mostly, the best solution was invisibility, but sometimes even this was not an option. Her body devised an exquisite double-binding torment. The most unacceptable aspect of her was her gender, but after puberty she suffered severe period pains which generated nausea and vomiting that could not be concealed. This most visible sickness demanded attention from others—the very attention that was even more agonising than the physical pain. The sickbay in school offered no privacy. It was simply a curtained-off couch in the hallway outside the headmistress's office. This counter-attack from the id created the most appalling dilemma: how to be invisible, inaudible, to not exist for others in a body that was roaring its existence with mortifyingly public vehemence. She was dimly aware that her body was trying to vomit her self—and in particular her femaleness—out of her.

Brenda was poisoned by her mother's view of the nature of women: powerless victims and doormats whose sole virtue was silent, uncomplaining suffering, and acceptance. As the only daughter amongst five sons, she was singled out for this humiliation. What was even worse for Brenda was that her mother believed that this was not just how things *were*, but how they *should* be, and she created all sorts of excuses and rationales to justify keeping women weak and disempowered. Brenda's mother thought women should be paid less, shouldn't take *men's* jobs, shouldn't sit on juries, it was a waste of money to send girls to college and she wouldn't have a female doctor ("she wouldn't come out on call at night"). In consequence, Brenda told her mother nothing that mattered about her private and personal life. Her entanglement with her mother is illustrated by Brenda's insistence that she would never be like her: she would never marry, have children, or put herself into a man's power. Unfortunately, in following this strategy, Brenda was only a little more free and self-determining than if she had complied with her mother's beliefs. In therapy, she was desperate to extract mother from her psyche, but her persistent image was that of a multi-branched vine growing throughout her body with extensions in every cell. This growth was so profuse and resilient that she couldn't hope to pull it out. As any gardener knows, you pull on such a weed, the root breaks and the plant grows again—even more prolifically. At the time she had fears— that she has since lost—of cancer invading and metastasising through her body. Brenda had no boundary against her mother or her mother's views: despite her ego's outraged defiance, she was as immersed in her mother's hatred of the feminine as she was in the air she breathed. This open wound extended into her relationship with the world, and there were constant horrifying fantasy intrusions of people or animals being tortured, buried alive, or burned alive. In her teens, she prayed for the protection from suffering of everyone she knew, all of mankind, the entire animal kingdom and back through more primitive phyla to bacteria. Her prayers had an obsessive quality, a fear that if she left anybody or anything out of her net of protection, she would expose them to even greater risk. In her adult years, she had a recurrent dream of being chased by torturers. They caught her by pressing a knot like a button in her spine, and she awoke each time with an agonising spasm in her back.

How did Brenda manage to escape from the torturing secret police and her nightmare prison cell?

Ironically, reading feminist classics just made her more angry, and inflicted further wounds on her self-esteem as she realised just how extensive was the hatred and contempt for women. Working in IT, she achieved some degree of self-respect for the false self she was creating. Various forms of help came in her thirties: through co-counselling she met and surrounded herself with empowered and self-respecting older women and went on the thrilling and creative rollercoaster ride of self-discovery and self-development. Through co-counselling too, she met a man who loved her without competing, comparison, or put-downs. Brenda started one-to-one therapy after the co-counselling adventure came to an end. She found therapy dull by comparison. She didn't know how to use it and floundered in her own spaced-out void. With time it became apparent that she had two boundary settings. When alone in bed she was wide open to invasion by the world's sufferings. With her therapist, she dissociated into a bland, polite persona unable to expose or even access her deeper layers. When, in time, she did manage to get in touch with herself in her therapist's presence, it was only with her eyes closed and her face covered. For many years thereafter, she lay on the couch for her therapy sessions, away from the danger of eye-contact. Her therapists—there was more than one—were no doubt often as bored and frustrated as she was, so little did she present to work with. It took years for her to bridge the gap between the surface of her life which had all the boxes ticked and for which she felt she should be grateful, and the underlying reality of her deep unhappiness, self-hatred, fear, and depression. Her therapists' sensitivity, acceptance, patience, and self-restraint were stretched to the limit.

* * *

This chapter investigates the interconnections between boundaries and the self. Strong but flexible boundaries enable us to minimise frustration, shame, guilt, horror, and powerlessness and to live with autonomy, spontaneity, and open to relationship. But what *are* boundaries, how do we create them, and what is the impact of inadequate boundaries? How can they become thicker, yet flexible and dynamic so that we cease being puppets controlled by others and no longer live in flayed agony in the face of the world's suffering?

Boundaries define systems

Life is an emergent property that depends on boundaries to vivify non-living organic molecules. Organic molecules must be concentrated in the same space for reactions to occur that facilitate the production of more complex molecules. Thus, the great step forward in the creation of life was the formation of the simplest cell membrane—the first boundary—which enclosed part of the primal soup and facilitated proximate chemical reactions. Fast-forward a few billion years and we see another boundary forming—the developing human embryo; initially part of the mother's body, it becomes more differentiated but still bound to and dependent on the mother as the months of gestation pass. After birth it is physically separate and will survive her absence. Material boundaries separate the two, who meet at these borders, skin to skin and eye to eye.

In the more gradual *psychological* birth of the human infant, an invisible boundary forms that encloses the child's self. As long as mother is in a state of primary maternal preoccupation, more or less predicting the baby's needs, the baby can be deluded into thinking that he and mother share a mind. But later, as mother begins the necessary business of frustrating the child, the toddler gradually develops a theory of mind, as he realises that mother and he have different agendas, different feelings, and different thoughts. This process is believed to begin in the second six months after birth (Rayner, Joyce, Rose, Twman, & Clulow, 2005, p. 62) but does not reach completion until about the end of the preoperational stage around the age of six or seven. Then, as Piaget showed experimentally, the child is able to realise that mother does not know what he knows if she is not present to observe what he has seen—the child is now able to see situations from other than a personal perspective. The preoperational child, by contrast, is unable to distinguish between the objective—how things are, and the subjective—how they appear to the child (Kegan, 1982, p. 30; Sugarman, 2001, p. 84).

The process of development is a gradual differentiation out of embeddedness (Kegan, 1982, p. 31), like the emergence of a statue from the marble during sculpting. We are embedded successively in the reflexes (sensorimotor stage), the perceptions (preoperational stage), and the concrete (concrete operational stage) (p. 33). This continues with the adolescent moving away from merger with family to identification with the peer group and subsequently, as a young adult, by physical distancing from home and family of origin to become more embedded in the bigger society. Likewise older, retired adults frequently distance themselves from society—anticipating their removal by death—to re-enter what Washburn calls the dynamic ground (Cortright, 1997). With each differentiation and emergence from an old union comes a new matrix of embeddedness.

Development from womb to tomb encompasses the central themes of differentiation and separation. But the drive towards separation away from one communal state is always accompanied by movement towards a new union—as well as some degree of non-separation from the old matrix. Boundaries mediate this dialectic between contact and separation. The semipermeable membrane round a cell both separates the cell from its environment and enables transfer of nutrients into the cell and secreted products out of the cell. "Wherever and whenever a boundary comes into existence, it is felt both as contact and as isolation" (Perls quoted in Polster, E. & Polster, M., 1974, p. 102).

With every step in differentiation, another boundary is formed. We form boundaries between me and you; subject and object; my family or property and not mine; past and present; inside and outside; narrow, near focus and distant, broad focus; id, ego, and superego; the conscious and unconscious; or between thought and feeling. At the same time as we are differentiating in our personal experience, we are also categorising the world outside ourselves into people and animals, living things and the inanimate world, the earth and other planets, planets and stars, different countries and races, different languages, etc. Indeed the entire history of human knowledge rests on a founding grammar of such distinctions. However, the fundamental boundary is between self and not-self, and all other boundaries depend on recognising your own separate existence (Wilber, 1985, p. 46).

Boundaries define systems: "For there to be a system, there must be a boundary that delimits a space within which certain operational rules can hold sway and a certain function be performed" (Wright,

1991, p. 202). The image of a membrane surrounding a cell suggests a relatively unchanging—though semipermeable—boundary, but the reality is that boundaries change all the time. A family is a clear system as long as the members all live together, but if we think of a father who travels for a living, a young adult child who returns home only for the occasional weekend, the mature child who has left home "for good", or the family member in a state of cut-off from the others, it is clear that boundaries are highly flexible and some elements are more embedded in the system while others move in and out. Gestalt psychology recognises the movable feast of the boundary epitomised in ambiguous images, such as the one that can be perceived as either an old hag or a young girl (Perls, Hefferline, & Goodman, 1972, p. 27). The line that defines the cheek and chin profile of the young girl in one viewing is the boundary of the Roman nose of the old woman in another viewing. Unconsciously, the mind selects the meaning in the lines of the drawing. Likewise, in life we are constantly selecting and creating patterns out of our perceptions and experiences with a succession of figures emerging out of the ground of the inner and outer environment. This is brilliantly illustrated by the other famous Gestalt picture (ibid., p. 26): if black is perceived as the background, the figure observed is a white chalice; in an inverse viewing, the figures are two heads in profile silhouetted against the white background. Gestalt psychotherapy builds on this perceptual flux in its awareness that our moment by moment experience is a constant flow of one figure after another emerging out of the ground. This is particularly evident in meditation where there is little or no change in the external environment, yet the internal moviemaker throws up an ever-changing array of emotionally charged memories, fantasies, and sensations—what the spiritual teacher Catherine Ingram refers to as the ravings of the mad woman in the attic. Each of these fleeting thoughts is a figure with a boundary round it. A figure is really a fleeting system or gestalt.

Boundaries and contact

Just as Winnicott noted that there is no such thing as a baby (without a mother), there is no such thing as an organism without an environment. We are always in an "interacting field" (Perls, Hefferline, & Goodman, 1972, p. 228), so that feeling and reasoning, for example, are always responses to something external, whether current or as internalised imagos of past situations. Boundaries cannot be separated from contact any more than they can be separated from the self. They form the edge of the self and, as Perls emphasised, they are the place where contact with the environment happens. For true contact to be made, attention must be spontaneous, not laboured or fixed (ibid., p. 63). Contact with the inner world is mediated by proprioception and imagery, while the outer world is received through the senses: by touch, vision, hearing, smell, and taste. This contact is one-way with the material world and most non-mammalian species: we take in, but there is no sign—apart from an avoidance reflex—that we are received. Only with the higher animals is there a potential for two-way contact, the vast bulk of which occurs with other humans. This is where difficulties can arise.

A boundary surrounds the foreign other, which can therefore be noticed as it emerges as a figure against the ground of the environment. Without this boundary, there would be "no awareness, hence no excitement, hence no contact" (ibid., p. 118). In a state of confluence, we cannot see though there is nothing wrong with our eyes; we cannot hear though there is nothing wrong with our ears; we have nothing to say though there is nothing wrong with our voices. Confluence "is the condition where organism and environment are not differentiated from each other" (Clarkson, 1989, p. 55). Many people confuse confluence and social contact. In fact these are opposites, because it is rare to have genuine contact while colluding with stereotypical good manners (Perls, Hefferline, & Goodman, 1972, p. 152). "Primarily, contact is the awareness of, and behaviour toward, the assimilable novelty; and the rejection of the unassimilable novelty" (ibid., p. 230). Perls defined contact as creative adjustment of the organism and the environment. This occurs in contact–withdrawal cycles which may last for a minute, the duration of a therapy session, months, years, or a lifetime (Polster, E. & Polster, M., 1974, pp. 176–184). Abnormal psychology is "the study of the interruption, inhibition, or other accidents in the course of creative adjustment" (Perls, Hefferline, & Goodman, 1972, pp. 230–231).

Boundaries then are the border, more like a fence than a wall, across which contact occurs—with other parts of the self or with the living or non-living world. Gestalt therapy is concerned with increasing contact, and it views contact as vitalising (Polster, E. & Polster, M., 1974, p. 128). Contact is both necessary and sufficient for change because "appropriating the assimilable or rejecting the unassimilable novelty will inevitably lead to change" (ibid., p. 101). True contact may be defined as that which leads to change by assimilating something new. We build self from successive experiences of contact across the lifespan.

Damaging contact

In the world of psychotherapy, particularly humanistic therapy and most explicitly Gestalt, contact is viewed as a good thing, whereas poor contact is understood as a sign of psychopathology. However, there are two problems with this belief system: first, the latter part of the contact-withdrawal cycle—withdrawal—is often ignored and, second, the object of contact is not clearly defined.

Let us remind ourselves that contact is that which leads to change by the assimilation of something new. But it does not follow that "the something new" is experienced in a positive way, or that the experience of contact is reciprocal. Indeed most contact difficulties arise out of previous damaging contact with other human beings. Many of us are caught in a double-bind: we need other people but, at the same time, we have had repeated negative experiences of contact that are bruising, aggressive, blocking, alienating, flooding, invasive, excessive, confusing, disrespectful, non-mirroring, projecting, ignoring, and one-way— to name only some of the unsatisfactory kinds of contact. My client Tom divides engagements with other people into two classes: those that add to the self and those that take away. If others converse in your presence exclusively on topics about which you have no knowledge or interest so that you are excluded, that takes away from self. If others have very different beliefs and values and (even if only implicitly) disparage yours or fail or refuse to see them, you are likewise diminished.

Extending the relationship model of transactional analysis to the chakra system of distinct energy centres helps clarify which interactions are nourishing and which are damaging. If the same chakras in each person are activated, all is well: my head (intellect) talks to your head; or your heart (loving feeling) talks to my heart; or our gut instincts or sexual chakras have mutually agreeable interactions. But if I reveal my feelings to somebody who deconstructs them with reductive logic, I will feel abused and react with hurt and anger. The individual who wants no-strings sex doesn't match well with somebody who wants a love affair. When disembodied left-brain thinking meets embodied intuition, they are likely to feel mutual contempt, though the former will have the power advantage of being backed up by education, statistics, evidence, and other socially validated "proofs". However, embodied intuition is likely to be closer to the truth since it actually perceives what is in front of it, rather than being a self-enclosed system of logic that is closed off from whole swathes of reality (see Chapter Three). This is the kind of mutual incomprehension and self-certainty with which different branches of therapy meet each other: for instance Freudian thinking or CBT occupy a different chakra (head) from body psychotherapy (gut). Likewise, Gestalt is a gut therapy that is viewed with disapproval by some person-centred therapists who aspire to come from the heart centre, while the Gestalt practitioner may feel impatience with the "niceness" of the Pollyanna PCT practitioners. Overall, different chakras don't communicate well with each other, the heart centre being particularly vulnerable to anything other than another heart centre. Cross-chakra conversation may represent contact, but it is not nourishing and it is not genuine communication, where the intention should be mutual comprehension. It is cross-chakra contact that is responsible for Tom losing self in social interactions. This is, of course, true for everyone, but given his developmental history, Tom has a particular need for others to meet him from the heart where it will be safe for his own heart to thrive.

Even when we communicate via the same chakras, another problem can arise when there is unequal investment on either side of an episode of contact. One person may see and hear something that profoundly influences them, while the other may be unaware of what is happening for the listener. The differences in memory between individuals present at the "same" event are clear evidence that we all take in the world according to our *current* wishes, needs, expectations, what we are *capable* of experiencing emotionally, intellectually, and physically at that moment, and according to the self-buttressing narratives we have devised.

Gestalt therapy, being highly phenomenological and external, pays little attention to the inner process and contact with the self. Jung, on the other hand, viewed the internal world as more real than the external: "He who looks outside dreams, he who looks inside awakens". Jung was acutely aware of the need for a sealed container to facilitate inner transformation. His metaphor of the alchemical vessel or vas as the space in which we balance our functions and meet our opposites (the sacred marriage) suggests that—insofar as this is possible—boundaries are erected against the outer world in order to initiate this individuation process. For this inner, nourishing contact, we need stronger boundaries against the outside, not more contact. One reason for this reversal of emphasis may be that Jung was a self-declared introvert, whereas Perls appears to have been an extravert, albeit a largely self-centred one.

The ego and boundaries

For aware contact, I must first be in contact with myself as well as the other. Therefore, we must define internal as well as external boundaries; this in turn begs the question about where the ego and the self are located.

If the conscious ego manifests as this river of figures constantly emerging and disappearing, how then do we delimit the ego? Perls, Hefferline, and Goodman (1972, p. 462) suggest that the two sides of the boundary are: what we identify with and what is alien. Perls claims that "the boundaries, the places of contact, constitute the Ego. Only where and when the Self meets the 'foreign' does the ego start functioning, come into existence, determine the boundary between the personal and the impersonal 'field'" (quoted in Polster, E. & Polster, M., 1974, p. 103). In psychodynamic terms, only when the baby is frustrated by mother does theory of mind, differentiation, and ego development start. According to Wright (1991, p. 124): "the ego is the realm of transformed structures—that is structures that have accepted the incorporation of limiting boundaries and distances that satisfy the requirements of social reality". These theories, therefore, define the ego as the realm of the personal or non-foreign (Gestalt) and the realm of the socially acceptable (psychodynamic). We will return to the link between boundaries and self in a later section.

Polster, E. and Polster, M. have defined "I-boundaries" as the limits of permissible contactfulness (1974, p. 108), which can be described in several different dimensions: boundaries of the body, of values, familiarity, self-expression, and exposure (pp. 115–127). These are all different overlapping ways in which we manifest our identity and the limits of what our ego considers acceptable. If our sexuality is unacceptable, we may be in touch only with our heads, believe sex outside of marriage or homosexual sex is wrong, stick to conservative sexual acts, be disengaged from sex and liable to impotence and be excessively embarrassed and ashamed at being observed in sexual behaviour. In Joyce's *Ulysses*, Stephen Dadalus has rigid boundaries round the body and sexuality; he is all air: intellect and religious scruple. Leopold Bloom, on the other hand, is more earthy: sensual and embodied, but also with the mind integrated and highly engaged with the world. The boundary regarding exposure depends on our levels of trust in others and, not surprisingly, Brenda has an exposure boundary like a bombshelter. She disappears the moment a camera appears and will have nothing to do with more recent variants of exposure such as social network sites or reality television. She is disturbed by the spread of extensive surveillance in current society through CCTV, identity cards, and the capacity to track an individual's location via one's mobile phone.

Boundaries—inner and outer

I-boundaries may be divided into internal and external boundaries: the former governing our relationship to ourselves, the latter our contact with other people.

We are not just single cells bathed in an environmental soup. Psychologically, we are more like the multicellular organisms that we are biologically. We don't just have boundaries to separate us from the world, we also have internal boundaries keeping inner compartments separate from each other. For example, many people are confused about boundaries within the body, so that they may be unable to tell if they are experiencing hunger. This inability to notice or interpret body sensations indicates an alienation from the physical self (Clarkson, 1989, p. 76).

We can also see these inner boundaries operating in repression or suppression and a host of other ego defence mechanisms (Bienenfeld, 2006, pp. 51–53). These boundaries optimally protect us against hyper- or hypoarousal by separating the internal environment from the conscious mind. When a memory or fantasy pops onto the screen of my inner cinema, I may have an aversive reaction and act to remove that picture from the screen, distract myself with something else, hurry other images into view or simply close my eyes and space-out or even fall asleep. Whatever the defence, whether of the sympathetic nervous system fight or flight variety or the parasympathetic freezing mode, there is an increase in contraction and rigidity. If, on the other hand, I receive the image with a faith in my ability to process it, my armouring can melt a little.

Kenneth Wright (1991, p. 125), coming from a more psychodynamic perspective, conceives of inner boundaries and limits as that which imposes greater differentiation and structure onto early childhood's impulse-driven relation to objects. Some of these boundaries come from the nature of the material (the walls, doors, and windows keep us from running into the garden to chase the dog) and the biological (the child can't fly, must sleep, etc.), while others are set by the social world. Here the id impulses gradually become constrained by the dictates of the parents and, subsequently, the internalised superego.

However, if we accept that full contact manifests as a sharp figure against a well-contrasted background, we must conclude that the inner boundary of most relevance to contact is that between the conscious and unconscious minds. In crude anatomical terms, these may be located in the left and right cortical hemispheres respectively (Schore, 2010), with the corpus callosum as a connecting bridge. Ego defence mechanisms may then be conceptualised as different kinds of rigid inner contact boundaries. Let us examine their aetiology in the case of Brenda.

Despite her experience of having a thin skin with respect to the outside world, Brenda does have inner boundaries. However these are rigid, and thereby characteristic of avoidant attachment. Here the child has to compensate for the unresponsive parent and thus becomes excessively reliant on self-regulation (Siegel, 2012, p. 203), but in the distorted form of emotional repression. As for her external boundaries, they too are rigid in terms of releasing her own energy when interacting with the world: that is, she is overbounded, as we saw in Chapter One. However, her external boundaries function poorly at keeping out the pain and horrors of the world or the demands of other people. This is because her mother, who herself was in confluence with the world, was unable to filter out impingements, and thereby protect her daughter. At the same time, Brenda acquired, by a process of osmosis, the undefended absorbency modelled by her mother, thus replicating that same confluence with the environment. The ambivalent attachment that *underlies* the avoidant also contributed to her open boundaries (Pollard, 2005, p. 206). Here the internal working model of attachment is filled with uncertainty, so that the child is excessively responsive to its unreliable parents (Siegel, 2012, p. 204). If we understand that anxiety underpins the apparent nonchalance of the avoidant child, then it makes sense that weak external boundaries are coupled with strong internal boundaries.

We commonly experience our outer boundaries only when they are infringed. The father or mother who "drop by" their adult daughter's home without warning or invitation and who watch the comings and goings at her house are invading her boundaries as they attempt to control her life. The adult son whose parents demand his attendance at the Sunday family gatherings and who phone repeatedly for him to explain himself is having his boundaries infringed. The child in a fused family who won't or can't fit in with the culture of enmeshment will find his weak boundaries constantly challenged. These are all cases where the young adult is trying to differentiate away from their family of origin, but is blocked and stymied, guilt-tripped or threatened at every turn. This refusal to permit differentiation blocks the formation of boundaries in the first place and generates an adult child who is either insensitive to the boundaries of others because they haven't got any themselves, or—like Brenda—is hypersensitive to impingement because their boundaries are so fragile.

The child who is unaware of boundaries will live out of a false "self" and may be prone to depression—what one client calls "suffocating", as she struggles to invest her life with any meaning or sense of authenticity. Those with fragile boundaries are extremely vulnerable to what the family therapist Murray Bowen calls "cutoff" (Nichols, 2013), where the non-compliant individual cannot tolerate contact with some or all family members and removes himself emotionally, and sometimes physically as well. This is the case for Brenda who decided that she was better off outside the family than in, that any possibility of support was far outweighed by the likelihood of abuse and damage to her self-esteem. Indeed, she was all too aware that when she experienced difficulties in her life, she had to expend extra energy and attention on hiding this from her family. At best, she would receive pity; at worst taunts, contempt, or blame.

The individual who impinges on a sibling's social space, who steals their friends, moves in next door against their wishes or gets a job in the same institution, is blind to the needs of the other and highly invasive of boundaries. Likewise, the parent or older sibling who believes they are "head" of the family and have the right and the capacity to determine the lives of others is intruding on the space of those others. Physical invasion, surveillance, or attempts to control the lives of others are all ways of infringing their boundaries. One client, an only child, had a very close and loving but enmeshed relationship with his mother. When he attempted to leave home in his thirties, she alternated guilt-tripping and faux independence (pretending she was too busy with her golf and social life to have time for him) with setting a private detective on his trail—or so he said. This man suffered from a paranoid type of narcissism where he imagined every negative conversation he overheard at work was a coded criticism of him, and that many of the memos to his team were covert messages to himself alone. When his mother brought him to Mass, he believed that the priest's homily was directed at him personally. It was as difficult for me as for him to distinguish between the real and the imagined. As graphically emerged in our work together, boundary invasion and inhibition of boundary formation can devastate the self. This young man withdrew more and more from relationship with others in an attempt to substitute physical distancing for poor interpersonal boundaries.

Resistance to contact

Contact is not always nourishing. It can be destructive when an unarmoured part of one person (heart) is attacked by an armoured part of another (head): where, in Buber's words, there is an I-it interaction. Experiences of negative contact with one's environment can lead the individual to *expect* hurt, anger, resentment, fusion, frustration, and many other feelings we prefer to avoid. Consequently we may learn to resist contact in any of five different ways: introjection, projection, retroflection, deflection, and confluence (Polster, E. & Polster, M., 1974). The authors describe this resistance in terms of blocks to contact with the *external* environment: the introjector indiscriminately and passively incorporates, the projector disowns, the retroflector reinvests his energy back into a separate intrapersonal system, the deflector weakens contact with indirectness, and the confluent individual yields to whatever way the situation is tending (p. 71).

Perls conceived of the way the self develops through streams of contacts as akin to how the body grows through the consumption, digestion, and assimilation of food. Introjects are elements of the environment taken in but not digested, and therefore not incorporated into the matrix of self. He argued that introjection arises from the blocking of oral disgust in the infant and that the solution is to remobilise disgust (Perls, Hefferline, & Goodman, 1972, p. 199). Joyce (1968) who is also an adherent of the feeding metaphor, particularly in the Lestrygonians chapter of *Ulysses*, has Bloom entering the Burton restaurant:

> Men, men, men.
>
> ... wolfing gobfuls of sloppy food ... A man with an infant's saucestained napkin tucked round him shovelled gurgling soup down his gullet. A man spitting back on his plate: halfmasticated gristle ... Bolting to get it over. ... Bitten off more than he can chew. ...
>
> Smells of men. His gorge rose. Spaton sawdust, sweetish warmish cigarette smoke, reek of plug, spilt beer, men's beery piss, the stale of ferment. (pp. 168–169)

Bloom backs out and goes back up the street to Davy Byrne's where he gets a (vegetarian) gorgonzola sandwich and a glass of Burgundy. Here is a visceral example of how Bloom filters his environment: disgust plays the role of a transport-closing system in a semipermeable membrane; hunger the role of a pore-opening system.

Brenda's two main ways of resisting external contact are retroflection and confluence, though she does some introjecting as well. She shows the appearance of keeping people out (retroflection), which, however, overlays a vulnerability to confluence with the environment. The rigid boundaries were provoked by her angry and hostile father, the fusion by her confluent mother. I am retroflecting when I do to myself what I would like to do to someone else or what I would like someone else to do for me. I may blame myself for being a pathetic wimp instead of blaming the other, or I may soothe or pamper myself and expect nothing from others: either way, I am living in a self-created universe (Polster, E. & Polster, M., 1974, pp. 82–89) and resist contact with the outer world by getting parts of *myself* to play the part of the outer world. This is what the rigidly-boundaried part of Brenda does in relation to the social world, and she fantasises about the ultimate retroflection of becoming a solipsistic hermit. Her confluence has been kept in place because of the rewards she gets from participatory merger with the natural world. Similarly, when swimming in the nourishing waters of a good novel, she revels in her easy absorption. However, she just as easily incorporated the toxin from the marinade of her fusion with her mother. She could defend herself against her father's active aggression in a way she was unable to keep out her mother's shame and masochism. She reacted to this passive incorporation of toxic material with literal nausea and vomiting. Her somatic assimilation of her mother's beliefs and values meant that Brenda initially experienced her "bilious attacks" as vomiting out who she herself *was*—her femaleness—rather than her mother's masochistic beliefs about women. Only by removing herself physically from her family and re-marinating herself in an environment that affirmed women was she able to heal her self-hatred— and her monthly vomiting.

As young babies, we are all in a state of confluence with our surroundings and therefore cannot but absorb whatsoever is on offer emotionally and physically. As we become aware that parts of us are unacceptable or that adult figures are unavailable for contact, we generate the more sophisticated defences that depend on the development of the superego. We may then utilise one predominant defensive style, though we may occasionally use other approaches as well. In families where there is a culture of blame, some members—the projectors— will blame others who are forced to swallow the blame—the introjectors and retroflectors. (Virginia Satir's classification (Satir, 1978) shows how defences become communication styles in a family setting. Satir's blamer is Perls's projector; her placater is a mixture of Perls's introjector, retroflector, and confluent individual; Perls's deflector combines Satir's computer and distracter.) The particular defensive style will depend on a complex interaction of factors such as the child's temperament, the roles played by parents, the child's relationship to them, their place in the family, the roles played by the older siblings, and so on. In showing nothing of herself, Brenda's avoidant/dismissing mother made it difficult for Brenda to differentiate herself from the environment.

We resist contact with the external world through a variety of defences, described by Perls and summarised above. But parts of the internal psyche also resist contact with each other. If we see the great realm of the unconscious as the inner "environment" of our conscious mind, how would these kinds of resistance look in terms of contact? In this case, confluence would refer to our inability to form sharp figures in our internal worlds. We are not willing to deal with struggle between our different subpersonalities, and so we remain largely unaware of our inner dynamics—we are entirely unconscious. Many avoidantly attached people have this lack of psychological-mindedness, but here Brenda differs from them in being somewhat willing and able to reflect and mentalise—a capacity developed, she believes, by her reading of classic novels.

Introjection implies a failure to discriminate between the nourishing and the noxious and the indiscriminate swallowing of both.

Whenever, whether in the interests of honesty or courage or in the grip of compulsion, Brenda replays terrifying fantasies or bad memories that diminish her self-esteem, she fails to deconstruct and re-envision the values of her upbringing and so continues to eat from the poisoned dish. But sometimes self-protection must come first: the old inner imperative of taking it on the chin has to be challenged and the masochism named.

We may ascribe cruelty or capriciousness to the unconscious and regard it as not part of ourselves. Freud projectively conceived of the unconscious as a seething cauldron of unstructured and unregulated desires and madness. In contrast Jung, having learnt to be comfortable with the messages of his own unconscious, saw it as a place of nourishment and the most fundamental part of every human being. The projector is in denial of some aspect of himself and keeps this cruelty, hatred, ugliness, etc. well repressed. While Freud feared the unconscious and believed it had to be tamed, he didn't deny that it was part of him. Somebody who identifies only with their conscious and thinking mind and believes that the unconscious has to be controlled ("starve the feelings") is projecting out their irrational and feeling side. In McGilchrist's terms, the right-brain master is banished and the left-brain emissary runs the show (2009).

I am retroflecting when I do to myself what I would like to do to someone else or what I would like someone else to do for me. But how would this play out in the inner world? I ask parts of my conscious to play the role of the unconscious so that I don't have to deal with its frightening and unpredictable otherness. When Richard Dawkins and his ilk pretend that science can provide the numinous wonder of religious experience, they are in the grip of this kind of left-brain retroflection.

"Deflection is a manoeuver for turning aside from direct contact with another person" (Polster, E. & Polster, M., 1974, p. 89). If we over-rationalise, minimise, or laugh off our dreams or pay little attention to them, we are deflecting contact with the unconscious.

The inner and the outer combined

The outer world is experienced inside; but *what* is internalised depends on our prior, but currently active, inner world which itself is the product of previous internalisations. If I am in the midst of paranoid memories, I am far more likely to be paranoid in my current interaction. In voluntary solitary confinement in a sterile and unchanging physical environment, where little contact with the outside is possible, we could continue to have a rich, though not necessarily comfortable inner life. The memories of our past, our daytime fantasies, our night-time dreams, our attempts to think or imagine all continue to bubble away, one figure replacing another and generating a continually changing self. The hermit may find that processing this backlog, as well as dealing with his experience of God (which he might perceive as either internal or external) is sufficient for a lifetime. Small amounts of change in the external environment, such as a fly landing on the wall, will provide food for contact which would be ignored in a richer environment. An overly rich environment creates the opposite problem of demanding a constant rigorous filtering and exclusion.

Our contact with the environment and our defences against it depend very much on the nature of that environment. In regard to the social world, Brenda claims, provocatively, that she would like to live in a solipsistic universe, and she has learned through therapy to erect strong and impermeable boundaries against other people. (Not quite the result most therapists aim for!) Brenda's greatest joy is to sink into the natural environment which she experiences as benign and nourishing. Perls would argue that her confluence with the natural world does not amount to contact because contact implies a boundary that must be bridged. However, as was argued in Chapter Two, this merger may permit—and is experienced by Brenda as—valid participatory consciousness: she *knows* the natural world through identification. But unfortunately for Brenda, she finds she cannot restrict her defences against contact to one realm. As she has become more defended against people, she is less open to the natural world.

I would question whether what Gestalt therapists label as resistance to contact does in fact constitute resistance. These kinds of "resistance" seem more like residues of partially completed development. Thus we all start in a state of confluence and we then develop defences of increasing sophistication as we progress through childhood (see Bienenfeld, 2006, pp. 62–63 for a psychodynamic view of the maturation of defences). Distortion of contact may be a consequence rather than—as implied—the cause of these defences.

Personal space and claustrophobia

Brenda suffers from claustrophobia in closed-in or crowded spaces and one of her most persistent terrors concerned being buried alive. She puts her claustrophobia down to getting stuck in the birth canal—though she doesn't actually know anything about her birth. Another possibility is that her fear of small spaces is connected with her insecure attachment style(s). The kind of interpersonal boundary discussed above does not depend on proximity, but on an internal representation of the other. We have another kind of boundary—a physical one, which nonetheless extends further than the contours of our skin; this ensures we keep an appropriate distance between bodies in physical proximity to each other. Optimally, we can sense the energetic aura of the other and do not infringe on their space and, equally, we dislike our own space being invaded. Our experience of these energy boundaries is determined by the parts of the brain that sense the body in space. Proprioception refers to our "sixth sense" which receives information about our body position, movement, and posture. Proprioceptors in the muscles, tendons, joints, and ligaments send impulses to the brain which then sends signals back to the muscles telling them to change position or stop moving. Much of this information (e.g., for maintenance of balance) is processed unconsciously by the cerebellum at the back of the skull which controls movement. Conscious proprioception, on the other hand, passes through the thalamus and ends in the parietal lobe of the cortex (under the crown of the skull), which is devoted to generating maps of our bodies and our position in space. This processing by the sensory cortex permits decision-making in response to body information about the length, tension, and pressure in the musculoskeletal system (Carter, 2009, pp. 102, 160). The large size of the parietal lobe suggests how important this orientation in space is for our survival.

Matthew Longo and his team at Birkbeck College have created a way of measuring personal space or near space—the space surrounding the body. When bisecting horizontal lines, healthy adults display a leftward bias in near space, but a rightward bias in far space. The rate of this shift can be used to quantify the extent of personal space. Investigating within the range of normal individuals, they found that those with a larger personal space reported a greater fear of claustrophobia (Lourenco, Longo, & Pathman, 2011). Long arms also correlate with personal space independently of claustrophobia, and the extent of peripersonal space can be manipulated with tools: holding long tools such as a rake increases personal space, whereas heavy weights on the wrist shrink near space (ibid.). Likewise, stimulating the arm muscles with vibrators generates the sensation of arms moving inwards, thus creating the subjective illusion that the body has shrunk (Carter, 2009, p. 172). It remains to be seen whether wrist weights or vibrators could be used to alleviate claustrophobia.

It is not yet clear whether the sense of physical boundary, manifesting as claustrophobia at one extreme, is inevitably connected with social boundaries. Not surprisingly, avoidant/dismissing attachment types are more uncomfortable than others when other *people* are too close (Howe, 2011, p. 108), but whether they are generally more claustrophobic with respect to the material world is not known.

Introversion, shyness, and weak interpersonal boundaries

Both introversion and shyness appear to lie at one extreme of social-boundary sensitivity. The degree of extraversion is substantially genetic in origin, with a heritability of about fifty per cent (Plomin, DeFries, McClearn, & McGuffin, 2008, p. 244). Compared to introverts, extraverts need more environmental stimuli to feel energised in the neural circuit that keeps the brain aroused; this includes the dorsolateral prefrontal cortex, the anterior cingulate cortex and the thalamus (Carter, 2009, p. 196). Thus, the neuroscience of introversion/extraversion fails to show any direct overlap with the neuroscience of physical boundaries. However, it seems highly likely to me that they are indirectly connected, and I would expect that introverts have greater personal space requirements than extraverts. A connection between physical and emotional boundaries has been revealed through brain scans of meditating individuals, where diminished activity in the parietal lobe during deep meditation has been shown to correlate with an emotional no-boundary experience (Hay, 2006, p. 176).

As a recovering shy child who has to some degree mastered this handicap, Brenda no longer finds an excessive amount of contact with others as stressful as before; however, as an introvert, she finds it boring, dispiriting, and pointless. She longs to get away and read a book or sit in silence watching the light change over the valley from the top of a mountain. Childhood shyness/inhibition is one of the most genetically determined of the personality traits, with a heritability of seventy-five per cent (Plomin, DeFries, McClearn, & McGuffin, 2008, pp. 234, 237), but little is known about the neuroscience of shyness or its relationship to separation anxiety (heritability of forty per cent) or adult introversion.

In introversion, the inner boundaries are relatively open and the external boundaries relatively closed as compared with extraversion where the opposite state pertains. Whatever one's personality type, inner and outer boundaries tend to open alternately: when intense attention is given to the inner process, outer contact is cut off and vice versa. One example is the proverbial absent-minded professor who is so absorbed in a book he steps off the library ladder into mid-air.

Boundary dysfunction

Perls defined mental health as "the formation of *complete* and *comprehensive* Gestalten" (Perls, Hefferline, & Goodman, 1972, p. ix, my italics). In neurosis, and more so in psychosis, there is often rigidity in (fixation) or a lack of (repression) figure formation. Thus, "confusion, boredom, compulsions, fixations, anxiety, amnesias, stagnation and self-consciousness are indicative of figure/ground formation which is disturbed" (ibid., p. ix). Brenda, as we have seen, engages with the world by absorbing it indiscriminately. However, this mode of being quickly becomes very stressful, so she regularly protects herself by what she calls "spacing out". This is a state where she represses figure formation; she may feel calm and peaceful or stagnant and bored, but she is not really living and has no memories of such periods beyond a foggy haze.

Ease and vitality can coexist only when figure has differentiated from ground with full clarity, that is, when a complete gestalt has formed. In the absence of this awareness of contrast between figure and ground, excitement is experienced as anxiety, which may be defined as constricted excitement (Polster, E. & Polster, M. 1974, pp. 33, 179). One possible reason is that full contact with the figure is necessary to bind the excitation and process it in a complete contact–withdrawal cycle. When this does not happen, the excitement is free-floating and not understood or capable of being harnessed into action.

For fluidity, spontaneity, and depth of contact, there is a time element which ensures boundaries of optimum flexibility. Boundaries may be obsessive and rigid where unfinished business from the past dominates the person's life. The successful man who never completes the cycle to become fully aware of his own success goes through life achieving more and more, but never being satisfied: he is still living out his childhood struggle with his more favoured brother. This individual may experience his life as sterile or stressful and is usually boring in his monomania. Miss Havisham is the great fictional character who cannot let go of the unfinished business of the past—being jilted on her wedding day. Her entire subsequent life is motivated by the need to get even through the daughter she adopts and brings up to entrap and hurt men just as she has been abandoned and humiliated.

Polster, E. and Polster, M. (1974, p. 38) also point to the other end of the spectrum: labile individuals who cannot maintain contact for long enough to complete the cycle and achieve meaning. Where the obsessive cannot let things go, the labile person skims through life, not landing long enough to reach the end of anything, whether it is a conversation, a degree, or a marriage. Alternatively, they may complete tasks in the world, but never settle into moments of contact with people or other elements of the environment which would facilitate *depth* of engagement. The protagonist of Kundera's *The Unbearable Lightness of Being* is one such fictional individual: always able to let go because he has not formed a deep bond in the first place.

Ogden and colleagues examine in practical detail the loss of boundaries in traumatised individuals. They note that most trauma occurs in the context of interpersonal relationships, so that it includes boundary violations as well as loss of autonomy and self-regulation (Ogden, Minton, & Pain, 2006, p. 23). Trauma may result in fight or flight (hyperarousal), or if neither of these are possible, as is usually the case for abused children, then freezing (hypoarousal) is the only option available (p. 97). While the boundary violation may be most apparent in the behaviour of the hypoaroused, it is there too in the hyper-vigilant or over-aggressive individual who responds reflexively and without awareness to invasion of his personal space (p. 227). Alternatively, the overboundaried will be physically and/or emotionally distant in relationships, while the underboundaried fail to set limits or make demands and are too compliant and "nice", resulting in a huge stress load (p. 286). The authors distinguish between, on the one hand, a cognitive or emotional understanding of boundaries and, on the other, somatic boundaries, in which the individual has a felt sense of safety (pp. 226–227). Many people have a cognitive sense of rights and boundaries which they cannot back up with a felt (somatic) sense of preferences or entitlements (p. 286). Until the "no" is located in the body there is no safety, and the greater the incongruence between the cognitive and the somatic boundary the more blame and anger may be felt—towards self and others.

Terrifying images of torture and people being burnt or buried alive and dreams of being pursued by torturers plagued Brenda from her teens into her forties. These intrusions appear to have derived from internalised relational trauma, so that Brenda treated herself as would a torturer. When, as a result of therapy, she gradually began to be more forgiving and less demanding of herself and to lead a less stressful life, the intrusions and nightmares all but ceased. She feels safer now while still being aware of the horrors of torture in many parts of the world—in the present as well as in the historical past.

A client Tom who has a lot of childhood trauma, generally manages to regulate his arousal levels. However, agreeing to go on an adventure holiday with his girlfriend triggered panic attacks. These were then exacerbated when he tried to meditate his way out of them: this melted his already weak boundaries even more. This in turn led to his hippocampus pathways being overwhelmed by the firing of the amygdala, which cannot be directly controlled by the rational mind. Here the boundaries are defined, not by anything like a fence, but by the fact that neurons that wire together fire together. As a result, separate neural networks are formed which are triggered in the two distinct conditions of normal arousal or hyperarousal. Only the removal of the immediate threat—the holiday—and the use of an anxiolytic drug calmed him enough to restore normal arousal and thereby make therapy on boundaries possible at all. His task was of course to find his "no", whose absence was signalled by his sunken contracted diaphragm. Unfortunately, saying "no" is associated with early threats and fears of being abandoned, so Tom is caught in a double-bind: terror is the outcome whether he says "yes" or "no". Traumatised people inevitably have some degree of disembodiment. This is damaging for them because it is *somatic* boundaries that are critical in building protection against re-traumatisation. They can be generated by actions with the arms (blocking, pushing, or circling) or legs (kicking, walking away) or finding the physical source of the voice and gradually building its strength or volume in response to trigger statements, all of which contribute to re-embodiment.

Therapy of boundaries

Our first psychological boundaries form as we emerge out of a state of confluence and introjection, and they depend on our process of separating being met by parents with respect, confidence, and a sense of our entitlement. If my differentiation is encouraged and valued, I will develop healthy boundaries; if not I will remain in confluence. If parts of me are considered unacceptable, I will develop the later kinds of boundary defences already described. It follows from this that one crucial foundation for healing boundary infringement is a reparative relationship of mutually non-impinging respect, in which the individual must at the same time learn to take responsibility for their own life and decisions.

Brenda needed to detoxify herself of all the old noxious input she had absorbed through confluence by embedding herself in a healthy environment. At the same time she had to remove herself from all communication with her family who continued to serve up the same contaminated dish. She was also an introjector, and therefore needed to learn to distinguish and filter out the toxic from the nourishing in her interactions with others. Her membrane needed to become *semi*-permeable. The retroflection defence has two components. When it comes to doing for herself what the other could do for her, Brenda needs to distinguish who she can trust to do the job better than she can. In terms of blaming herself instead of blaming others, part of the journey of her recovery has involved her beginning to project out anger and responsibility. Switching from retroflection to projection has been a necessary step to clear the way for congruent contact.

Creating boundaries out of confluence amongst adults is neither easy nor pretty. In two novels depicting couples breaking out of fused relationships, we see the ugly destructiveness and tearing pain of the emerging self demanding release from control by the partner, simultaneous with the loss of love and support from the other. Psychological birth can be as terrifying and bloody, but also potentially as liberating, as physical birth. In the brilliant and terrible contemporary Israeli novel, *Husband and Wife* (Shalev, 2002), the appallingly codependent couple scream unjust, hate-filled accusations at each other in their unconscious desperation to free themselves from the stifling stranglehold of their confluence. Eventually, he—with the help of a Tibetan healer—takes the initiative and leaves, whereupon she falls apart but is later reborn from the ashes. On the other hand, the psychological birth in an earlier (1961) novel *Revolutionary Road* (Yates, 2007) is a stillbirth. April performs an abortion on herself to rid herself of the unwanted baby her husband manipulated her into keeping—not because he wanted the child, but because of his need for power over her. She dies in the attempt, but the note she leaves makes it clear that there was an element of suicide by Russian Roulette in her action—or at any rate, she would prefer to risk death than carry on as they have been, a state of affairs that would have been cemented by the advent of another child. If the first half of the nineteenth century was an era of courtship novels (ending with "Reader, I married him"), the second half focused on the problems of marriage and adultery. The novels of the late twentieth and twenty-first centuries, along with the society they reflect, have moved on to the next stage—the individual's need for self-discovery though separation and the breaking of social bonds.

The confluent or fused individual has an undeveloped self and a large compensating "pseudo self", to use the terminology of the family therapist Margaret Hall (1981). This pseudo-self is an amalgam of other people's opinions, beliefs, and values, absorbed without any conscious evaluation or commitment to them. The boundaries of the pseudo-self are endlessly negotiable because of the terror of abandonment which is based on the (outdated but still present) belief that loss of the other equals death. Thus do men and women remain in emotionally or physically violent relationships, both strangled in their dependence on the other and hating the other for that dependence. One way whereby things can move is by hitting rock bottom in the abyss of the codependence, so that one of the couple makes a desperate bid for freedom. Both partners are then in danger of grabbing hold of the lifebelt of a similar relationship unless they find appropriate alternative support. The other way to break out is to gradually form other connections in parallel with the relationship, so that the total dependence on the other is spread round a larger circle.

Codependence in relation to a partner is a particularly destructive example of a general phenomenon. Anything we incorporate into our personal boundaries becomes part of the central core that is the self. Yalom (1989, p. 85) writes of a client who identified heavily with his profession. Criticism of any aspect of his work was felt as a mortal assault to which he therefore responded with the viciousness we mount against anything that threatens our survival.

Gestalt therapy requires the development of awareness and the experiencing of the somatic and emotional block or void, followed by experimenting on it to mobilise the fixed boundaries. Perls suggests that the difference between vitality and neurosis is continuing creativity in the face of an inner obstacle as distinct from a state of confusion, inner division, or insensitivity. "The neurotic begins to lose contact with the actuality … What he must learn is to recognize sharply when he is no longer in contact, how he is not, and where and what the actuality now is, so he can continue contacting it" (Perls, Hefferline, & Goodman, 1972, p. 465). Ogden, Minton, and Pain (2006, p. 171) write of a rape victim who found herself freezing in the presence of her long-term therapist. She realised that the therapist was wearing a similar sweater to the rapist's, and ultimately, that her freeze response was a signal that she needed a personal boundary. She was able to begin generating this somatically with wide circling movements of her arms.

Tom experienced the social world as one where he was at the mercy of other people. He reacted by becoming increasingly isolated, punctuated by rare but bruising forays into social engagement. On these occasions, he concluded that any gain to self resulting from contact was more than outweighed by the loss of self from handing over power to others. It was only when he realised that he had a role in *creating* his environment that he began to challenge his withdrawal. He discovered that he could shift the conversational agenda onto topics of interest to him, that he didn't have to offer his vulnerability up as a kind of sacrifice in the interests of openness, and that there was no point in looking for approval from somebody who envied him for his gifts.

Creating strong impermeable boundaries—which are really defences— initially feels like a great relief if we have been overexposed to the world. But they ultimately leave us isolated and lonely. The trick is to have flexible permeable boundaries where we both stay in touch with our own self but are also open to the other. Brenda found that therapy led to a building of defences which protected her against invasion by others, and largely shielded her against inner intrusions such as terrifying dreams and fantasies about torture. However, the downside of this armouring is that her capacity to immerse herself in nature, drama, music, and literature was reduced. She was now cut off from this source of nourishment, while still operating her old avoidant style of relating. The new bleakness of her inner world made her more open to friendship when it was offered, by warm open-hearted people who entered her life when she took up a new job. Her love for them has been a huge challenge to her: it has rescued her from isolation in her fortified castle, but threatens at every moment (every phone call) to steal her autonomy. Worrying about what other people think is the great attack on boundaries. Only as she is taking on the full otherness of the other—their quiddity—and realises that she does not know what they are thinking, that she cannot control their inner world, and that this inner world has very little connection to her—only now is she developing boundaries that allow her to breathe. She is moving beyond her old narcissism about her place in the world of others and discovering that she is at the edge, not the centre of their lives. With this awareness of the unknowability of others, she finds that she might as well act in a way that suits her and stop thinking of the consequences to her relationships. She cannot control them, but it is scary not to try. She feels like the baby bird jumping off the cliff and having faith that she can fly, though she has no experience that this is so.

Writing about what she calls the "spiritually sensitive person", Judith Blackstone's description of herself uncannily matches how Brenda experiences the other:

> All my life I had found that the presence of other people disrupted my inner contact with myself—my ability to hear my own thoughts or know my own feelings. When I related with others, I usually felt merged with them. I seemed to have no barrier, no cushion between myself and the world around me, and I often had the sense of actually being pulled out of myself into my surroundings. (Blackstone, 2012, p. 5)

Blackstone distinguishes spiritual sensitivity from sensory-processing disorder or sensory-integration disorder which is viewed as a pathology of the nervous system (p. 88). In contrast, people with the gift of spiritual potential are high-functioning and do not have the symptoms of severe psychological wounding. Rather they are innately more open to others. The positive side of this is the gift of empathy, the negative is the dislocation of the self by others. Blackstone's solution (p. 91) is not to become more dense or avoidant, but rather to become even more sensitive and open—but crucially from a place of full embodiment. When you inhabit the body in tandem with the development of sensitivity, stimuli can pass through your consciousness without disturbing it.

Boundaries and the self

The ego boundary is constantly shifting: unlike the membrane round a plant cell with its rigidly enclosing cell wall, but more like an amoeba, throwing out protoplasmic extrusions towards food sources or withdrawing from what is toxic. On the inner side of this boundary is who I am—reaching out to or withdrawing from the world, letting some experiences in and keeping others out. We experience our muscular armour softening when we become more receptive, as we allow a more emotional engagement with the world. This is equally true when we relax our inner boundaries: when, for example, our superego permits more id expression, or when, in Gestalt terms, we allow more organismic satisfaction and authenticity.

The self is a much bigger entity than the ego. Perls, Hefferline, and Goodman (1972, p. 463) criticise psychoanalysis for its definition of the state of a healthy self as a system of ego-boundaries, which Perls conceives as only a stage—and an emptied out one at that—in the development of self. For Perls, the self is the "system of contacts at any one moment" (p. 235) and is therefore flexible and various, like the existential definition of self. The self is the integrator which finds and makes the meanings we grow by. In Jungian terms, the goal of the Self is fulfilled wholeness—individuation to Jungians, self-actualisation in humanistic therapy, or role-expansion in psychodrama. The boundaries of the realised Self are ever-expanding as we develop more and more aspects of our potential. Or, perhaps they are not so much expanding as throwing out new growth, while the old retracts by a process akin to programmed cell death that is part of structured development. At one age, sex is the most charged of fantasies, while at a later life stage it loses its fascination and is replaced by a move towards the spiritual. We appear to advance by a process of replacement *and* integration of the old with the new. According to Perls, we are in a state of psychological health when we identify with what he called the "forming self", but if on the contrary we try to conquer our movement and spontaneity, we find life "dull, confused and painful" (p. 235).

Leopold Bloom in Joyce's *Ulysses* is the great literary example of the endlessly forming self. He drifts semi-purposefully through the streets of Dublin in ever-changing contact with the world about him. As he observes and meets and greets, he remembers, wonders, imagines, fantasises, and empathises. He is part of the Dublin society of 16

June 1904—but not in confluence with it, aided in this by being Jewish and therefore an outsider, despite having been born and raised in the city. In his peregrinations round Dublin, we see his boundaries functioning to separate him from others but still remain in contact. We see him avoiding being drawn into the confluence of drifting to the pub with the others in the newspaper office. We hear his thoughts as he avoids lending a suitcase to somebody he meets along the way. He invites in contact too, but usually maintaining clear boundaries, so that we hear his inner commentary alongside his outer pleasantries. When he bumps into Mrs. Breen and she notices his funeral attire, he thinks "may as well get her sympathy" (1968, p. 156), and then reminds himself to ask about the husband (p. 157). Likewise, as he chats warily to Nosey Flynn, he counters the unstated but underlying poking and jeering about his cuckoldry with his own partially accepting, partially disgusted observation of Flynn's scratching and his dripping nose (pp. 172–173). At other times, Bloom's contact is more spontaneous and without the splitting between direct experience and inner commentator—the kind that Perls regards as genuine contact. This is the case for his sexual fantasies or his reading an ad about a Zionist colony (pp. 62–63), as distinct from his social encounters, where he is more driven by politeness. But Bloom can also be drawn into momentary empathy, when he imagines Mrs. Purefoy "three days bad now" (p. 158): "Three days imagine groaning on a bed with a vinegared handkerchief round her forehead, her belly swollen out! … Child's head too big: forceps. Doubled up inside her trying to butt its way out blindly, groping for the way out" (p. 161). Or the animals killed for food: "Wretched brutes there at the cattle market, waiting for the poleaxe to split their skulls open" (p. 170).

Boundaries and the self are coincident: we can't have one without the other. Boundaries contain the self; the expression of the self generates strong but flexible boundaries. Thus, Brenda may be unassertive and compliant with friends whom she fears to antagonise, but when she has a long-term goal or passion driving her life (as when she returned to college), the importance of the other person fell away and she could be ruthless about not answering the phone during study hours. Here the goal that is an expression of self firmed up her boundaries, while both goal execution and boundaries led to the consolidation and expansion of self. The self may be viewed as a thing with rigid boundaries or a process with flexible boundaries (see also Chapter Eight). The body therapist Nick Totton has pointed out that human beings live in constant self-regulating movement between these two poles.

> Symptoms are how stasis moves into process, and edges are how process moves into stasis. So if someone becomes too rigid and resistant to change, they tend to develop a symptom, an irritation which destabilizes their boundary; conversely, if movement and change go too far and too fast, the person will develop an edge, which stabilizes the boundary. (Totton, 2005, p. 181)

The mother who is well attuned to her infant gives permission for the creation of healthy boundaries. She is not so invasive as to over-impinge on the developing self of the child. However, the mother who—at a later stage—fails to frustrate the growing child, does not communicate the message that mother and child are different and separate. Such a child may not experience the grit on which the formation of the boundary pearl depends. For strong but flexible boundaries, therefore, the child must receive optimum levels of encouragement and mirroring on the one hand and adequate levels of frustration and challenge on the other: a constant interplay of unconditional acceptance for the child's current true self and stimulating challenge for the potential self he might become. This is, as we saw in Chapter One, the kind of attunement that leads to secure attachment, and strong but flexible boundaries are one manifestation of the securely attached self. Avoidant/dismissing parents tend to overdo the frustration of the child and lead to the kind of frustrated self with which Brenda battles.

Intersubjectivity

Daniel Stern found that infants aged seven to nine months begin to become more self-conscious in their social interactions and to realise that other people can share the same feelings and intentions as they do—what Stern called intersubjectivity. The infant's excitement about his rattle is matched by mother's excitement about his excitement, creating a sense of mutuality. While Margaret Mahler's theory of separation-individuation emphasises the separation of the child away from mother in its psychological birth, Stern's theory focuses on the enhanced capacity for mutual sharing and appreciation that separation brings. Intersubjective theory brings into the foreground the context of relationship in which two subjectivities engage. The foundations of our intersubjectivity may be seen in the early reciprocity of gesture between mother and child, the attunement and entrainment within the same rhythms in the "conversations" between a mother and her pre-verbal baby. Jessica Benjamin (1990), in reworking object relations, shows that "intersubjectivity reorients the conception of the psychic world from a subject's relations to its object towards a subject meeting another subject" (p. 20). This places a different emphasis on our interactions with others: away from contact with another monad across our two sets of boundaries towards what happens in the "field" of self and other "distinct but interrelated beings". It is recognition by the other that tells us who we are. The other not only mirrors us as Winnicott pointed out, but we also recognise ourselves in the other. They are both mirror and model for us and show us that "my mental representation works" (Stern quoted in Benjamin, 1990, p. 21). Intersubjectivity, then, challenges the dualism inherent in the Gestalt theory of contact across boundaries and introduces a tension between the idea of a boundary and the idea of an interactive field.

Intersubjectivity in psychotherapy practice is 180 degrees away from the psychoanalytic perspective of the therapist as blank screen. It is also very different from the person-centredness of Carl Rogers, where the therapist or teacher provides core conditions for the growth of the other, but puts his own self aside and thus turns himself into an object for the client's use. Intersubjective therapy, on the other hand, involves two people in a mutual, interactive relationship, where the client has the opportunity to recognise the being of the therapist just as much as the therapist mirrors and values the client (Staunton, 2008). Person-centred therapy depends on the therapist providing the core conditions of empathy, congruence, and unconditional positive regard without which, Rogers argued, the client cannot grow in the direction of self-actualisation. This works well for certain kinds of clients in the earlier stages of the therapeutic process. The person-centred therapist is highly respectful of the client's boundaries—but the problem with this is that the client doesn't get the chance to strengthen or become flexible in his boundaries or to respond appropriately to the boundaries of the other. More recent developments in person-centred therapy incorporate the ideas of intersubjectivity, where the therapist is present as a person in their own right, not simply as a provider of core conditions to the client; rather they share their own thoughts and feelings, so that the therapy is relationship-centred rather than client-centred (Mearns and Cooper, 2005). This kind of client-therapist relationship is a better reflection of how we live in the world. As Rosalind Pearmain puts it: "there is no brain without a body, there is no body without an environment, there is no sense of self or meaning without others to share it" (2001, p. 12): we form part of an interconnecting *field* of contact. For the client with boundary issues, whether the highly defended, the schizoid, or the narcissist through to the thin-skinned client whose boundaries are fragile, the intersubjective therapist works with this continuous exchange between subjects. Patrick Nolan describes the intersubjective field as a third element in therapy in addition to therapist and client. "Because the intersubjective element of the relationship resonates energetically with what is happening in therapy, when we attend to it we strengthen our attunement to the client and what occurs between us" (Nolan, 2012, p. 87). He cites examples where he picks up on the client's unconscious or pre-conscious process through his own responses: his observations, feelings, and images. When these are brought into the dialogue, the client's process moves forward.

Brenda's experience of blank-screen therapy—in which she would include some person-centred therapy—was not good. With her first client-centred therapist, who said very little, Brenda felt as if she was floating in outer space, a sensation she recognised from having tried but failed to bring her mother into contact. The latter showed nothing of herself; she was buried in a safe place deep within, which even she herself could not access. Brenda's mother was so accustomed to giving way to the other that she literally did not know how she felt or what she wanted. There was nobody there to engage in an interactive relationship. Thus, therapy as an empty space for the client to fill was the worst possible model for Brenda. She needed a therapist who would engage in a robust manner, but without impinging, controlling, or judging. She needed *all* of the relational elements that Nolan (2012, p. 33) prescribes for a therapist: mirroring, empathy, containment, and lack of pressure or impingement. With the blank-screen therapist, she got the last two elements (the two absences), but not the containment, and she wasn't sure about the mirroring and empathy since the therapist responded so little. She got on much better with a later, more interactive and playful, therapist.

Early psychotherapists of very different stripes, from Freud to Winnicott to Rogers, conceived of relationships as necessary because of what we receive from the other, whether that is feeding or mirroring or positive regard respectively. David Brazier (2009), coming from a background in person-centred therapy and subsequently Zen Buddhism, goes further and suggests that the fundamental human need is not to receive but to *give*, and what we want to give is love. From this premise, he goes on to develop a theory of other-centred therapy. Brenda was familiar with this frustration of her desire to give. Her mother found it impossible to receive gifts or compliments or help, indeed love in any of the forms in which it manifests. Because she felt unworthy to receive, any attempt to give to her seemed to elicit pain, embarrassment, or poor self-esteem. Brazier maintains that "love is the primary drive in human life" (2009, p. 1), but whether we have a greater need to give or receive may depend on what was most frustrated in the parent–child relationship. Brenda's partner John who minded his needy and frightened mother in childhood—and continued codependent caretaking of others into adulthood—is exhausted with giving. What he really needs but feels unsafe in negotiating is some love for himself; as a surrogate, he desperately tries to feed himself nourishment through the beauty of the soprano voice, which he experiences as "love" directed at him. Brenda, who wanted to love her mother, felt her love was not noticed. Equally, she wanted to give to John, but he rebuffed her offers. She has even given up on buying him presents because they were never right. In trying to meet his own desperate need for accurate mirroring by choosing his own presents, John has extinguished Brenda's already-weakened impulse to give. They have become more extreme in their polarity with John as the giver and Brenda as the receiver in the relationship.

Empathy

The capacity for intersubjectivity depends on empathy. How can we distinguish this from confluence or sympathy? Confluence is the absence of a boundary between self and some others, which may equally be understood as the sharing of a boundaried space with these others. In other words, there is a boundary against foreign others who are not part of your family, tribe, or ethnic group, who are not followers of your football team or who do not share the same beliefs. Sympathy is based on a partial confluence—you feel for the other who has a problem with which you can identify. Or sometimes you merely recognise the existence of a problem but don't actually feel much for the other, being too busy with your own issues.

I propose that *empathy*—experiencing other people's feelings from *their* perspective, even if they are very different from our own reactions—derives from the concrete operational stage (aged six or seven), whereas *sympathy*—sharing those feelings of others with which *we* can identify—is present from pre-birth and is a function of pre-separation merger with others. The fictional Jack (aged five) can identify Ma's feelings but doesn't understand why she feels that way: "Her face is gone flat, that means I said a wrong thing but I don't know which" (Donoghue, 2011, p. 17). True empathy requires the ability to both recognise our own feelings and to voluntarily melt the boundaries between self and other, so that we can tap into their feelings also and experience these as if they are our own. In *Middlemarch*, George Eliot explicitly asks the reader to do this: to empathise, not just with her heroine Dorothea, but with all of the more minor and less sympathetic—indeed sometimes repulsive—characters.

Empathy depends on the ability and willingness to step into another's shoes and be sensitive to their changing meanings and feelings, despite their lack of personal resonance for you. It incorporates a mixture of the cognitive, affective, and somatic (Cooper, 2008, p. 106). McWilliams distinguishes between empathy as a state of feeling with the other, and sympathy which emerges from "a defensive distancing from the suffering person" (quoted in Nolan, 2012, p. 33). In extreme cases, you may be able to empathise around an issue you could never imagine supporting, but nevertheless can walk in the other's shoes temporarily. Nolan gives an example of such empathy—and the necessity for it—in working with a sex offender (pp. 101–104). In another example, the therapist may empathise with the pain and low self-worth of a man whose fragile identity depends on putting down women, while being repelled by his views and the abuse on which he believes his ego survival depends. You repudiate the acts while empathising with the buried feelings that underpin the acts, and you are then in a position to help disentangle the motivation from its current consequences.

Brenda experiences empathy as a temporary opening of a gate in the boundary fence and a stepping into the space of another who has also opened their gate to allow you in: it entails abandoning herself in order to be with the other. But this kind of "empathy" is really a willing absorption into the other and plays no part in intersubjective engagement because only *one* subjectivity—that of the other—is present. Judith Blackstone (2012, p. 175) opens up another path to empathy. She raises the possibility of entering into the space between me and the other. This does not involve leaving my own body, but rather spontaneously attuning to the interpersonal space itself: the terrain of intersubjectivity. She enables her clients to achieve this by becoming embodied and experiencing their own personal space as *continuous with* the space of the environment and the space of the other.

Empathy, which is one of the core conditions of person-centred therapy and a foundation for virtually all forms of counselling and psychotherapy, has the considerable healing powers of making the client feel understood, validated, and mirrored. More assertive clients will quickly pick up on the difference between empathy and sympathy. They will feel used and exploited by your sympathy. A group member speaking of her father's death in front of her colleagues quickly made it clear that my sympathy was not wanted; she needed to contain her feelings by strengthening her boundaries, not re-experience them in a public space. My sympathy with this young woman was blind to what my empathy could have shown me: that she needed me to understand, not just her grief and loss, but also her need for privacy and containment.

Empathy is one of the relational factors that most contributes to the effectiveness of psychotherapy and counselling, whatever the orientation, and it may be considerably more significant than any "techniques" used (Cooper, 2008, p. 107). However, little has been said about how empathy is generated and to what degree and how it can be developed during the course of a therapy training. The variation in our ability to empathise is partially determined by our genes (Plomin, DeFries, McClearn, & McGuffin, 2008, p. 249). Autism is an extreme example of a deficiency in relational contact (including empathy) and is largely hardwired, having a heritability of greater than ninety per cent (ibid., p. 228). However, in most cases, empathy depends to a great extent on the quality of our early relationships. Having sensitive, attuned caregivers in our first year or two facilitates the development of the orbitofrontal cortex (OFC) and other parts of the social brain, which permit us to feel for others (Pearmain, 2001; Gerhardt, 2004). Romanian orphans deprived of all but the most basic caring needed for physical survival failed to develop an OFC at all (Gerhardt, 2004)! Empathy may also depend on mirror neurons in the emotional brain. This class of neurons fires not only when you experience something yourself, but also when you perceive another person experiencing the same thing. It is possible, therefore, that students in therapy trainings who have little ability to empathise may be able to develop this capacity by experiencing reparative attuned relationships with therapists or by observing and experiencing fellow trainees exhibiting empathy in group process.

Boundaries and spiritual practice

St Paul wrote of the developmental movement of the child open to the world, to the adult closed off, and then to a more spiritually mature position where the boundaries can be dissolved:

> When I was a child, I spake as a child, I understood as a child, I thought as a child: but when I became a man, I put away childish things. For now we see through a glass darkly; but then face to face: now I know in part; but then shall I know even as also I am known. (1 Corinthians 13:11–12)

This passage presages by 2,000 years Ken Wilber's hierarchy of spiritual development from prepersonal engagement with the world face to face in participative consciousness, to the personal defended or boundaried world to the transpersonal world of no boundary.

Much meditation practice is aimed at dissolving boundaries between self and not-self to move towards unity consciousness where subject and object become one. "To be sure, any and all boundaries are obstacles to unity consciousness, but since all our other boundaries depend upon this primary boundary, to see through it is to see through all" (Wilber, 1985, p. 46). A team of neuroscientists in Philadelphia examined patterns of brain activity in people who had at least fifteen years' experience of Tibetan Buddhist meditation. Before meditation, the scans showed high activity in the left superior parietal lobe of the cerebral cortex. This is the region of the brain that recognises the physical limits of our bodies: this gives me a sense of where I stop and the rest of the world starts (see above). During deep meditation, activity in this part of the brain was reduced, coincident with the meditators experiencing a loss of separation between themselves and the environment (Hay, 2006, p. 176). These expert meditators possessed strong boundaries, yet had also developed the capacity to melt those boundaries.

What about the effect of this kind of meditation on people who have never developed adequate boundaries in the first place? Tom was diagnosed as having borderline personality disorder, which Cozolino (2010) has classified as a kind of complex post-traumatic stress disorder where "early attachment was experienced as traumatic, emotionally dysregulating, and possibly life threatening" (p. 281). Tom has the boundary dysfunctions expected of such disorganised attachment, and clings to successive alarming women in his life in a re-traumatising pattern. Interestingly, given the above link between interpersonal and physical boundaries, he also had difficulty in orienting himself in space, so that he couldn't go for a walk with his partner without repeatedly crashing into her as if in a gravitational field with her. Tom spent some months practising meditation, which had the effect of eroding whatever rudimentary boundaries—along with power and assertiveness—he had. As we saw, he then volunteered to go on an excessively challenging adventure holiday with his partner that resulted in weeks of panic attacks and months of slow recovery from re-traumatisation even after he had withdrawn from the commitment. As this shows, boundary-softening, "expansive" meditation is dangerous for those who lack firm boundaries in the first place. For Tom, what helped was subsequent embodied "focusing" meditation. This helped him to build cortically-supported (hence the "focusing") internal boundaries against the overactive and unregulated amygdala that was the legacy of his trauma. At the same time, such meditation enabled him to experience himself as a body, for example, walking *in* his legs rather than experiencing his legs as stilts on which he (i.e., his head) balanced precariously. He had viewed his body as a capricious and potentially attacking other which belonged not to himself but to his mother and, later, to a succession of partners. It is crucial that meditation teachers begin to recognise the difference between people who need to build somatic boundaries and those who are heavily defended and would benefit from temporary melting. Boundaries are critical to the build-up and retention of personal power: without them we are at the mercy of the other. Lack of boundaries is a consequence of trauma, and so the removal of already fragile boundaries can only generate (further) trauma.

Sara Maitland writes about the two opposite outcomes of a practice of silence. Religious silence, whether within a Buddhist or Christian tradition, aims at self-emptying. On the other hand, Romantic poets who have sought solitude in nature seek the opposite:

to shore up and strengthen the boundaries of the self; to make a person less permeable to the Other; to assert the ego against the constructions and expectations of society; to enable an individual to establish autonomous freedom and an authentic voice. Rather than self-emptying, it seeks full-fill-ment. (Maitland, 2008, p. 251)

Maitland suggests that the empty expanses of the desert promote inner emptiness, whereas solitude in a richer, mountainous environment promotes a boundaried self primed for creativity.

All spiritual work embodies a paradox. We must close down our contact with others and seal off the alchemical vessel in order to contain the inner transformative process that makes possible the achievement of a no-boundary experience of unity. Jung did this in his own inimitable way through actively engaging with the images and psychic demands produced by his breakdown or spiritual emergency. Others take a different path via intensive meditation. In my own case, unboundaried states have emerged spontaneously following release from intense mental or physical effort, such as climbing a mountain or a sustained ten hour focus writing a research paper. Just as the compressed gas in a refrigerator turns ice cold on expansion, so when intense focus and striving cease, the mind suddenly expands into a state of relaxed receptivity. This is the nirvana of no striving, no attachment, where it is possible just to be. The sense of hearing which has been out of awareness suddenly becomes a source of exquisite pleasure, vision moves from near into distant focus. Hearing birdsong and watching the light colour the clouds feel sufficient for a lifetime. There is the same open presence to the world, especially sound perception, that I once got on hashish in the Rif mountains when no more stimulus was necessary than the sound of goat bells.

I have already suggested the ways in which we create inner boundaries against the unconscious. Another way of conceptualising this may be to think in terms of boundaries against the God within. For John Cottingham (2012), contact with the other can transform us. In this light, "belief" in God emerges intersubjectively "from the individual human experience of how we respond to the action of the gracious Other by changing in ways we could never have achieved on our own." Those who know God have been granted the grace of the softening of their boundaries against this internal Other and have thereby been transformed.

Summary

This predominantly theoretical chapter has examined boundaries and contact mainly through the lens of Gestalt therapy. Brenda has thin, over-permeable boundaries that are ineffective in protecting her against the horrors of the world, despite being overbounded with respect to the availability of her own energy. Boundaries define systems, including the self and the ego: they are the place where contact with the environment happens. Gestalt theory's understanding of the nature of contact and our resistance to it has been described. We have explored how this thinking can be extended to a concept of inner boundaries, primarily between the conscious and unconscious mind. Damaging contact has been defined in terms of crosstalk between incompatible chakras (energy centres). The relationship between boundary weakness and claustrophobia, introversion and shyness has been examined. Boundary dysfunctions, including trauma, and the therapy of boundaries were discussed through a variety of modalities. The opening and closing of flexible boundaries has been explored in terms of intersubjectivity, empathy, and spiritual practice.

CHAPTER FIVE

Time, space, and silence: regaining our capacity to experience

The time–space–silence continuum

In childhood, at her grandmother's house, there was an infinity of time, space, and silence. The hours and the days stretched expansively ahead, not empty but without the impingements of struggling, clashing egos. The men on the farm seemed to work without an inner battle between what they wanted and what they should or had to do. It was midsummer, so the hay was cut, dried, and stacked in the barn or in hay cocks or ricks in the fields. It was late summer, so the combine harvester appeared and the barley was cut and threshed and the baled straw was brought in. It was morning, so the hens and pigs, dogs and cats were fed and the hens were let out into the comparatively fox-free safety of the daylight hours. It was midday, so the cattle were counted and the men came in for dinner. It was evening, so the animals were fed again and the hens locked up for the night. The rhythms of the day and the season determined what one did so that few existential decisions had to be made. Furthermore, in her memory, there was no jostling for dominance: every man had his place and all were valued and accepted in their differences. Just as the time and space were not empty but felt infinite, so the silence was not absolute but felt abundant. In reality, the empty canvas of bedtime silence was painted with the waking sounds of cows lowing mournfully and her grandmother moving about in the kitchen, sometimes with the caramel resonance of the old honeycomb wireless. Later there were bees humming drowsily on the plum trees, the jet-fighter whine of a horsefly before it stung, her grandmother's whoops of laughter, the men's wry jokes, the pigs grunting, the hens clucking peacefully, while the Massey Ferguson tractor exploded into life.

Brenda is exhausted and stressed with her over-permeable boundaries and inner conflict. Consequently, she is vulnerable to impingement and feels bombarded by speed, crowding, and noise. She looks back on her childhood idyll in the country as a paradise lost. She longs for time, space, and silence—all distinct concepts objectively, but subjectively each in plenitude carrying the promise of peace. The experience of each of them expands, calms, and activates the parasympathetic nervous system. But now in urban adulthood, Brenda knows a lot more about noise than silence, about busyness and time squeezed than expanded time, about contraction rather than space. All three are in short supply in urban society. The absence of any one of them—being rushed, in a tight space, or a noisy environment—creates a kind of synaesthesia of stress. In synaesthesia, stimulation of one sensory or cognitive pathway automatically triggers another. In stress, speeding-up time leads to an experience of constriction and anxiety. Constricting space generates speediness, which is experienced as inner noise. Noise impinges, batters our boundaries, and narrows our sense of space. Pressure of time creates inner cacophony; while noise triggers the sympathetic nervous system—a flight reaction where speed is of the essence. A sense of *inner* space follows from the time and silence quotient. The inner space that is cramped, unquiet, or speedy is particularly sensitive to external impingement. The most destructive noise in our lives is the internal cacophony that emerges out of self-judgement, shame, guilt, fear: the consequences of conflict with others or the demands we make on ourselves. This is felt as a lack of not just silence but space and time.

As I look at my laptop screen, a flashing mustard-coloured notice aggressively demands space for a Java Auto Updater. Likewise, a dial-up eircom connection insists itself into my consciousness every time I turn on the computer and keeps reappearing however often I cancel it. I cover the flashing mustard sign with a yellow non-flashing sticker and wonder how I can access gentler needs in such an intrusive age. Perhaps I should write with a pen. But my handwriting went into reverse evolution when I acquired my first PC twenty-five years ago. What I am talking about here is the need to escape the impingements of our barbarian invasions: the computer with its own importunate personality, the press of other bodies and cars and machines and noise and pollution, the hundreds of unwatchable TV channels, the muzak, the talk, the parties, the concerts and films, the daily jollity, the "craic", the unending expansion of perfectionism in work, the daily, noisy, pushy output of more bureaucracy, more forms, more technological "solutions" to problems we didn't have prior to their solutions, the computer updates, the phone apps, the new journals and books and ads, the Facebook demands, emails, phone messages, texts, the vast adrenalised human infestation with every year the evidence of more breeding manifesting at the school gates. We are bombarded with input, with the busy-ness of others, with the demands for equal busy-ness in ourselves.

Why do we voluntarily subject ourselves to such a barrage of stimulus? What gives (some of) us such sensory hunger that, as a society, we feed ourselves into overload? Raymond Tallis (2008) regards this as the libidinous hunger for life of the voracious child at the breast. But these yang hungers are highly addictive because the opposite balancing yin needs are being ignored. We may sometimes have to go out and *get*, but we also have needs for stillness and receptivity that are neglected. For Brenda as for Freud, nirvana is a state of being free of need and impulse, including freedom from the need to defend against the other or the environment.

A blackbird sits on a laburnum branch outside my window and I watch, and am held by the watching.

Silence

How can I conjure up solitude and silence?

Picture a lonely cemetery on a mountainside where you might come across:

> a little stone angel or cupid, finger on lip ... the genius of the place—
> the genius of a silence so definite that it was less a negation than
> a refutation of speech. The silence it guarded was far from being
> empty of content or character. (Mann, 1960, p. 321)

Silence that pulses and hums, the silence of the moon, the hush in the ocean depths or an abandoned mine, the creaking silence of the empty house, the silence at the still point of the revolving sound. A microphone in the mud bed of the River Liffey revealed the humming, clicking conversations of the resident invertebrates, the sound of a world devoid of humans. How to write about an absence: all the silent places, the sounding quality of silence in nature, human noise, and nature's sounds, the quality of not-talking silences between people, what it means, what we project onto it, the listening silence when alone, what silence does to us, inner and outer silence, silent religious orders and silent retreats. Solitary confinement and the silenced disempowered. The intense holding of hypnotically quiet films: *Into Great Silence* (Philip Gröning); *Spring, Summer, Fall, Winter … and Spring* (Kim Ki-duk); *The Sheltering Sky* (Bernardo Bertolucci); *Beau Travail* (Claire Denis); *The Thin Red Line* (Terrence Malick); *Of Gods and Men* (Xavier Beauvois)—some literally without sound, others generating a meditative state through the non-impinging voice, music, and image.

In a world of relentless and meaningless inputs, we are starved of silence and waiting, of the opportunity to experience ourselves, to know how we feel, to find what we truly desire. Or simply to repair our bodies in the face of an overextended sympathetic nervous system: to learn to breathe deeply, to calm our fluttering hearts, our quivering stomachs and shaking, sweaty hands, to slow down our movements, speech, and overexcited reactivity.

Opening to silence takes courage, for it may not immediately bring the peace we long for. Rather, it reveals *whatever* is within. But the absence of external noise provides a space in which we can access and fully experience and process our inner state—whether this is frustrated, joyful, irritated, calm, loving, or hopeless—with all its attendant stories and physiologies. The greater the inner clamour and racket, the more we need external silence as an antidote and healing space. If we do manage to generate inner quiet, again this can be experienced as a positive or a negative thing; we are unlikely to move straight to the state of the advanced meditation master. Inner silence may be experienced as peaceful, calm, and rich with meaning: the kind of presence evoked by reading Proust. Conversely, the quiet inner landscape may be a bleak existential void: an absence as portrayed in Beckett's silence-strewn plays. There is the pathological quiet of the under-stimulated and the depressive. The under-stimulated child of unavailable parents is in sore need of nourishment—mental, emotional, and relational. For them, unlike most urban people, more stimulus not less is called for. The depressive, on the other hand, may be defending against an excess of negative feeling such as shame, anxiety, grief, or poor self-esteem, the suppression of anger or assertiveness, or from an unmirrored real self and compliant false self. They wait, like the Fisher King, in a wasteland of despair, but Parsifal does not appear or does not know how to break the spell.

Between people, silence can signify almost anything: a comforting familiarity where nothing is required; or an empty familiarity bled dry of hope and interest; the impulse-free zone after catharsis; a state of cogitation, or one of anxious grasping after words that won't offend or incite; a time when nothing can be said that will help, or where everything has been said; children should be seen but not heard; the speech that is not heard. The multiple meanings of silence are evident to the psychotherapist sitting with her various clients. There is the torpid silence of the client with flattened affect, whether self-generated as a defence against anxiety or resulting from medication with antidepressants There is the compulsive talker with their terrified sprinting over the cracks in the pavement where silence beckons and threatens. For some, of course, speaking is healing, as they reveal, for the first time, what they feel but has not been accepted or allowed in their social milieu. Whether speaking is healing or not depends on what is habitual for us: as Perls said: "only the novel is nourishing" (Perls, Hefferline, & Goodman, 1972, p. 230). It also depends on the level of the self from which the speech arises. There are some things we regret saying and others we regret not saying. Optimally, there are the clients who know when to speak and when to wait: those who have found the *pause* which Tara Brach (2003) describes as a place of refuge and renewal. She cautions us not to confuse spontaneity, a place of creativity, with impulsiveness, which keeps us in a compulsive loop. This pause—in talking or active thinking or egoic engagement with the other—opens the way to mindfulness. We interrupt the alienated verbalising so that we can come into the full presence of the experience.

Winnicott was aware of the buds of true self whereof we must not speak because they are still in the process of forming. Premature revelation and the probable inaccurate mirroring of the other would distort or abort the development of something precious and true. Adolescents are particularly submerged in the unsayable as their identities struggle towards a shaky formation, like newborn foals finding their legs. Because of the fragility of that nascent process, Winnicott believed that adolescents need to remain hidden and do not wish to be understood. Indeed, as he said, "adults should hide among themselves what they come to understand of adolescence" (quoted in Frankel, 1998, p. 118). Sometimes, inappropriate speaking is not so much premature as a failure of boundaries. Nowhere is this more true than in the deeply personal and painful stories people reveal to an anonymous public on radio or television. The sympathy, empathy, or mirroring that are hoped for may be countered by hostility, contempt, misunderstanding, or exploitation.

Silence, then, can mean anything, depending on the individual and their inner state. It is a non-impinging space in which we can experience whatever is happening for us, whether labelled as good or bad. But, if we can stay with the silence we can dive down through aqueous depths of varying currents or stillness, zones of warmth or cold. For those who flee from inner experiences, silence is the means of bringing them into contact with the self. In active relating to another, silence may provide a comforting refuge for the ego ("tell them nothing and they will have nothing to use against you") or, conversely, an exposure of the true self when the talking defence is dismantled. One Buddhist teacher in the early stages of Alzheimer's disease was addressing an audience when he suddenly blanked out and forgot what he had intended to say. He went through layers of fear, effort to remember, imagining what the audience was thinking, more anxiety, until he finally reached acceptance. Each painful step was verbalised and shared with the audience, such that one of them later said that he had never before experienced such a deep transmission. The inability to speak removed the persona, revealing the greater truth beneath.

We may torment ourselves in seeking silence. There are always some noises out there: the hum of machinery, children at play, distant traffic, the bleating of sheep or the barking of dogs. Eckhart Tolle (2005) and other spiritual teachers recommend that we listen for the silence in the midst of the sounds. We become what we attend to. We create inner silence by paying attention to outer silence. We create inner stillness by watching the stillness of the space in which the tree waves its branches. In Gestalt terms, we must learn to attend to the ground instead of the figure or, as Tara Brach (2003) puts it, identify with the ocean rather than the waves.

Just as meditation is deepened on a retreat, Proust knew that inner connection and transcendence depended on Marcel's external life becoming more tranquil.

> But for a little while now, I have begun to hear again very clearly, if I take care to listen, the sobs I was strong enough to contain in front of my father and that did not burst out until I found myself alone with Mama. They have never really stopped; and it is only because life is quieting down around me more and more that I can hear them again. (2003, p. 40)

He also understood how objects are saturated with memory and meaning: "The past is hidden outside the realm of intelligence and beyond its reach, in some material object (in the sensation that this material object would give us) which we do not suspect. It depends on chance whether we encounter this object before we die" (p. 47). Proust needed silence to write and had his rooms lined with cork to shut out external sounds. It is hard to imagine how a Proust could emerge today in our discontinuous and uprooted lives. Too much change, too much noise and stimulus, too little solitude would saturate his antennae and block retrieval of the past, along with its depths of richness and meaning.

Perhaps the greatest demand for silence emerges from the need to honour the ineffable at the centre of religious experience, or as Wittgenstein put it: "whereof we cannot speak thereof we must remain silent". All spiritual traditions access depth through silence, none more so than Buddhism. While spoken prayer, chanting, or singing may generate a community of worship, it is silent meditation and prayer that open the space for what Heidegger saw as "the presencing of Being" (Levin, 1988, p. 272). The non-theocratic traditions place most value on the esoteric spiritual path, but even the more exoteric religions like Christianity and Islam have their esoteric branches where you access God through inner prayer and contemplation. Even the very practical tradition of Quakerism, which is strongly oriented towards social justice, explicitly values silence in its meetings: you only speak when you are moved to speak. The path of silence has always been intrinsic to spiritual revelation. Karen Armstrong argues that it was achieving "mental stillness that made the experience of unknowing a numinous reality" in the lives of early Christian mystics (2009, p. 111). This tranquillity was attained through apophatic or wordless spiritual practice by desert monks. The contemplatives were grounded by the unchanging daily tasks and disciplines of community living, which combat "the excitement and drama that is inimical to the authentic religious experience" (p. 113). Heidegger, despite having no time for the traditional God, nevertheless knew that we could experience Being through "a listening, receptive attitude, characterised by silence" (Armstrong, 2009, p. 268). Similarly, Eckhart Tolle writes: "The Unmanifested is present in this world as silence. This is why ... nothing in this world is so like God as silence" (2005, p. 113). In his terms, the Unmanifested is "the Being within all beings ... a realm of deep stillness and peace, but also of joy and intense aliveness" (p. 108).

Solitude

> We should set aside a room, just for ourselves, at the back of the shop, keeping it entirely free and establishing there our true liberty, our principle solitude and asylum. Within it our normal conversation should be of ourselves, with ourselves, so privy that no commerce or communication with the outside world should find a place there. (Montaigne, 1993, p. 270)

Brenda experiences her life as a house built below the tideline on the beach. With predictable regularity, the foundations flood, and unfailingly she reacts with rage and an impotent flinging of sandbags round the boundaries of the submerged walls. When she first named the problem so baldly, she thought she must seem insane or at least pretty stupid; her behaviour is outrageously out of character with her image of herself as a supremely rational person. Why has she not moved to a house unlikely to flood? She hadn't realised that she could live in a different house. She could see that others do, but their lives look miraculous to her, something to which she couldn't possibly aspire. She believed that their houses were subject to the same floods, but that they had some mysterious inbuilt powers to either resist or tolerate the inundations.

The floods are, of course, the impingements and demands of other people, and the house her self at the beck and call of others. After a shy, lonely, and rejected adolescence where she had no friends within or outside the family, she acquired the semblance of friends in her twenties. But these were relationships on other people's terms; the real Brenda was buried while in company. In her thirties, she began to have contact with others where she felt acceptable as herself. But friendship continued to be difficult. She strayed into bullying relationships in which she had been chosen by the other—an honour she thought, but in reality she was selected for victimhood as surely as the children targeted by the Incas for sacrifice to their god, the Sun. Now in her fifties, in a transition that seems miraculous to her, she has loving friends, close enough to unconditional in their acceptance. But she still fears their loss by stepping out of line or being unavailable. How many relationships have perished through neglect or not bothering? So she is overly compliant. When a friend suggests a walk or lunch, Brenda replies: "and when would it suit *you*?" No matter that she has been working five days at a stretch and desperately needs some time alone. No matter that lunch or a walk will so disrupt a free day that she will not have the focused time she needs for her new obsession: water-colour painting. And so her life is put on endless hold and her perception of genuine loving friends is reframed as a series of unwelcome chores that have regularly to be serviced. So grateful is she for the self-esteem, stimulus, and joy that friendship brings that her relationship pattern has veered from avoidant to compliant.

Jung claimed that extraverts were object-seeking, whereas introverts were object-avoiding. Brenda is an extreme introvert on personality tests, but viewing her as simply as object-avoiding misses part of the truth. Storr (1989) shows how an apparent introvert can actually be an extravert who has a great need for solitude. He argues that the compliant or placatory type of object-seeker operates from the false self in the company of others. Only in solitude can they reconnect with the true self, and in the absence of sufficient alone-time they become depressed. Brenda recognises this: she only feels connected with herself, centred, and relaxed in the absence of what she experiences as the clamouring demands of others. And yet, she thought she had stopped burying herself in company—quite literally burying during her early days in co-counselling, when she would crawl under a beanbag to avoid being looked at by her counselling partner. At a head level, she thought she was now—two decades later—being herself. Certainly her ego can be fairly unrestrained with friends, and she can be opinionated, argumentative, and angry—and then guilty and fearful. But her body knows that there is another part that does not breathe when in company, that sleeps under the covers in the basement while everyone parties upstairs. Who is that invisible spectre in the cellar? It's the incompetent part, boring, useless, confused, stupid; also the impatient, hostile, contemptuous, bored, intolerant, exhausted part, the one who has let everyone else speak and has despaired of the opportunity to speak herself. In short, the two shadow energies of weakness and other-rejection, but especially the latter.

The development of the capacity to be alone depends on the baby being able to be peacefully alone in the presence of the mother, without anxiety about either abandonment or impingement by maternal expectations (Winnicott, 1990). This beingness facilitates the infant in getting in touch with his deepest impulses, needs, and feelings. Brenda is caught in a cruel dilemma. With her own tightly regulated energy and thin boundaries against the world, she feels burned by the laser of John's intensity, or crushed by his unregulated releases of energy. On these occasions, she craves solitude, but she cannot rest when she finally is alone because she feels so stripped of aura and uncontained. John provides good containing when his own energy is contained, but when he is distressed she cannot rest without him, yet feels annihilated in his company.

Jessica Benjamin (1990) describes the mother whose dominant need for a response from her baby overrides her ability to attend to the infant's needs. This leads to a power struggle, what might be called an anti-attunement battle. Such a child attempts to withdraw from mother's unwanted stimulation, but at the same time must remain vigilant to mother's attempts to draw him in. He is thus trapped between separateness and union where neither is fully possible. "In [such] a negative cycle of recognition, a person feels that aloneness is only possible by obliterating the intrusive other, that attunement is only possible by surrendering to the other" (p. 28). In other words, being present to yourself is only possible when literally alone. Benjamin's detailed description of the impact of a mother who has herself been deprived of attunement explains the aetiology of the individual who falls between object-seeking and object-rejection, who is neither a clear introvert nor an obvious extravert. The fundamental—and non-pathological—need is for contact with self, where you are not being forced to attend to the other. While some fortunate people may be able to achieve this in the presence of others, for many some degree of solitude is required—whether a few hours per week or per day, or a more permanent arrangement.

We all have opposing drives: towards closeness with others and towards separation and independence. In young children, the beginning of separation is assisted by a transitional object, which is emotionally charged with comfort and safety and therefore can replace the mother in her absence. Thus, as discussed in Chapter Two, transitional objects help us develop the capacity to be alone and also mediate the beginnings of imagination. As we saw in Chapter Three, Winnicott believed that "it is creative apperception more than anything else that makes the individual feel that life is worth living" (Winnicott, 1991, p. 65). According to Storr, this creative living depends on "colouring the external world with the warm hues of the imagination" (1989, p. 71). In its absence we feel depression and despair. If we cannot imaginatively engage with life, but merely see it as something to which we must adapt, life will feel futile and empty.

Today there is a taboo against object-avoidance, and more so against object-rejection. Sara Maitland refers to "a profoundly personalist culture, in which only relationships, feelings and psychodynamics are allowed full significance" (2009, p. 33). Nowhere is this more true than in the world of counselling and psychotherapy and the other helping professions. Anthony Storr (1989), in his forgotten little gem *Solitude*, has tried to correct the imbalance in psychoanalysis. He argues that solitude is every bit as important as relationship—especially to introverts as well as to overly-compliant extraverts. However, nobody else in the therapy world has picked up the baton, and there is an overwhelming emphasis on relationship—both within and outside the therapeutic dyad—in therapeutic writing, training, and practice.

I suspect that Brenda is not especially adaptive in relationship, compared to other women at least. For society to function smoothly, there are times when we all have to smile when we would prefer to snarl, to engage when we want to withdraw. Yet Brenda gets no recognition from friends when she says she needs alone time; instead, she fears that they become offended. Is Brenda's need for solitude exceptional? Her need is indeed partly based on the exhaustion brought on by relationship. But she also has an increasing inner demand for time alone to place order on her life through some act of creation, which is what triggered her desire to paint. Many of the most satisfying times in our lives depend on solitude, including most creativity, intellectual work, spiritual sustenance, and receptiveness to beauty and nature. Lip-service is paid to the need to separate as well as to connect, but this is often seen as just a part of the contact–withdrawal cycle. Little serious attention is given to the joys of solitude for its own sake. Rather it is often viewed merely as a jumping-off place for more contact—a kind of *reculer pour mieux sauter*. No wonder burnout is such a huge problem in the helping professions.

An increased need for solitude may accompany ageing, and the self-confessed extravert Sara Maitland writes of her withdrawal from society at the age of fifty: not as a running away from people or even noise, but a running towards "the positive power of silence" (2009, p. 30). Jung believed that the tasks of the first half of life were to learn how to live in the world, making relationships, creating a family, building a career: the outward arc. The task of the second half was to transcend the ego and connect with the soul: the inward arc. Solitude is a way into time, space, and silence; but there's nothing immediate or inevitable in the outcome. It can just as easily lead to depression, excessive sleep, the flourishing of addictions and compulsive activities, or a cacophony of inner voices. What does this depend on?

It is clear that we cannot benefit from solitude in the absence of good boundaries against the other: if we carry others with us into solitude we will be deafened by the internal din. In the words of Montaigne (1993): "We take our fetters with us; our freedom is not total: we still turn our gaze towards the things we have left behind; our imagination is full of them". If solitude is a way of compensating for poor boundaries, then we will need a long processing period to work through the internalised relationship dynamics that we carry within us. Only when this is done can we find the peace we strive for.

We all have very different beginnings in life, so it is not surprising that we differ greatly in both our need for and our capacity to use solitude and silence in adulthood. Thus the spiritual path may be far more fraught for some than others. As Jung himself knew, tranquillity and oneness may be preceded by terrifying demons, and we must pass through our own shadows before we can emerge into the light: "One does not become enlightened by imagining figures of light, but by making the darkness conscious" (Jung quoted in Stevens, 1990, p. 45).

Time

Subjective time

Time has of course an objective dimension. The earth rotates on its axis and revolves round the sun at constant rates. Thus we have the basis for the definition of the spans of a day and a year. Clocks have been devised to take care of the shorter time-span of hours, minutes, and seconds within a day. Subjective time is another matter entirely; it is, like Dali's melting watches, flexible. In undeveloped countries and in Western culture until the early modern period (fifteenth to seventeenth centuries), time was marked by the cycle of light and dark. Once clock-time is introduced, with its demands for punctuality, people feel squeezed and harassed (Hoffman, 2009, pp. 131–132; Krznaric, 2012).

The speed at which time seems to pass correlates with the rate of neuronal firing, which is determined by the balance between excitatory and inhibitory neurotransmitters. Stimulants like coffee speed up the brain allowing more external events to be noted so that time seems to stretch out. The brain clock (Carter, 2009, p. 186) that registers subjective time depends on dopamine flowing between the substantia nigra (where it is produced), the basal ganglia, and the prefrontal cortex, so the sense of time passing is altered in disorders such as Parkinson's disease and schizophrenia, which are associated with abnormal levels of this neurotransmitter.

Subjective time coincides most with objective time when our attention is directed outside ourselves, taking in many stimuli (Hoffman, 2009, p. 72). However, when our attention is directed inwards, there is enormous variation in the perceived passage of time, and we often create the very thing we are trying to avoid. Some individuals have an overall slower perception of time than others and childhood time is much slower than adult time. But all of us have an even greater variation within ourselves depending on the emotional and physiological conditions in which we find ourselves. The cliché is that "time flies when you're enjoying yourself", but it's not at all as simple as that. Time seems to go slowly when in physical or mental pain or boredom when we are urging it to move faster, like Proust's sick man who awakes and believes the light under his door signals morning, only to realise that it is merely the servants going to bed and that "he will have to suffer the whole night through without remedy" (2003, p. 8). But time equally moves slowly in a state of calm, when we are not fretting about time moving too fast or too slowly, but in a state of acceptance and being-ness, possibly achieving a lot or not, but, crucially, not worrying about what we are getting done. We sit in the garden soaking up the sun and time stands still. Or we work in the garden, moving from one task to another, but without agenda, and again time does not race by. There is a sufficiency of time and we are relaxed and without hurry or worry or the pressure to get X amount done today.

William Faulkner observed that "only when the clock stops does time come to life" (2012, p. 82), and indeed it is when we are immersed in life, in a state of flow, that time stands still. Subjective time has been shown to slow down in states of extreme concentration such as meditation (Hoffman, 2009, p. 73). Conversely, when we don't enter deeply into a task but simply skate along the surface of it, we are not concentrating and time speeds up. We enter a vicious circle that connects lack of time with lack of concentration. The curtailing of time generates the stress of time shortage both in the short term—only a day left till the deadline—or in the longer (but still too short) term—the span of our life is limited and ends in death. Fighting time for less of it—as when we are sick, lonely, or bored—slows it down unpleasantly. Fighting for more of it—as when we are busy or pressured by thoughts of mortality—speeds it up unpleasantly. It is our non-acceptance that generates suffering.

An over-awareness of time shortage leads us to try to cheat time by multitasking. However, the more we multitask, the more we try to fit in, the faster time goes by. Multitasking is the result of refusing to make decisions about what matters in our lives and wanting to "have it all". Not only do we suffer, but we do not gain time by multitasking. When measurements were performed on the time taken to perform two mental tasks simultaneously, it was discovered that it took the subjects more time to perform each task. Likewise, when two physical activities were alternated, they were done less well and took longer (Hoffman, 2009, p. 71).

We may be delighted with what we have achieved at the end of a rushed day, but we will not have *experienced* that day. In achieving externals, we have actually wasted a day of our lives. Herein lies the double-bind within which Westerners battle out their existence. We cannot decide whether to settle for a life fully experienced and therefore rich from within, or a life of achievement lived from an external locus of evaluation—for "perfection of the life, or of the work", as Yeats put it ("The Choice", 1974). The "achievement" may be something we do for the sake of our egos, either directly as in gaining promotion at work or pushing our children to succeed, or indirectly by doing things for others for the sake of their gratitude. Alternatively, we may be run ragged by our empathy for the suffering of the destitute, refugees, migrants, or laboratory animals or our concern about the future of the environment or some other cause. While there is still a crisis in the world, can we justify taking time for ourselves and having a rest? In either case, we are treating ourselves as objects—to be admired by others or to be used in the service of others. As objects we give ourselves no respect: we ignore our body and emotional signals which tell us that we need rest or sleep or a change or balance or something more suited to who we are.

The poet David Whyte talks about working for a charitable organisation as a young man, and becoming exhausted because the world was never saved and there was always more to do. He sought advice from a Benedictine friend who said the answer to exhaustion was not rest: it was being himself, finding his vocation in life. When Brenda worked in IT, she was always rushing. She hurried through her duties to create more space for "the real me". She hoped she could live outside her life in a well-paid, respected profession; but at the same time, she longed to live inside herself, expressing who she really was, where her passions actually lay. Time is intimately entwined not just with such major long-term decisions about our lives, but also with the moment-by-moment decisions. She wants to teach, she wants to go horseriding, she wants to climb mountains, she wants to read, she wants to bake, she wants to paint: "I want, I want, I want, I want", she cries self-mockingly. When you combine all this libido with other contradictory needs—for freedom *and* containment, for solitude *and* contact, for fitting in as much as possible before she dies *and* slowing down and having an inner life—inevitably, there are loud clashes of self-generated stress where you want everything at once. Brenda is reminded of her god-daughter, aged six or seven, whom she took to the Christmas pantomime. But there was snow on the ground, so they made a snowman in the garden first. They had to break off this activity to go to the theatre, to the tragic disappointment—tears and protest—of the child. Her god-daughter lived in the present, for her the future did not exist. For Brenda, the future may exist, but it is extremely unreliable, so everything has to be accomplished instantaneously. Her awareness of death hampers her enjoying life in stages: she tries to multitask her entire life.

We can only experience one thing at a time, so choices have to be made. The problem with choices is that one decision precludes another. Having decided to write this morning, I cannot also garden; or in the longer term, having decided to be a psychotherapist I cannot continue being a scientist. Failure to make such clean decisions and back them up with a no-regrets policy leads to literal multitasking or to inner multitasking, where you appear on the outside to be reading, but on the inside you are filled with self-recrimination or guilt that you are not getting some physical exercise. Or the young mother who has returned to work, but whose attention is always divided between the new baby and the career, feeling guilty about the one when taking care of the other. Thus we generate splits within ourselves that mean we are unnecessarily stressed and wasting our lives: rather than fully experiencing each, we fall into the cracks between one activity and another. We must become aware of being dragged along by the unstated philosophy that more is better. We need to realise that there is an alternative: that depth of experience is better (Krznaric, 2012). This dilemma is clearly about time and a sense of panic over the shortage of it. Brenda is acutely aware that life is finite and that we do not know the day or hour when it will be over. In her youth, she didn't question that life would go on for ever. But somewhere in midlife she realised that time was not infinite and that she had better start living *her* life, not some arbitrary, patched-together simulacrum that happened to land at her feet.

The anxiety generated by having a limited lifespan is mimicked in small scale in situations where the time for something desired is restricted. Thus, during the therapy session, we can translate the meaning of the anxiety from time into money: "I am paying one euro a minute for this. I have sat in silence for five minutes unsure how to proceed; that makes five euros (paper money!) wasted that I could have spent in a cafe or a second-hand bookshop. I have the illusion of money falling through the slot as in public payphones or old-fashioned gas or electricity meters. I cannot take the time to find my bearings because it costs too much: but is blabbing out the first thing I think of a good enough use of the money?" The anxiety about whether we are getting good enough value out of our lives can be seen in microcosm in the therapy session. Am I using the object optimally? Underlying a kind of greed here is anxiety about life slipping through our fingers.

Psychopathology and time

Brenda has lived through duty or what would bring kudos or glory in the eyes of others, as well as from what has landed at her feet. This is because she lacked the imagination and courage to envisage a path that is right for her. She has deferred *her* life long enough, and so she is panicked that she will get sick, have an accident, become mentally or physically disabled or die before she drinks it to the full. But as Yalom said: "Existence cannot be postponed" (1980, p. 161). Time is now at a premium, life is suddenly urgent, and she is becoming ruthless about time-wasting. So each week is a clash between painting and baking, training for climbing in the Alps and revising her school French and maintaining friendships and doing some work. She focuses on the present and the near future and worries that her life won't last long. Our engagement with time is highly individual, so that some focus more on the past, others on the present, some find time hangs heavy, others that it speeds by, while yet others seem largely unaware of time. Some seem incapable of being on time, while others anxiously attend to their arrival five minutes early or somehow always arrive bang on time for an appointment. For each of us, we live at a pace that is suited to our temperament, and so it is painful for us to be in the company of those with a much slower or faster pace than ourselves—a rarely acknowledged but potentially highly significant element in relationship conflict.

There are pathological extremes to our experience and management of time. In some conditions, the gap between subjective and objective time widens dramatically. In depression, time slows down; in mania it speeds up; in schizophrenia all connection to external time may be lost, so that time may speed up or go backwards (Hoffman, 2009, pp. 94–95). The role of dopamine in the brain clock partly explains some of these time distortions. Schizophrenia is associated with high levels of dopamine which would explain time speeding up. Conversely, in catatonic states the flow of dopamine slows down so much that the brain clock is barely "moving" and the individuals lose all sense of time (Carter, 2009, p. 186).

Other temporal disorders are characterised by the focus being largely confined to or excluding of the past, present, or future (Hoffman, 2009, pp. 96–103). If the psyche becomes arrested at a traumatic or painful point in the past, it utilises a range of defence mechanisms to block out the pain (e.g., repression), or unconsciously revert to it (e.g., repetition compulsion) as in the flashbacks of post-traumatic stress disorder, where a past event is repeatedly experienced as happening now. Disorders of the future include denial of the passage of time or anxiety about what is to come. Contraction of time to the present is seen in narcissistic personality disorder, where the narrative self is fragmented. In the interests of narcissistic gratification, the individual exists in a permanent now without the depth and integration that awareness of past and future would bring. Such narcissism is becoming more of a norm as society fragments in the face of incessant and headlong change, and culture and the media become more and more shallowly obsessed with novelty for its own sake (Frosh, 1991; Elliott, 2002).

Time and the lifespan

Young children live in an eternal present. Until the hippocampus develops around the age of three years, we do not establish explicit memories. But an understanding of objective time takes many years more to develop, as we know from the impatient child asking repeatedly how much longer he has to wait for the longed-for treat to materialise. By early adulthood we have developed a strong sense of objective time, and mostly we have acquired the discipline of living within that framework. We have not yet developed that sense of chronic time-shortage that becomes more pronounced the older we get and the faster life seems to flash by. This is partly explained by young people having more excitatory neurotransmitters (Carter, 2009, p. 186), so that they register more external events, which leads to a sense of time stretching out. Older people—at least those who haven't drunk their morning coffee!—with their slower brain clocks, register successive events (e.g., moments in a rapid movement) as single rather than multiple occurrences; this is associated with the subjective sense of time speeding up. This difference between young and old people also explains the greater ability of the young to cope with faster external events, and, hence, with change.

Time and rhythm

Our engagement with time starts at birth. Colwyn Trevarthen's observation of infants and mothers along with the work of Daniel Stern and Allan Schore shows that the primary element of infant care is the ability of the mother to enter a state of affective attunement to the baby's non-verbal communications. Mother responds "with varying degrees of synchrony with the movement, rhythms and phrasings of the infant" (Pearmain, 2001, p. 23). These reciprocal interactions "involve matching of form, timing and intensity" (Nolan, 2012, p. 5), so that the caregiver and child enter a state of entrainment or rhythmic coupling. Nolan cites studies which suggest that these early rhythms underlie verbal communication in adults.

The body psychotherapist Roz Carroll (2005b) shows how rhythm is intrinsic to every aspect of body organisation in dozens of circadian and ultradian rhythms, including hormonal, metabolic, and neural cycles, and sleep-waking patterns. Many of these rhythms underlie our lifestyles, activities, and habits. They form the basis of how we relate to others and include rhythms of breathing, heartbeat, muscle tension, gait, gesture, posture, eye contact, the pace and cadence of speech, and taking-turns, matching and de-synchronisation in conversation. Carroll maintains that rhythm is self-organising: "When we connect to our internal rhythm, we know who we are. How we connect to the rhythm of another defines our relationship with them in that moment" (Carroll, 2005b, p. 91). We need regularity of self-rhythm and entrainment with others, but we also need the new and surprising that permits reorganisation.

One way of encapsulating Brenda's frustration is that she jerks from one mode of timing to another: from rigid, blinkered rush to deadened lethargy, rarely in tune with a foundational energy rhythm. Her gait, for example, is rigid and fast—she can't wait to get to her destination—or alternately flopping and exhausted—she has given up hope of getting there. She knows that she is far too focused on arrival and not on the process along the way. She challenges herself in this, but under stress regresses to her habitual patterns. In relation to others, she frequently has difficulty establishing a rhythm, either unable to find her way into the conversation and feeling obliterated, or having awkward starts, stops, and silences with others as tentative as herself. She feels the need for a master of ceremonies who will establish when and for how long each person will get the floor. She often comes away from these exchanges with breathing restricted and muscles clenched, needing vigorous exercise to unwind from the stress. It is clear that, when alone, her pace and rhythm are quite different from her patterns with others, when she feels that who she is would be quite unacceptable. Carroll (2005b, p. 92) maintains that rigidity—Brenda's basic pattern—is a sign of fear of relating: it is thus to be expected from the avoidantly attached. Unfortunately, Brenda uses the relational dissonance as a further reason to give up trying.

Time, memory, and identity

Time is the thread on which the beads of our lives are strung. Unlike most animals, we humans do not just inhabit the present tense; we are as likely to live in the past or the future or to range freely between the three. Our identity is crucially tied to our ability to remember. The hippocampus is the region of the brain needed for transforming short-term perception into long-term memory; if it is removed, the patient can remember events prior to its removal, but not after. In the absence of memory formation, we live in the permanent fragmented present from one isolated incident to another, not remembering what happened a minute ago. There is no thread holding sense or identity together, and so all the beads of perception scatter and evaporate the instant they come into being. Identity depends on memory, and a good memory contributes to the individual having a rich experience of life—indeed of having had a life at all. Our perceptions of each instant depend on our accumulated past memories, because each new impression is not merely added to, but shaped by memory networks already in place. In *Four Quartets*, T. S. Eliot (1974) captured this concertina nature of time, whereby the past and the present are contained in the future and the future in the past. Thus, our experience of the present is influenced by the past and will in turn influence the future, as has been argued by philosophers such as Husserl (Hoffman, 2009, p. 65), neuroscientists like Edelman (p. 69), and the entire field of psychotherapy.

But the telescoping of time implies an ongoing continuity that is increasingly being challenged by the worldwide increased pace of change. The smooth passage of subjective time and identity accumulation can be interrupted. My experience of emigrating at the age of twenty-five was of a dislocation that separated the before and after. The new Californian experiences were not filed in the extant system, but rather those files were stamped "outdated" and placed in storage. I began to live from scratch in a phenomenological world: one perception succeeding another, rather like the continuous present of childhood before the filing system has been established. Eventually, of course, a new model of what Edelman calls the "remembered present" (Hoffman, 2009, p. 69) was established, but it remained un-integrated with the previous filing system. My memories of before were rarely visited, so that when I returned to Ireland four years later many of them had been lost—not just autobiographical memories, but semantic memories associated with home, such as Irish poetry and indeed the Irish language. Other semantic memory less intimately part of my old identity (e.g., my school French) did not suffer to the same degree. I experienced similar dislocations through other changes: of partner, career, home, friends, and family losses. Much greater change than this is becoming common-place, as refugees, economic migrants, and employees of multinationals find themselves in radically unfamiliar cultures where they don't speak the outlandishly foreign tongue (or even recognise the alphabet). Even if we don't literally move to another part of the world, the rate of change where we already live may be so great that we are constantly adapting to the unfamiliar: new jobs, new bureaucracy, new townscapes, and particularly new technology and broken and blended families. In the future, the unrooted, fragmented, ahistorical, and culturally dissociated individual may be the norm. All of this change radically affects the frayed thread of continuity in our lives that permits a cohesive narrative structure and identity to take form.

Part of the magic of Proust's masterpiece is that Marcel revisits the same places and people and perceives them from multiple time-perspectives, through the receptive eyes of the time-less child or the defended, sophisticated adult. There is a kind of disbelief that this could be the same person, and a constant revisiting in wonder. There is a sense of time's infinity which exists completely outside the realm of death anxiety. For example, Marcel's ability to access involuntary memory, to expand it into a child's moment of eternity, depends on some constancy of stimuli: the same cake and tea, the same bell tone, the same gate latch. Thus, the sound of the bell brought him into his own depths and "the whole of that past which I was not aware that I carried about within me" (Proust, 1996, p. 450). For Proust, despite the fact that he lived with poor health and was aware that his life would be cut short, knew that we occupy "a place ... prolonged past measure ... in Time" (ibid., p. 451). An infinitely rich meaning arises out of the interplay between the macrocosm and the microcosm and the capacity to use the *moment* as the gateway into *eternity*. Thus has Proust transcended the limitations of life through a subjective experience of the infinity of time, but this is achieved precisely by the most intense attention to the evanescent. Redemption for Proust comes when he uncovers the ground of his being and thereby experiences the continuity of his self. In doing this he encounters his essence which is outside of time and change, and thus immortal.

Cultural time

We are all intersubjective beings, even the narcissistic individualists among us. We live with others in a common culture that affects us all, however much we try to resist it. Thus, I may want to live at the pace of a desert nomad or a South Sea islander, but unless I move there that is going to be difficult. I become what surrounds me. The structuring of time, the pace and rhythms are transmitted to me, just as much as are language, knowledge, beliefs, values, and expectations. Indeed the more implicit the message, the harder it is to resist. So while I may disagree with some of the values of my society, it is much harder to shake off the bodily stamp of pace and rhythm. As Proust noted "the information [voluntary memory] gives about the past preserves nothing of it" (2003, p. 46). It is involuntary body memory—what neuroscientists call implicit memory—that holds the emotional texture of our lives. We enter into a kind of dance with those amongst whom we live, reflecting a process that was initiated by our caregivers mediated through their handling of our bodies and of our being: loving, irritated, bored, calm, anxious, speedy, intrusive, respectful, gentle, distracted, present, engaged, playful, efficient. Suppose that I, as an urban Westerner, went to live in Africa. This would not be impossible; but neither would it be easy and unstressful to adapt to a greater inertia, because my relatively fast and impatient pace flows through all aspects of who I am, including my assumptions, expectations, needs, and even moral beliefs—for instance, that things can be changed for the better.

In urban and economically advanced societies the world over, there is a faster pace of life than in their rural and undeveloped equivalents. In the West, there is a longing for a slower pace of life while still retaining a Western standard of living. Whole series of "life-change" television programmes have portrayed couples and families uprooting from urban environments in the UK and Ireland that are ugly, noisy, speedy, and with depressing grey weather to boot. Even before the publication of Peter Mayle's *A Year in Provence*, there has been a trend of moving to the sun, beauty, and slower pace of life of Southern Europe—or of voyeuristically watching other people do this on television. Unfortunately, these transplants apparently have a half-life of only two years, after which loneliness and lack of purpose drives the emigrants home again: a reminder that we all need a *balance* between stimulus and peace. But a longing for slowness in midlife is gaining ground as a counterweight to the speed and noise beloved of the young. This is exemplified by a slow movement (Bakewell, 2010, pp. 72–73): slow food, slow holidays, slow (Tantric) sex, downshifting, and transplantation to slower cultures. One aspect of speedy life that people are leaving behind is the sheer selfishness of cultures where time is as valued as money and, therefore, just as unlikely to be shared with others.

Civilisations and families go through trajectories. Where there is a background of poverty, material well-being is at the top of the hierarchy of needs—most of the major developers who ruined Ireland came from small farming backgrounds. Several generations later, when wealth or sufficiency is taken for granted, spiritual needs come into play. Thomas Mann's novel *Buddenbrooks* portrays this trajectory: the first two generations become rich and then richer merchants and the third generation, taking material wealth for granted, seek their life's purpose through art and aestheticism. Similarly, the 1960s counterculture emerged against the background of material prosperity in Western Europe and the USA after the Second World War. However children who have grown up on communes or in other self-consciously downshifting environments often return to the mainstream materialist culture. Today, while in developing cultures there is an overwhelming move towards increased speed, in the West there is a small movement of people who are sufficiently secure in material terms to long for time.

Time and death

Hovering over this discussion of time and choice is the Grim Reaper, the spectre of death. With the decline in religion and the loss of belief in an afterlife, our minds have become more focused on time limitation. When I first read Yalom's tome on the four major existential issues of isolation, freedom, meaninglessness, and death, it was the challenges of freedom and meaninglessness that spoke to me; and indeed it was on these topics that I wrote my first article for a therapy journal some ten years ago. Now, both of these concerns have been subsumed by the one that underpins all of them: death. Since various friends have had ailments and injuries that were either life-threatening or that preclude certain activities, I now have an even more urgent awareness of the shortage of time. We all have a last time when we will experience various things: the last time we will run or even walk, the last time we will climb a mountain, travel abroad, work, have sex, drive a car, live independently, experience unproblematic health, the last moment we will be alive. Even young children have last moments: for example, the last day of freedom before starting the relentless discipline of school, which is followed by more school and then work for ever and ever. This is what Brenda felt as a four-year-old, having been "tricked" into starting school by her older brother who said she could leave if she didn't like it! The most precious things in life are mostly those we take for granted while we have the capacity for them and which we appreciate only as we mourn their absence. And yet knowing this is not helpful, because it is difficult to enjoy things fully if we are over-aware of them, because to think about them is to raise the spectre of their loss. But the real existential cruncher is that this knowledge of last-times is something we gain only in retrospect. Of nothing is this more true than the last day of living. This generates an inherent existential stress that pursues us through life, particularly once we pass through the midlife realisation of life's finitude. Indeed, Cicero said that "To philosophise is to learn how to die" (Bakewell, 2010, p. 13).

Yalom quotes a patient who exuberantly declared that "cancer cures psychoneurosis" (1980, p. 160). Brenda, who is healthy, has slumped in depression beside a friend who has multiple health problems but is vibrant with life after recovery from cancer. Our mortality forges an indissoluble link between time and purpose. Heidegger has examined the existential meaning of time, where death serves as a "boundary condition" (Weixel-Dixon & Strasser, 2005; Cooper & Adams, 2005). We have multiple defences to keep us in denial of death (Becker, 1973; Cooper & Adams, 2005; Yalom, 1980), but Heidegger believed that if we face up to our "being-towards-death", our lives can acquire orientation and meaning. Sartre, on the other hand, believed that the arbitrariness of death made our lives similarly arbitrary and absurd (Cooper & Adams, 2005, p. 81). In a meeting with Freud, the poet Rilke shared his feeling that human affairs were meaningless because they all end in death. Freud, in an unusually optimistic moment, maintained that it is precisely because we know things will pass that we cherish them (Hoffman, 2009, p. 113).

How is it that transience paralyses or depresses some into nihilism (Rilke and Sartre), while it provokes others into valuing life precisely because of its transience (Freud and Heidegger)? Life is short and uncertain, so there is no point in taking it seriously—it could be snatched away from you within the hour or the week. Or, life is short and uncertain, so we must cherish it while we have it. This dichotomy smacks of two different kinds of attachment: secure attachment generates sufficient trust in the relationship with life that we value it while we have it and mourn it when we are in danger of losing it. The alternative worldview, it seems to me, comes from insecure attachment, where we either anxiously cling on to life (ambivalent variety) or we pre-empt the abandonment by pretending it doesn't matter (avoidant variety), labelling it as absurd and meaningless. The clinging ambivalent attachment that underlies Brenda's predominantly avoidant style determines her attitude towards mortality and time: she panics that she will never live out either the life or the work that elude her.

But Proust had a deeper understanding of our relationship to time and mortality. He knew that in slowing life down so that we become fully present to ourselves, where the present telescopes into the timelessness of childhood, we transcend time:

> ... [Marcel's being] was likely to find itself in the one and only medium in which it could exist and enjoy the essence of things, that is to say: outside time. This explained why it was that my anxiety on the subject of my death had ceased at the moment when I had unconsciously recognised the taste of the little madeleine, since the being which at that moment I had been was an extra-temporal being and therefore unalarmed by the vicissitudes of the future. (Proust, 1996, p. 223)

When we find ourselves at "the still point of the turning world" (Eliot, *Four Quartets*, 1974), time stands still.

* * *

One approach to slowing down time is to remove oneself psychically rather than physically from one's culture through meditation, but this necessitates considerable discipline and willingness to face one's demons in the process. Mindfulness meditation is particularly geared towards the problem of speed and aims to slow us down enough to actually *experience* our lives. For what is at stake in the crisis of noise and speed is nothing less than the capacity to experience.

We have one chance at a life and, for many of us, it is flashing by as meaninglessly and wastefully as money flushed down the toilet. We are failing to enter into the moment, to absorb and integrate our experiences and sensations: the scent of a musty room, birdsong outside the window, the feeling of our breathing deepening and our bellies expanding as we settle and ground in our bodies in the present moment. In a less demanding and impinging world, we could attend to the gifts of the other in trivial exchanges, we would notice trouble before it becomes a crisis, we could explore—feelings or thoughts, a conversation or a path through the woods—without knowing where any of it might lead and without seeking any guarantee of outcome, but enjoying the not-knowing. In a slower, less noisy life, we would experience at a pace and rhythm which permits the savouring of the past as well as the present and their interweaving with each other. In short, we would be feeling, experiencing humans instead of efficient, successful robots who act out when their circuits overload. We would live at a pace that is human rather than one fixed by the speed of technology or the demands of the economy. The reduction in stress would undoubtedly have far-reaching effects on not just our individual but also our social lives. There would be fewer causes for marital discord and family instability, as well as less social unrest, conflict, violence, and, even, war and terrorism. John Calhoun's research, which showed that overcrowding of rats led to murderous violence and sexual and mothering dysfunction (Calhoun, 1962; Ramsden & Adams, 2009), should warn us that as our planet becomes more and more overcrowded these questions can only become more urgent.

Summary

Our capacity for full and deep experiencing depends on adequate amounts of time, space, and silence. Immersing ourselves in solitude and silence may well not bring immediate peace, but rather will expose us to whatever is within. However these conditions will enable us to process what is there and, ultimately, open us to what Heidegger called the presencing of Being. Chapter Five examines the developmental roots of an inability to be present to the self in the company of the other as well as the positive and non-pathological power of solitude and silence. The ability to be alone in a state of peace and creative engagement with life depends both on having developed the capacity for being in touch with who we are, and on being able to imaginatively bridge the gap between inner and outer worlds.

The existential issues thrown up by our mortality are reflected in our subjective experience of time. The psychology and neuroscience of our relationship to time are described in the context of memory and identity, states of concentration and multitasking, different stages of the lifespan and psychopathology.

PART III

THROWNNESS AND LIMITATION: NAVIGATING THE SOCIAL WORLD

CHAPTER SIX

Competitiveness as the struggle for recognition and respect

And we are here as on a darkling plain
Swept with confused alarms of struggle and flight,
Where ignorant armies clash by night.

—Matthew Arnold, *"Dover Beach"*, 1867

Out there, under the shining vault of heaven,
Men tell each other: 'Man, be thyself!'
But in here, among us trolls, we say: 'Man, be thyself—and to Hell with
the rest of the world!'

—Ibsen, *Peer Gynt*, trans. M. Meyer, 1994, p. 65

The political and the personal—Brenda's story

In all of us, the personal and the political are intertwined: individual and social change may support or may undermine each other. In Brenda's case, her self-esteem was, in her youth, crippled because of the denigration of women in her family and the wider Irish society; later, the success of the feminist movement was vital in supporting her personal work towards developing self-worth. Our current climate of competitive individualism generates status anxiety in the young, and causes Brenda to feel alienated from the larger society. Status based on gender along with class, race, and other group labels has been replaced by worth based on "individual" achievement and/or visibility—what the new media call "presence". I will however argue here that the injustice of any such hierarchy of regard harms us all.

For Brenda, the political that has most impinged on her life was the institutionalised contempt for and exclusion of women and the feminine that she grew up with in her family and in the wider environment of school, the workplace, and the culture as a whole. There was no dramatic abuse to complain of, just the slow drip of ongoing insults and humiliating messages and interactions. Brenda's mother decided that the available money was reserved for sending her brothers to university, but she rejected the despised option of becoming a secretary. She was fortunate that her aspirations were soon met by new political forces: the appearance of *The Female Eunuch* and *The Feminine Mystique*; the founding of the Irish Women's Liberation Movement when she was in her teens; and the advent of free third level education in the 1970s, just in time for her to avail of it. She attended early meetings of the IWLM in her school uniform, but a political movement was no place for one so disabled by shyness. She felt her fragmentary shreds of self drowning among the overwhelmingly self-confident journalists and professionals who had founded the IWLM: she saw no way of taking her place among them. Thus her pain and anger remained trapped inside her, and the only way she felt capable of contributing to the "revolution" was by setting a feminist example. She would achieve as much as she could through success at work; she would storm a male bastion—the up-and-coming field of computer science. This was her sacrifice—often compromised by the personal—but nonetheless a sacrifice of many decades.

In retrospect, she is embarrassed and scathing about her "pathetic" schoolgirl naivety. What seemed like a revolutionary stance in the context of her family and school, turned out to be as ordinary as doing nursing. Only one other person from her year in her all-girls school went on to university, but the computer science degree in her college was crowded with girls. She had an abnormal amount of ambition for someone with a modest ability and very little interest, but her hunger for success was recognised and she got some good opportunities at levels where women were invisible. For a time she was the only female manager in an IT company, but her fundamental disinterest in the subject, tipping into impatient boredom, meant she would never make the grand feminist statement she had hoped for. It was, she now thinks, a sacrifice without meaning—nobody benefitted and nobody was even aware that a sacrifice was being made. She comforts herself by saying she was *part* of a movement in history.

But the irony is that, by frustrating her deepest impulses, her isolated guerrilla action for freedom actually led to her enslavement. She had striven to be valued, but it was the false self of her professional persona that was respected and recognised. Her will-driven discipline to succeed in an alien world left her soul dried up and despairing; in the words of Yeats: "too long a sacrifice/Can make a stone of the heart" (1974, *Easter, 1916*). In her dismissal of "mere feelings" her avoidant attachment again raised its inhibiting and controlling head, thereby blocking any likelihood of developing a fulfilled self. Her belief that she could override her feelings and *make* herself commit her life to something so repellent damaged her libido almost beyond repair. In its place her will became the slave-driver, whipping her spirit into subjection close to death. Nothing in her experience had shown her that it was possible to be aligned with her true self, while still winning respect in the world. This acceptance and feeding of her true self was what she had put off in her interior battle for professional success, as we saw in Chapter Three. But as the Harlem Renaissance poet, Langston Hughes ("Dream Deferred", 1994) asks: "What happens to a dream deferred?/ Does it dry up/Like a raisin in the sun?" Brenda lived with the consequences of her sacrifice—the frustration of her true self—in her desiccated heart.

All political struggles, from Brenda's feminist dream to the struggles of Irish nationalists and Black Americans, are ultimately about respect and recognition. Perhaps the respect can be enjoyed by the second or third generation, but the generation at the front line of a civil rights movement, a war, or economic migration will always be marked by the wounds of their origins and of their struggles. The message here is one about limitations and compromise. In one lifetime we can make only limited changes and the external and internal may not march in step. The inner journey depends on being true to oneself, but the outer requires a compromise if the movement is to influence the dominant culture. In order to achieve on society's terms, Brenda had to become someone she was not. If the first wave of feminism (the suffragettes) gave women the vote and the second wave in the 1960s and 1970s provided further equal opportunities for women to live like men, then the contemporary third wave needs to be about women being respected for being and living like women in all the variety and complexity that entails, including considerable overlap with men. True respect and recognition arise only when there is no single power or way of being to be emulated—such as white middle-class males.

The problem of the meritocracy

Nowadays hereditary privilege—white middle-/upper-class male to white middle-/upper-class male—has to some degree been replaced by a meritocracy. Many who should know better seem to regard meritocracy as an acceptable alternative to privilege. Jenni Murray the Radio 4 Women's Hour presenter, in an interview with the *Radio Times* (9–15 July 2011) at first questioned whether her receipt of a DBE was fair. After all, she just does what she enjoys. She then bypassed her qualms and expressed herself thrilled that the UK is now a meritocracy where a working-class girl could rise to such heights. This is a problematic view. She has done a job for which she is talented and suited and is well rewarded already by recognition and financial remuneration. However, she has not created the inherited or environmental attributes that enable her to do this job well. The political philosopher Michael Sandel made just this point in his televised Harvard lectures: we cannot take credit for our gifts, whether of good health, extraversion, confidence, supportive parenting, position in the family (eldest children are more successful—Conley, 2004), or good education. Whatever her qualities, Jenni Murray did not create them; she acquired them through genetic predisposition, a supportive upbringing, a good education or opportunities becoming available. She simply used this cornucopia of gifts in a way that brought her satisfaction. She misses the point of radical equality–that it is incompatible with a meritocracy.

Who is honoured?

Of course, race, gender, or class should not preclude you from your chosen path in life or from the satisfaction of expressing your gifts. But let's not pretend that people should be rewarded for their self-expression—the satisfaction is its own reward—or that those who happen to be well adapted to certain public niches are more worthy of reward or recognition than others. Careers in the public eye in media, politics, entertainment, or sport are of no greater value to society— indeed, arguably, far less than the less visible careers of mother, carer, farmer, doctor, nurse, or policeman. It is nonsensical to further honour people who are already well rewarded with public recognition: you might just as well give prizes for extraversion. Most of the world's work is done by people who own a tiny fraction of the world's wealth. Where would our society be and how would its great achievements have been realised without them? By far the most obvious example would be a genuine valuing of the unglamorous job of mothering: it takes exceptional gifts and skills to do the job well, and with no other endeavour is society more affected by the outcome. But people are mostly blind to the existence of traits such as empathy, attunement, gentle encouragement, and limit-setting. Yes, lip-service is sometimes paid to mothering— except when mothers are being blamed for the world's evils—but nobody really *sees* the job they do. This is recognised by the title of a book by Naomi Stadlen, *What Mothers Do: Especially When it Looks Like Nothing*. The societal implications of not valuing mothering have been explored by Sue Gerhardt (2004, 2011). In societies where community has broken down, where mothers are unsupported or rushed and harassed, where they are working and unavailable or not working but isolated and depressed, it is impossible for them to provide an attuned, empathic, holding relationship. Depending on other circumstances, this leads to anxious attachment, stress, depression, self-harm, narcissism, and a host of possible psychopathologies—all of which have multiple detrimental spin-offs for society at large. But we cannot simply replace the kudos of being a good sportsman with admiration for good mothers. We must recognise that it takes all of us to generate a society.

More contentiously, I would argue that people who excel at particular careers—whether public or private—are of no more value than all-rounders. As a society we favour and reward the extremes. But very talented individuals may be polarised, so that academic prowess, for example, may be teamed with poor emotional intelligence. How many high-flying businessmen are good fathers? It would make more sense to encourage *balance* rather than specialisation. How are people to optimise all of their capacities if some are so clearly favoured by society over others? Would we regard such favouritism as acceptable in a family setting? Imbalance, no less than inequality, guarantees frustration.

Interconnectivity

In deconstructing the ideology of who is honoured, we must begin to understand how the apparent achievements of one individual depend on the contributions of a complex system of interactions and supports. Jenni Murray is only the front-woman of a large team of producers, researchers, and support staff. The high-achieving alpha male often thanks his wife for her support, but such better-half tokenism never sounds less than patronising and hypocritical. What I am talking about is a genuine awareness of interconnectivity. I have to laugh (OK, it's more like a snarl) when I see a politician taking the credit for "opening" a new building in which they will not work and that they have not conceived, designed, built, or paid for. When it comes to art or sport, it may look as if the individual has achieved all alone, but great artists or sportsmen have received great gifts from their genes, their family and social environment, or from God, if that is how you view it. (It is only in recent times that the creator/performer has taken credit for God's gifts.) They have also been helped by innumerable family members, teachers, editors, agents, managers, coaches, even the cooks in restaurants where they eat, the farmers who grow the food, or the railway, car, or plane manufacturers or pilots or ground crew that allow them to travel.

Tokenism

The need to be valued is the ultimate motive for political struggle. But in the fight for that valuing, many are co-opted into the dominant culture and allowed to achieve only on the terms of that culture. Yet, the dominant culture itself does not change. Thus women and working-class, ethnic, and other minorities are allowed to make themselves in the image of the white middle-class male, but only at some considerable cost to their own truth. Meanwhile, the culture does not expand to include the values, beliefs, and motivations of the full heterogeneous spectrum of womankind and mankind. So long as the culture does not change, we remain in a position of tokenism. The few token women who can tolerate the male political culture will join it, but there is no genuine intention to make politics inclusive, i.e., fifty per cent female, or to balance masculine values with feminine. We may have working-class women getting the odd knighthood, but we are no closer to genuine egalitarianism where there is equal respect and valuing for *all*.

The very principle of meritocracy keeps competitive individualism in place.

Recognition and the hierarchy of needs

We have seen how Brenda was divided against herself because of her need for recognition from others for her achievements. She forced herself to become what she was not. What can this self-contradictory statement mean? The contradiction is explained by the fact that two fundamental needs of the self were in conflict: the need for esteem and the need for authenticity. The part of her that was recognised and rewarded by society was what Winnicott (1990) called the false self: the part of us that adapts to the requirements, beliefs, and values of others. She developed this adaptive self specifically to gain self-worth, but the self that was valued was the false self. Meanwhile the true self was frustrated. It languished unnourished and unseen, with a conviction—based on her childhood experiences—that it was shameful and unworthy of respect. Her false self was the polar opposite to her true self, a masculine ego in opposition to a feminine soul, which had a terror that its existence and activities might be, like a spy's identity, uncovered.

It is clear that for Brenda her need for esteem was given priority over her need for authenticity. That authenticity could be treated in so cavalier a way reveals that the requirement for self-worth is fundamental. The humanistic psychologist Abraham Maslow (1970) constructed a theory of motivation with a hierarchy of needs, in which the lower level need must be satisfied before a higher level demand can be pursued. The most basic needs are those for physical survival; these are followed, sequentially, by needs for safety (emotional security); relationship (love, belonging); esteem (social status and recognition); and finally self-actualisation (authenticity and becoming all that I can be). Self-actualisation is similar to Jung's concept of individuation and must be viewed as a *process* or tendency rather than a destination, as the end point is probably unattainable. Thus it is the process of becoming what we are intended to be that constitutes the true self in Winnicott's terms. Clearly there can be no self-actualisation without authenticity, although authenticity alone does not amount to self-actualisation. For all of us, a society of competitive individualism that is structured to deny our esteem needs will inevitably frustrate our innate tendency towards actualisation of the self. This is particularly true of the avoidantly attached, because the hostile parenting that generates this type has already damaged the self-worth of the child before they enter the brutal competitiveness of society at large.

We need to start generating genuinely respectful and nourishing social relationships—based not on competitiveness, admiration, and envy, but on respect and empathic, accurate mirroring, where we, as it were, greet the God in one another. In calling for greater fairness in the distribution of esteem in our society, it is hard not to sound like the young child with one of its earliest cries: "it's not fair!". But moral philosophers Susan Neiman (2008) and David Kleinberg-Levin (2005) argue that morality—what *should* be as distinct from what is—is based not merely on reason but, ultimately, on just such emotional discomfort and bodily feeling. We may live in ethically-debased times, but "the body's capacity to register by sense and sensibility what is good and right has not been destroyed" (Kleinberg-Levin, 2005, p. 119). Societal favouritism is a kind of injustice that we take for granted in our culture, but it creates status stress and anxiety, with consequent low self-worth and depression that damage the whole society (James, 2008; Wilkinson & Pickett, 2009). The need for accurate positive mirroring in building identity (discussed in Chapter Two) begins in childhood but continues throughout adulthood, as recognised by therapists and philosophers such as Kohut (in Lessem, 2005) and Sartre (1957). Respect for the other does not simply involve being vaguely "nice" to them; it also entails *seeing* them, recognising them for who they are.

As is so often the case, it is Winnicott (1991) who has delved into the depths of our psychic structures to discover what such recognition of the other entails. In his essay "The Use of an Object" (pp. 86–94), Winnicott distinguishes between two ways of relating to the other. In what Winnicott calls "relating", we experience the self as an isolate and the other as a "phenomenon of the subject". In what he calls "using the object", we experience a "shared reality" in which "the object's independent existence" is vital. In earliest development, the object is "related to" and still experienced as under the subject's omnipotent control, but subsequently the object is "used" when it is recognised as an independent and external entity. In order to recognise the object as independent of our control, we must destroy it inside while observing that it has survived outside. As Jessica Benjamin has pointed out, Winnicott has reformulated the solution to Hegel's master-slave paradox: "in the struggle for recognition each subject must … struggle to negate the other". However, "if I completely negate the other, he does not exist; and if he does not survive, he is *not there* to recognise me" (Benjamin, 1990, p. 38). Once we have differentiated from the other, we no longer need to destroy them. It appears that Western society as a whole is dominated by people who are not yet certain of their own separate individuality. They must continue to destroy the other through ruthless competition in order to assert their own identity. However, they must not completely destroy the other or he won't be eligible to recognise them: what "winner" cares about praise from a "loser"? This is the dilemma of the narcissist.

Narcissism

Primary and secondary narcissism were first described by Freud. The former constitutes a normal state prior to the infant's distinction between self and other, the latter a substitute for the painful awareness of separation. Narcissistic personality disorders have been viewed as originating in the transition between the two stages, where the child remains stuck in the state of omnipotence (the early developmental "relating" stage described above), because of the carer's failure to respond empathically to the child during the omnipotent period (Frosh, 1991). Alternatively, such disorders can arise from the failure of the parent to provide a wider context of social relations into which the child can separate (Elliott, 2002). Nowadays, however, narcissism is so rife that we can no longer ascribe it to individual parenting and have to look at the wider social conditions.

Margaret and Michael Rustin (2009) examine narcissism as a response to impoverished relationships within our society. When individuals feel that others are indifferent or threatening to them, they "can become absorbed largely in themselves, and withdraw feeling and attention from others" (p. 209). This can give rise to the defences of hyper-individualism or pseudo-collectivism. The hyper-individualism reflects an excess of self-love and indifference to others except in their role as admirers, as exemplified by the hunger for celebrity status. Narcissism is not just a response to an empty and alienated society; it also helps generate it. The downgrading of the individual superego associated with the permissive society has led to a narcissistic acting out in the sexual sphere, so that other forms of love become contaminated with or eroded by the sexual (Staunton, 2002, p. 73). There is, in addition, a destructive version of narcissism (Rustin, M. & Rustin, M., 2009) that can operate at an individual or collective level, where a sadistic inner subpersonality attacks elements of the self that it perceives as weak and arrogantly rejects the reality of its dependency on others—an extreme version of the avoidant personality.

Pseudo-collectivism and alienation

Narcissism can also manifest in identification with the collective in order to borrow strength or support for a damaged or fragile sense of individual identity. Thus the individual may identify with certain celebrities or become a groupie following a pop music group or football team; alternatively they may join ethnic or radical nationalist movements, terrorist groups, local gangs, or religious cults—anything that will prop up the weak ego. The extremity of the identification with groups is a reverse mirror of the collapse of social bonds that has helped generate the weak ego in the first place. Collective narcissism includes a splitting defence where your own group represents all that is "good", while all that is "bad" is projected onto the other side: thus arise prejudice and emotional and physical violence—and, *in extremis*, war. What Rustin, M. and Rustin, M. (2009, p. 225) call "pathological identifications" arise when "the elementary foundations of trust in others and in the wider society become eroded", as we saw in the street rioting in cities in the UK in the summer of 2011.

"This is the happiest day of my life since Offaly won the All-Ireland": a common enough sentiment on vox pops in Ireland, but one which is guaranteed to get up Brenda's nose every time. She recognises the All-Ireland as a male game—but is it Gaelic football, hurling, soccer or rugby? And, could she possibly imagine caring who won? She has at least five problems in identifying with such a stance. (1) Women's role is confined to washing the sweat and mud off the jerseys and conferring heroic status on her men as the detergent ads—those infallible indicators of the zeitgeist—remind us. (2) She can't imagine taking the credit for something in which she played absolutely no part. (3) Games are for playing, not watching—claiming an interest in sports has come to mean an interest in watching television. (4) Sport has become almost synonymous with competition. She enjoys non-competitive active pursuits that involve the sensuous pleasure of her body's strength or flexibility and the joy of feeling part of nature. Both experiences are destroyed by the competitive urge. (5) Sport has become a branch of industry. Her problem is that she is repelled and alienated by confluence (I am "my" team), competitiveness, financial greed (TV broadcasting rights), and male dominance. Collective narcissism thus generates problems not only for those who place themselves within the collective, but also for those who are on the outside.

Brenda concedes that nobody is *making* her watch the All-Ireland. But that doesn't mean that she and millions of others are not affected by this culture of fusion and competitiveness. The dominance of sport is simply an example of her problem in identifying with Western— becoming global—beliefs and values. She could just as easily have selected celebrityitis or reality television or the dozens of TV programmes devoted to winning and losing and consequent humiliation in fields ranging from business to, of all things, cooking. So what are the alternatives for the likes of Brenda who refuse to bow to mass culture? The life of a monad focused on self and a few friends and interests? This is how she actually lives, but it falls a long way short of meeting her needs. We all need community—but one with which we can identify, by which we feel enriched and to which we are motivated to contribute. The lack of this can only increase our frustration.

Interdependency

A physical and social environment that is secure, relatively predictable, and respectful creates a space for the development of strong individual identities, "sustained by a sufficiency of solidarity and a variety of collective identities which can be allowed to be complex and non-exclusive" (Rustin, M. & Rustin, M., 2009, p. 226). It is clear that the estrangement from the world noted by Starhawk (1990—see below) and the individualistic or collective narcissistic defences theorised by psychoanalysts are systemically interconnected in a mutually reinforcing circle, with estrangement leading to narcissism, narcissism to estrangement.

Oliver James (2008) argues trenchantly that happiness is not a matter of personal effort, but a product of environmental circumstances that include egalitarian cooperation. The very concept of interdependency has been under attack since the early 1980s via the ideologies of Reaganism and Thatcherism: "there's no such thing as society". Competitive individualism has subsequently been promoted as the precondition of economic survival, with no reference at all to the benefits of cooperation. Cameron's "big society" pretends to recognise and remedy the social fragmentation wrought by Thatcherism ("broken Britain"), but it is no more than sugar on the bitter neo-liberal pill, which continues to be prescribed in undiluted form—i.e., with ever-diminishing protection for the weaker sections of society. Back in reality, what the recent youth rioting in the UK manifests is, according to the cartoonist Martin Rowson (2011), the "big broken society". Howard Jacobson (2011), in a superb article, bridges the usual left-right or heart-head divide and engages with both the cause and the solution for the narcissistic fragmentation and lawlessness. How can we expect young people born into an underclass to respect property or the law when "that form of looting known as corporate larceny continues to rage unchecked"? However Jacobson, showing he is no wishy-washy liberal, adds that:

> Liberalism today lies in ruins, not only because it has indulged the cultural bilge that has given the looters their baseless sense of entitlement—welcoming their idiot hoodlum patois as a rebellion against conformity and government, and never mind the hateful brutality—but because it has failed, in its sanctimoniousness, to understand the necessary role illiberalism—*guidelines, example, authority, boundaries*—plays in the governing of society (emphasis added).

Such "illiberalism" is, precisely, part of the holding and containment essential to good parenting. The breakdown in social relationships and interdependency can happen in insidious ways that may be benignly though mistakenly motivated. For example, we damage valued relationships and pursuits and the self when we begin to manipulate them for instrumental purposes rather than cultivating them for their intrinsic value, as is happening in virtually all of our institutions, workplaces, and wider society today. In consequence, we either measure *ourselves* in terms of market attractiveness (Elliott, 2002, p. 63), or *others* audit and assess us as units of productivity. That this is happening even in the hitherto self-regulating counselling and psychotherapy professions shows how much this way of being is out of awareness. The professions that are founded on self-awareness and the primacy of the connection between sensitive relationship and individual mental health appear not to (want to?) notice that their training and regulatory practices have adverse effects on the mental health of the practitioners, and therefore of their clients. They seem unaware of a contradiction between the authenticity, individuation/self-realisation, respect, and relational depth they claim to espouse and the practice of training students in a largely academic manner and grading them competitively. They seem unaware of the contradiction between therapeutic values of empathy and care and the lack of trust enshrined in the paranoia-inducing rules of the regulatory bodies. Amid such a punitive atmosphere of distrust, the therapist's concern for their own survival outstrips concern for the best interests of the client: "In the absence of values and principles, ethics becomes merely legalism, restricted to situations and trans-actions, a matter of resolving dilemmas and drawing up contracts" (Foley, 2011, p. 89). As I have argued elsewhere, "The therapy world's move towards regulation, towards the *appearance, rewards* and *status* of professionalisation, is part of our culture of narcissism" (Dowds, 2008, p. 12).

Challenging biological determinism

A dominant feature of Western and patriarchal societies is the near-universal acceptance of competition as both inevitable and a good thing. I would like to challenge this ethos and examine whether it is possible or desirable to change it. Competition is driven by aggression, by the desire to achieve a higher place in the pecking order than others around you. The phrase "pecking order" reveals the origins of this drive: it is something we share with other animals including birds. There is no doubt that all of us, females as well as males, have—and need—some degree of aggression. The gender difference in physical aggression is innate and reaches a peak in young adulthood, its main use being com-petition for resources, including mates (Konner, 2010, pp. 262–263). This is explained by one of the principles of neo-Darwinism: "the sex that invests more in offspring will be a scarce resource for which the other sex *competes*" (Konner, 2010, p. 40, emphasis added). Females, however, are not just the passive objects or even victims of male aggres-sion; in fact it is common for female preference to guide male evolution. Competition in nature can be extreme, and virtually all animal species, not just humans, kill their own kind when their resources are threat-ened (Konner, 2010, p. 42; Garnett, 2008). High population density has been shown to increase aggression in humans and other animals, and also to increase the gender differential in physical aggression (Konner,

2010, p. 745). Until we come to grips with overpopulation, we will have to cope with the problem of aggression.

And yet, and yet, and yet, there is a big "however" coming up. An over-reliance on one interpretation of evolutionary psychology not only legitimates the ruthlessness and inequality of unregulated free market capitalism, it can make us forget the complexity, totality, and cultural potential of human beings. Such "reductive Darwinitis" (Tallis, 2011) denies our enormous variety and capacity for a full spectrum of values and behaviour from good to bad, elevated to debased, culturally sublime to little more—or even less—than animals. Indeed, I would argue that animals too are debased by what evolutionary psychologists project onto them. Primate societies are characterised not only by sex and violence, but also by empathy and altruism (De Waal, 2005), caring parenting and relaxed oneness with nature. Humans and other primates have mirror neurons that fire not only when we feel pain ourselves but also when we observe pain in another. This shows that our brains are wired for empathy and compassion. Gordon Allport (1961) has categorised people into six types according to predominant motivation and values. The primary goals are: truth, utility, beauty, relationships, power, and spiritual unity. Thus the power acquired through competitiveness is only one of a range of possible primary motivations for individuals: only one. This matters because the inflation of evolutionary psychology by some scientists and many in the media has an impact on us all: the outcomes are debasing, soulless, ugly, and nihilistic. Where are the equivalent celebrations of humankind's capacity for truth, beauty, creativity, altruism, and spiritual experience? They are lacking, arguably, because they sit less comfortably with the societal *status quo*.

In the science of evolutionary psychology, kin selection theory has long been used to explain altruism: it is asserted that cooperation between relatives helps individuals to promote their own genes. This theory has lasted for a half century and is still tenaciously adhered to by most evolutionary biologists in the face of the facts: altruistic behaviour— adoption, saving the life of another while risking your own—frequently involves *non*-relatives. Recently, the biologist E. O. Wilson (2012) has proposed that selection occurs not just at an individual but also at a group level. Group selection is invoked to explain situations where a random mutation generates cooperative behaviour that confers a competitive advantage over other groups. Wilson suggests provocatively: "Individual selection is responsible for much of what we call sin, while group selection is responsible for the greater part of virtue. Together they have created the conflict between the poorer and better angels of our nature" (p. 241).

Our behaviour is not caused solely by our genes or by hardwiring in our brains. Nor is it determined solely by environment. Nor even by the sum of the two. Rather, it is the result of a variety of complex *interactions* between genes and environment. The environment can modulate aggression in both the short and long term. In the long term, the degree to which our brains become wired for empathy and compassion depends on the quality of our upbringing (Gerhardt, 2004), and a competitive environment will not support the empathic attunement that parents must display to raise loved children who will become caring adults. Research has shown that young adults who had been abused or neglected as children twenty years before had a higher frequency of juvenile delinquency than controls, significantly more offences, and were younger on first offence (Konner, 2010, p. 559).

The environment also has an immediate, short-term influence on our biology and our behaviour. Women have greater empathic ability than men, and this was found to be impaired when they were given testosterone (Van Honk et al., 2011). Considering that testosterone levels in men change according to circumstances (e.g., increase after winning at sport and decrease after losing), it is clearly possible to regulate empathy levels in the population by providing a suitable non-competitive, testosterone-lowering environment. In the nurturing environment of baby-tending, men's testosterone and aggression levels decrease (Konner, 2010). In hunter-gatherers the gender differential in behaviour is reduced by mixed-sex playgroups throughout childhood but intensified by gender segregation or high population density (ibid., p. 745).

There are a number of studies that explicitly examine the interaction between genetic and environmental influences on behaviour. In a study of adoptees, a "criminal environment" was found to have no impact on the frequency of criminal behaviour in adopted children who were not genetically predisposed to crime, but it did increase the frequency in genetically predisposed children over and above their already elevated levels (Plomin, DeFries, McClearn, & McGuffin, 2008, p. 258). The field of epigenetics is showing how our DNA can be modified in response to the environment, thus affecting *expression* of key behavioural genes. Abuse in childhood has been shown to result in a heightened HPA (hypothalamic-pituitary-adrenal) stress response by modifying and down-regulating the hippocampal glucocorticoid receptor gene (McGowan et al., 2009).

We may conclude then that basal aggression levels and the gender differential can be modified by environmental conditions. In neurobiological terms, our brains are plastic: neural networks are formed and pruned according to our interactions with stimuli in our social, physical, and emotional surroundings (Cozolino, 2010). It is clear from the above and many other studies (e.g., Plomin, DeFries, McClearn, & McGuffin, 2008) that genes and environment interact in complex and dynamic ways to generate humankind's huge range of ever-changing individuals and cultural groupings. Some individuals, particularly men, are predisposed hormonally to be more aggressive, but this innate tendency can be modulated in appropriate environments. Our biological inheritance is almost never deterministic and can be modified: in childhood by upbringing and education; in adulthood by social and cultural environment, life experience, training, psychotherapy, and meditation. It can be shaped and policed by the legal and cultural framework, and can be channelled into appropriate spheres of activity.

Winning: a Pyrrhic victory?

Is there anyone not willing to barter health, leisure and life itself against reputation and glory, the most useless, vain and counterfeit coinage in circulation? (Montaigne, 1993, p. 271).

It is clearly possible to change levels of aggression and competition, but is it desirable? Whatever the arena—whether it is crime or legally and socially sanctioned activities such as sport, business, education, politics, the arts (!) or humiliation television, in a competitive culture everyone is ultimately a loser. The losers lose while the "winners" only appear to win. For theirs is a temporary and Pyrrhic victory; in the words of Robert Browning: "In triumphs, people have dropped down dead" ("The Patriot"). The winner can never relax. He must always strive to stay on top form; but however hard he tries, sooner or later a younger, fitter challenger appears and ousts him from the podium. We haven't come far in the thousands of years since the king was challenged each year by a new contender who, if he managed to kill the old king, could replace him on the throne (Frazer, 1963). "Glory and tranquillity cannot dwell in the same lodgings", said Montaigne (1993, p. 277), referring not just to the inevitability of being toppled from the pedestal, but also to the ungrounding effect of placing your self-worth in the hands of the other. As long as regard comes from the outside, we remain in a state of addictive craving for what in reality must emerge from a secure self. We are trapped in the realm of the narcissist, as has already been discussed.

The shadow of a competitive culture is of course failure. Indeed, as Colin Feltham has pointed out, most of us regard failure as the occasional exception in an otherwise successful or uneventful life. In reality "failure is everywhere" (2012, p. 6), as he goes on to demonstrate in pages of examples, both individual and systemic. Such is our denial about failure that there is no systematic study or science of failure (pp. 132, 134). Instead, "the cult of excellence and machismo pervading many organizations can work against admissions of weakness and failure" (p. 127). This makes it difficult to learn from failure. Mariana Caplan (2001) urges us to accept the inevitability of failure and shows us how we can use it as a spiritual path. However, our phobia about the F word becomes clear when we see that even she needed to soften the title of her book, *The Way of Failure* with a subtitle, *Winning Through Losing*! (my exclamation mark).

The Dalai Lama has expressed astonishment at the extent of self-hatred and self-rejection amongst Western people, something he had never encountered before beginning to teach in the West (Brach, 2003, p. 11). We take it for granted that this is an inevitable consequence of being human. It is not! It is a consequence of the competitiveness and judgementalism of our culture. These related characteristics are not innate human attributes, they stem, rather, from a specifically Western cultural problem. Competitive individualism creates a pandemic of shame, poor self-esteem, envy, rage, and depression (Sloman, 2000, p. 262) and blocks our self-realisation because our esteem needs are always in deficit (see Maslow's hierarchy of needs). It constantly proclaims that one person is better than another full stop, not simply better at one particular thing. It inhibits development of each person's unique combination of qualities—once again, a recipe for frustration. For, in Jungian terms, individuation is a matter, not of specialisation, but of the balancing of opposites within ourselves; we achieve this by working on our *inferior* functions as well as by incorporating the shadow aspects of our personalities.

A competitive culture is one in which the message is relayed daily that you are not good enough—you are not up to scratch in terms of intelligence, beauty, "pulling power", career development, success, knowledge, material wealth, etc., etc. There is almost no arena in which we do not compete, even the spiritual. An acquaintance—oblivious to its absurdity—once boasted to me: "I am a better meditator than my wife",—a perfect example of the "spiritual materialism" with which the West has contaminated Buddhism. A recent brochure, again without irony, advertised life-coaching (achieving goals and making your dreams come true) in the same breath as transpersonal consciousness— and all within the corporate sector! Spiritual development is about acceptance, not performance and goal-setting. As Woody Allen is credited with saying: "if you want to make God laugh, tell him your plans".

Television is littered with fabricated competitions. The most crude and pernicious are undisguised popularity contests. Others make more or less pretence at assessing skills. But all of them instrumentalise, inflate, and humiliate. Celebrity magazines then carry the winners off in their claws for bloody games of hide-and-seek, where the celebrity victim is pampered and preened before their inevitable public sacrifice. Politics is an arena in which popularity contests (aka elections) are viewed, without question, as meeting the common good. However, populism does not amount to democracy and the public have in reality almost no say in policymaking. Indeed, it could be argued that even national governments have less and less say in policymaking. Fukuyama may have been wrong when he proclaimed the end of history. But in our post-financially—regulated globalised world, we have arguably reached the end of democratic politics, when countries such as my own are controlled by the IMF and ECB, and others who supposedly have retained their national sovereignty make policy according to the dictates of the "markets".

Amongst the power-hungry who play the game of national or institutional politics many (not all) are compensating for weak egos by controlling others. This bid for self-worth must ultimately fail: they are no happier or at ease in power than out of it. Indeed, their paranoia increases (think of Stalin) since they are terrified of losing their only—however inadequate—compensation for their self-hatred. They have climbed to the top of a ladder, but—with apologies to Joseph Campbell—it turns out they should have been, not simply on another ladder, but not on a ladder at all. What they are really looking for is not power-over but power-from-within. They are attempting to compensate for their deficient ego development. (Of course these individuals compensating for their power-deficiency are in a different category from genuine leaders who have a flexible inner strength that inspires others to follow them without any coercion, arrogance, or display.)

The feminist writer Starhawk ascribed the power-over mentality to "estrangement". This is:

> because its essence is that we do not see ourselves as part of the world. We are strangers to nature, to other human beings, to parts of ourselves. We see the world as made up of separate, isolated, non-living parts that have no inherent value. (They are not even dead—because death implies life.) Among things inherently separate and lifeless, the only power relationships possible are those of manipulation and domination. (Starhawk, 1990, p. 5)

Since she wrote this in 1982, we have moved closer to environmental catastrophe (though accompanied by greater environmental awareness) while our public life has deteriorated further, with financial deregulation, globalisation, and a marked increase in inequality and the instrumentalisation of the populace, no longer even as workers but now as mere consumers. What Starhawk called "estrangement" is associated with narcissism and its accompanying weak (though sometimes inflated) ego and poor self-esteem.

Competitiveness, capitalism, and social malaise

For those of us old enough to remember the English-speaking world before Thatcher and Reagan, we remember a time of more cooperation and equality and less competitive individualism, when European countries espoused a mixture of regulated capitalism and socialism. Society didn't change because of an emergency but only because of the ideologically driven unleashing of greed and a dogmatic and fatal belief in unregulated finance, which has generated a widening gap between rich and poor along with the ongoing global financial crisis. As Berman (1990, p. 341) says: "We have inherited a civilization in which things that really matter in human life exist at the margin of our culture". Childbirth, child-rearing, a rich inner life, a vibrant, inclusive, and cooperative public sphere, connection with the natural world and respect— these all matter, while great wealth, fame and fashion don't. The most highly paid work—much of the work in banks, ratings agencies, public relations, television and cinema—not only concerns ephemera, but is often actively destructive to society: it is ridiculous that people are paid more to *act* being a doctor, nurse, or detective than to actually *be* one. Psychologists and psychotherapists have begun to call for more collective, cooperative, relational, and egalitarian principles in society. Sue Gerhardt (2011) shows that our current narcissistic society generates babies starved of empathic attunement. Based on current trends, the World Health Organisation has predicted that depression will become the second most widespread illness after heart disease in the developed world by 2020. Oliver James (2008) argues that market capitalism through competitive, materialistic individualism is a direct cause of emotional distress such as anxiety and depression. Drawing on the work of Tim Kasser, he shows how "selfish capitalism" generates insecurity and a pandemic of low self-esteem. Interestingly, in comparing first world countries, the effect is more marked in the English-speaking countries than in more egalitarian and collectivist countries such as Denmark and Germany.

A groundbreaking book *The Spirit Level* shows that in the world's fifty richest countries almost every social problem is exacerbated by income inequality—and that more equal societies are better, not just for the poor, but also for the higher-earning sectors of the population. There is a straight-line graph relating health and social problems to income inequality, with Japan at one end of the scale and the USA at the other (highest inequality, worst social problems by far). The authors, epidemiologists Richard Wilkinson and Kate Pickett (2009), show that *every* section of more unequal societies does worse than the equivalent section in more equal societies in terms of trust, lifespan, obesity, mental illness, teenage birth rates, infant mortality, literacy, crime, violence, and many other indices. The major overall explanation is that status inequality increases levels of stress and distrust throughout the social hierarchy. The stress hormone cortisol rises when people face evaluation from others, and this has a negative impact on physical and emotional health. The only exceptions to the rule were suicide and smoking, which are higher in more equal societies. Possibly, people living in an ethos of equality are more likely to take responsibility themselves when things go wrong rather than lashing out at others. A separate study needs to be done on inequality stemming from other sources, such as gender, ethnicity, age, disability, and sexual orientation. However, if the authors are correct in thinking that status stress is the underlying cause of our widespread social problems, then it is highly likely that these discriminatory prejudices are just as damaging as socio-economic inequality.

Many other studies have shown that personal income contributes to individual happiness and well-being only up to a plateau, after which increased income adds no further to happiness (summarised in Seligman, 2011). According to Seligman, well-being depends on positive emotion, engagement, meaning, accomplishment, and positive relationships. Following on from Richard Layard, he argues that GDP should no longer be the only serious index for how a nation is doing and that an additional well-being index should inform political policy (p. 227). Daniel Pink (2011) shows that motivation in the workplace is only minimally related to financial reward. In experimental groups around the world, it has been demonstrated repeatedly that the highest financial incentives led to the *worst* performance while medium and lower remuneration led to equally good performance. Bonus culture does not work! In work that requires conceptual and creative skill, workers were found to be motivated by autonomy, the desire for mastery, and purpose—in other words, making a difference.

To summarise so far: competiveness and the inequality, financial or otherwise, that results, don't make us happy or generate a deeper well-being or flourishing. They create status anxiety, shame, panic, envy, rage, depression, poor self-esteem, and self-absorption. As a consequence, they spawn a range of social and medical problems. They are associated with narcissism and a thin, precarious, detached identity that manipulates self and others. People are many and varied in their mix of motivations, and power and money score well down the scale. In order to flourish, we require non-instrumentalised, unconditional positive relationships. We therefore need community and collectivism. We have a need for autonomy, mastery, and purpose; because we seek meaning in our lives, we are enlivened and inspired by beauty, truth, and an experience of the divine. We know all this—in our bodies if not in our heads. But we have lost our way as a culture. We have lost the ability to distinguish between what matters and what doesn't. Science is distorted in the service of political ideology to reduce us to nothing more than aggressive, competitive beasts. In reality this is only a small part of who we are. Our genetic inheritance interacts with our environment to create a vast range of personalities, behaviours, and motivations, so it behoves us to create a society that brings out the best rather than the worst impulses in mankind.

The loss of objective values

The philosopher Mark Rowlands (2008) asserts that the Western worldview depends primarily on the tension between Plato's concept of objectivism and the Enlightenment idea of individualism. For objectivists, values exist objectively and are independent of the belief system of a particular culture. Individualism, the belief in the individual freedom to live as you choose so long as you don't harm anybody else, incorporates the two ideas of autonomy and self-realisation. Both ways of thinking can degenerate: objectivism into fundamentalism, when the corrective of reasoning is abandoned; and individualism into relativism, when the corrective of objective values is omitted. Rowlands argues that the Enlightenment project is currently in decline, and focuses on two symptoms of this that are consequences of an imbalance between objectivism and individualism. One is fundamentalist religion and the other is the rise of fame that is unconnected to achievement or excellence: the cult of celebrity, or what he calls new variant fame ("vfame"). In abandoning objective values, the neo-individualists actually thwart the Enlightenment project of self-realisation because they have no objective standard on which to base their development: thus acquiring a Gucci handbag becomes as valid as spiritual practice. The media who feign shock and awe at the antics of celebrities, the public who consume these media with relish, and all the relativists in university cultural studies departments (Britney is as good as Beethoven, just different) buy into and deepen this erosion of societal values.

What Rowlands doesn't examine is why this is happening now. In the section on narcissism, we saw how impoverished, instrumentalising relationships generate self-absorption and the demand for attention and admiration. But here I want to suggest that the rise of "vfame" may also be the shadow of the struggle for equality. I notice with dismay that young women are particularly susceptible to acting out on the public stage in the absence of any noticeable talent or valuable message, and that celebrity magazines are overwhelmingly the domain of female voyeurs. The desire for fame and success seems to be provoked by a craving to be respected and envied. Respect alone might be sufficient if it weren't for the fact that you don't know you're special unless you are getting more attention than others, so the specialness that provokes envy is part of the equation also. "Respect" doesn't seem like a big enough word to describe the motivation for the ravenous fame hunger of an entire generation; but "diss-ing" a young gang member is one of the most reliable ways of dying from non-natural causes, so we have to recognise that the need for respect is fierce and primal. Young, disinherited underclass males go the route of gang culture, while the slightly less disinherited young take to the stage and screen to earn respect. The sectors of the population previously despised for their gender, class, race, or whatever other "difference" could be invented, have now been legally and publicly recognised as worthy of the same rights and opportunities as the non-different, and are protected against overt discrimination or crimes of hatred. However, political correctness notwithstanding, they are not equally *respected*. Values will need to change considerably before this happens.

When it comes to reinstating values back into our culture, Rowlands focuses on how to recognise *quality*. He puts together Marx's labour theory of value with capitalism's supply and demand definition of value. Thus, he proposes, the value of a skill or talent can be estimated by the amount of *labour* that went into mastering it combined with the *rarity* of the gift. By both measures, he argues, Beethoven is much better than Britney. I am fully in accord with the need to differentiate between the high-carat gold of achievement and the tinsel of "vfame", and to value quality in the arts, professions, or any other endeavour. A good novel provides satisfaction that lasts both for the lifetime of the individual and over the course of generations. The reader can, for example, return again and again to reap new rewards from the beauty of the language, the complexity or balance of the structure, the originality or depth of the thought, or the richness and psychological profundity of the characters. To give a ridiculous example: we do not get this from *Fifty Shades of Grey*. Much of the music being produced by boy- or girl-band hopefuls may have little objective cultural value, but, as a society, we need to attend to the motivation underlying the obsession with "vfame". It is not enough just to write the music off as rubbish. We need to grasp that these people—like the young gang member—are desperately acting out to gain respect.

Recognition of objective value in the arts does not validate competitiveness in this arena. Writing, art, and music competitions are nonsensical when you consider the nature of these pursuits. They are about developing the unique individual voice, so that judging competitions is akin to comparing apples, oranges, pears, and plums. While acknowledging that you can get a full range of quality in any fruit, it is still the case that if the panel of judges is biased towards pear-lovers, then the pear will win unless it is badly blemished. In the arts, within the works that meet Rowlands' criteria for quality, the best pear is being compared with the best apple and the best plum. The outcome will depend on the personal preferences and prejudices of the jury. Men, for example, generally dislike women's fiction, whatever the quality of the writing. The subject-matter is often seen as domestic and male judges and critics write it off as trivial, failing to grasp that the power of these works lies in an emotional subtlety to which they are blind.

The valuing of quality that Rowlands promotes may be desirable in terms of cultural products, but it also plays into a form of competitive individualism, and hence a vehicle for unequal valuing of the populace. Thus, not only is Bach's *music* better than Britney's, but as a consequence Bach himself becomes a better person than Britney. However, there is no need to revere the creator or performer of distinction over all others; indeed it takes away from our capacity to respond to and be grateful for their work. Just as we can be humbled and moved to worship by the sublime beauty of the music of Bach or Handel, we can equally be awestruck by the soaring grandeur of a medieval cathedral without knowing who designed, built, or decorated it. We must separate the achievement from the individual who is credited with the creation. We do have a human need for reverence and worship, but to worship a limited fellow human is to downgrade the mystery and wonder of creation.

Valuing the person, not the producer

Our entire culture is crying out for respect and recognition, and we are locked in an unpalatable and self-defeating contest for this valuing. We still feel free to judge others for character traits—anxiety, shyness, unassertiveness, being "losers"—that may be as unavoidable as skin colour or gender, whether due to inheritance or early upbringing. There are infinite different forms of disadvantage that do not fit into the categories of political correctness. Despite having gone some way towards reducing overt discrimination based on gender, class, race, sexuality, or disability, we still reserve our particular admiration for those who compete well on the white, middle-class, male public stage.

How do we get beyond the apparent contradiction between valuing excellence of achievement and valuing everyone on the grounds of their humanity? I would like to extend Rowlands' male philosopher's view with a female therapist's vision of valuing who we *are*: the *being* that Buddhism regards as our true nature. What we need is for our essence to be respected and recognised, not the tricks we can perform on stage or the sports field. I refer elsewhere (Chapter Two) to *being* as a foundation out of which healthy *doing* emerges. In the absence of a healthy sense of being, our doing is a futile attempt to regain or maintain being. And yet, outside the worlds of psychotherapy and meditation, the quality of our being is ignored.

The lack of genuine respect for the other that is common in the West may be traced to the interlinked (according to Max Weber) effects of instrumentalising capitalism (see above) and exoteric religion. When God is located outside the person, we are separate from God and in a state of peril where God may or may not be on our side. The Irish greeting "Dia dhuit" (God be with you), while a kindly wish and certainly warmer than a blunt "hello", carries this implicit message of the external split-off God. The Indian greeting "Namaste" (the divine in me honours the divine in you) accompanied by a bow of respect may be associated with Hinduism, but it nevertheless reflects the thinking of esoteric religion: there is a divine spark in all of us, all beings are part of Brahman. In this way of envisaging humanity, it is difficult for genuine adherents not to revere the other. In psychotherapy, such a principle of respect is most foregrounded by person-centred therapy. Carl Rogers (1967) discovered the facilitating power of a relationship with a therapist who embodies the core conditions of empathy, unconditional positive regard, and congruence. Such a relationship enables the client to connect with their inherent but hitherto blocked tendency towards healthy development. As in therapy, so in life: we all thrive and contribute best to our family, workplace and society at large when treated with dignity and respect. The contemporary PCT practitioners Mearns and Thorne (2000) examine some of the contexts where personhood is denied: from being judged and shamed in education, treated as machines in the workplace, or subjected to the grossest terror, pain, and humiliation in war. Once the principle of respecting others for their full humanity is pushed into second or third place, there are no limits to the horrors that can be inflicted in the name of "standards", productivity, or the dominance of one person's claims over another's.

Alternative values

What are the alternative values, beliefs, and motivations that are currently rarely valued or mirrored—in the public sphere, at least? Some schools of psychotherapy divide our primary drives into the two central needs for love and power (McAdams, 1997). These may also be viewed as the attachment and separating motivations or, in Freud's terms, the life and death instincts. Cooperation, community, receptiveness, relating, and communion with something larger than the self are all part of the love theme, while individualism, autonomy, agency, aggression, and mastery characterise the power drive. No prizes for guessing which is more associated with males and which with females. Nevertheless, as individuals and as societies, we live in a tension between both these needs and must constantly strive for a balance. The Western world is dangerously unbalanced, overrun by the barbarian invasion of unregulated capitalism and competitive individualism: hostile takeovers; financial colonisation; trading on futures; betting on food stocks and creating famine; ruthless exploitation of the majority by the few; downgrading of public services; the plundering of the world's resources; destruction of indigenous tribes and other species; garbage culture; celebrityitis—the list could go on and on. At a personal level we are lonely, distrustful, anxious, angry, shamed, narcissistic, and self-absorbed. Even Mother Teresa, who must have encountered more physical and social ills than most of us, has said that our greatest ailment is not belonging (Brach, 2003).

I am not saying anything new here that hasn't been said many times before by many other people. But nothing changes. We have all been bought off by the little goodies of capitalism and replaced our real needs with addictions: drink, drugs, eating, shopping, meaningless sex, workaholism, noise and non-stop doing. Brenda's addiction of choice is over-activity, from which she slumps into burnout and depression, before starting the busyness–burnout cycle again. Why does she do it? Because, in the absence of busyness, she starts feeling that she doesn't exist and her identity and self-esteem drain away. And, indeed, she is outside of any socially supported existence when she stops the busyness, because everyone else is working, or travelling, going to workshops or films or concerts or book clubs, entertaining or at the gym, or doing further training. There is absolutely nothing wrong with any of these activities. The problem with them is their relentlessness. Tara Brach (2000) asserts that addictions are all attempts to run from or self-medicate against intense and pervasive feelings of shame and poor self-worth. These arise out of competitive individualism and are endemic in the West. The consequences of addiction, beyond the shallow and temporary relief from shame, are emptiness at the core of our being or the self-abuse of burnout. Thomas Merton has said that "the rush and pressure of modern life are a form, perhaps the most common form, of [contemporary society's] innate violence" (quoted in Andre, Foglio, & Brody, 2000, p. 91). The effects of this life on speed is evident in both those young people who are thin and wired and who speak like a tape on fast forward, as well as in others defended against the speed who are overweight, silent, and torpid: the two types are trapped in uncontrolled circuiting of the sympathetic and parasympathetic nervous systems respectively.

However much we resist the dominant culture, we are marinated in it, and it is poisoning us by a process of osmosis (through the media, entertainment, other people) and indeed forcing us to collaborate with it if we are to earn a living. A diet composed largely of manioc (cassava)—which is a major food staple in the developing world—results in protein malnutrition, and sometimes in cyanide poisoning. That describes our culture well: "food" that is a mere filler, not only without nourishment, but actively toxic as well. Our addictions are not meeting our needs. A prolonged recession in the West might be one of the best things that could happen to us—if and only if the recession is managed so that the economic losses are shared. Drinking, cocaine use, and suicide rates (which are associated with alcohol abuse) along with crime rates, have decreased in Ireland since the economic crisis began in 2008 (Lally, 2012). However, the burden of economic losses is not being predominantly carried by the rich.

How have I got to competitive individualism from a starting place of dreams, sacrifices, and petrified hearts? They are connected by the love/power dichotomy. Love dreams of justice, equality, inclusion, and respect; but the realisation of the dream demands power. Those who assume the mantle of power are easily seduced by power's own dreams, which can take the form of revenge, replacement of one power by another, or vanity/compromise: selling the revolution for an honoured seat at the table of the status quo. The first revolution is corrupted by the dictates of power politics, and its most successful external outcome is membership of the power elite for the previously disempowered. An internal side-effect of playing the power game is the compromised, compressed heart, worn out by struggle and disillusioned by the discrepancy between dream and reality. The second revolution demands a return to the values that initiated the first: the balancing of power with love, and a genuine inclusiveness of beliefs and values alternative to the dominant worldview.

A way forward?

History (French and Russian revolutions, Chinese communism etc.) has shown repeatedly that social engineering doesn't work and leads to new problems that are often worse than the previous ones. John Gray (2002) claims that utopia is an unrealisable mirage and he urges us to grow up beyond such childish expectations of justice and equality. But the fact is that societies don't just stay the same; they get better sometimes, and worse sometimes. One such transformation is the vast improvement in human rights and opportunities for women, non-white ethnic groups, and other minorities in the Western world over the past century. Another example is the creation of the National Health Service in the UK after World War Two. Other equally just changes did not materialise—at the time—such as Noel Browne's Mother and Child Scheme in Ireland in the early 1950s. Yet, a few years later, a similar piece of health legislation was passed without argument. Why one change and not another? Why later but not before? The sociologist Peter Berger has observed that ideas "do not succeed in history by virtue of their truth but by virtue of their relationships to specific social processes" (quoted in Berman, 1984, p. 35). Feminist advances in the 1970s depended on universal education and birth control, and perhaps on labour-saving household appliances. The feminist movement was able to take advantage of this time in history and push things further by consciousness-raising and campaigning, and it recognised that change would only come about through working at both personal and political levels.

What about our current problems, which are less explicit and harder to define? The enemy is unidentifiable: it is just "the System". Supposedly the most powerful man in the world, Barack Obama has made few inroads despite evident integrity and ability. Electing him in the first place was about as much revolution as the USA could encompass, and the blocks of conservative power opposing him in office are greater than he can shift. By at least a modest majority, the voting public seems to be more radical and more in favour of change than the non-democratic lobbies and power-blocks that have a greater voice in running the country than the elected government. However, even if a world leader (head of the UN, or would it be the IMF or World Bank?) were able to impose equality and cooperation on us, it would be of no use. This is a change that has to come from the bottom up. It will come with emotional and spiritual education. The current popular fascination with celebrities and royal weddings for women, soccer and political gossip for men, the materialist-reductionist bias both of humanist (and often belligerently atheist) and of scientific intellectuals, and the universal preoccupation with self-promotion all represent the shadow of real needs that are being expressed in debased form: needs for worship, beauty, heroism, and truth; needs to matter to and connect with others; and ultimately a need for meaning. The remarkable achievement of the Western world in providing some degree, however unequal, of universal material sustenance for the population in terms of food, water, shelter, waste disposal, hygiene, and medical care, and the provision of universal (cognitive) education must now be supplemented by attending to our emotional and spiritual welfare. We cannot return to the past—and it was a long way from perfect anyway. The way forward—unless our civilisation is plunged into dystopia by economic collapse, population overgrowth, climate chaos, fuel shortage, war, famine or pestilence—is to move up the hierarchy of needs. Our Western society meets our physical and cognitive needs well to varying degrees, but we need a lot more than calories and calculus to thrive and flourish.

The personal and the political are mutually reinforcing, and expressions of new spiritual awareness will probably appear in grass-roots movements equivalent to those that emerged among the dispossessed in a swathe of Arab nations, amongst the unemployed in Madrid, among anti-globalisation protestors, and in online groupings in Ireland such as Claiming Our Future. These movements are focused on equality and genuine democracy, just as earlier people's movements such as Greenpeace raised awareness of the natural environment. The kind of emergence I am envisaging in the future might be more explicitly informed by awareness of emotional and spiritual needs. In making such mass movements possible, new communication technologies are playing a pivotal role—ironically, not just as a source of alienation, but as agents of unification and contact as well.

What about the young Brenda's feminist dream? There have been vast changes in women's rights and the respect afforded to women in Ireland since she grew up. These sociopolitical changes, together with greater inner freedom brought about by therapy, the love of her partner John, and her refusal to expose herself any more to the judgement and contempt of her brothers, have all contributed to a transformation in her self-esteem. She is no longer a walking, pulsing wound, jumpy with stress in hostile environments and flinching away from every news report of women-hatred in Afghanistan or Saudi Arabia, Africa or India. She is aware how lucky she is.

Summary

This chapter analyses the role of competitiveness in frustrating the expression and development of the true self. The case is argued that equality is incompatible with a meritocracy and that competitive individualism is not only damaging to the individual but to society as a whole. Sociological research shows that almost every social problem is exacerbated by inequality, while evidence from genetics and evolutionary psychology shows that the social environment interacts with genetic predisposition to modulate aggression levels. Thus it is not just desirable but also possible to reduce levels of competitiveness. At the level of group psychology, a world where others are perceived as threatening or indifferent leads to the collective narcissism with which our society is infused. At the level of individual psychology, the need to assert one's own identity leads to the desire to "destroy" the other through competition. This implies that provision of social conditions that facilitate the development of strong differentiated egos is what will save us. In society as a whole we are trapped in a competition for self-worth, but even if we are winners this is a Pyrrhic victory. We have other needs—notably for a cooperation and community as well as for individual authenticity—that are blocked by our addiction to attention and admiration. Society does need to return to recognising objective worth, for instance in the arts; but such valuing should not be tied to esteeming high-achieving individuals over others. It is axiomatic that all people should be valued equally.

CHAPTER SEVEN

Activism versus integrity: resolving the dilemma?

First they came for the communists,
And I didn't speak out because I wasn't a communist.
Then they came for the trade unionists,
And I didn't speak out because I wasn't a trade unionist.
Then they came for the Jews,
And I didn't speak out because I wasn't a Jew.
Then they came for me,
And there was no one left to speak out for me.

—Attributed to Pastor Martin Niemöller

The time is out of joint;
O cursèd spite,
That ever I was born to set it right.

—Shakespeare, *Hamlet*, Act 1, Scene 5, ca 1601

Activism and the demand for action

Shortly before she finally decided to jump ship, the IT company where Brenda used to work was transformed into a pressure-cooker of stress and resentment resulting from newly-implemented and abusive management practices. Subsequent to the company having been taken over, a new culture was instituted of bullying and summary dismissals, reinforced by contracts that established slave-owners rights over the staff. Swingeing cuts in her department led to depression, burnout, and a plummeting in the quality of the work. After futile protests to her immediate superiors and a colleague even being driven to a suicide attempt, she was left wondering about complaining at higher levels, blowing the whistle to the Labour Court or even speaking to the press. But Brenda doesn't have the stomach for activism. The simplest solution would have been to ignore what was happening, yet her conscience would not leave her alone, nagging her with Simon Wiesenthal's dictum, "For evil to flourish it only requires good men to do nothing". She felt the pressure of this—and the resistance to it. She struggled between her stubborn refusal to let *them* get away with it and her desire to stay within her comfort zone. Behind her anger and frustration with the system, she was well aware of the relative pettiness of the conflicts within the company. However, she tormented herself with the concern that the ethos behind such small disputes can sometimes be the thin end of a wedge: today a company, tomorrow the country. Though it is some years since these events, Brenda still feels guilt and frustration, but also some pride and sense of personal achievement when she looks back to her response to this challenge. Her unresolved moral dilemma came back to her recently, when she heard that one of her students—an immigrant—was being bullied and exploited by his employer: once again, shouldn't she be doing something?

Protesting about bullying is effective only if the abusing organisation or state can actually be embarrassed by naming and shaming, and Brenda was convinced that the upper echelons of management would simply blame increasing global competition for their actions. She dreaded the re-triggering of her early wound of not being heard: her rage and frustration always escalate and remain trapped in the face of the non-receiving other. When challenged by colleagues, she realised she was being too absolutist here: the management would mind, but wouldn't admit to it. She had to have faith that her voice would be heard, but she would never know for sure what difference she had made. This is true even with the vastly greater challenge of the international stage. In Lynne Reid Banks' novel, *Fair Exchange*, set in late 1980s London, Judy is an anti-apartheid activist and communist who participates in a three-year vigil outside the South African embassy calling for the release of Nelson Mandela from prison. When the novel ends in 1990, Mandela has been freed and apartheid has ended, but Judy can't judge how far, if at all, her actions have influenced events. Furthermore, with the events in Tiananmen Square and the collapse of communism in Eastern Europe, she has to face how the ideals of justice and equality in communism could be twisted into totalitarian repression and human rights abuses. In the end, she appears to retire from activism, yet still misses the comrade-ship and sense of purpose that went with it. Inherent in all activism is a state of unknowing.

Michael Ignatieff (2012) believes that "with the exception of North Korea there appears to be no regime entirely immune to human rights shaming", but he acknowledges that human rights pressure is only one factor in what leads to political change. So it seems that someone who gives his life to protest must be content with a small, slow, and uncertain impact, and, as Ignatieff makes clear, his power will depend on collective action and on globalisation of resources and organisation. This is something that Brenda intuited: she would be completely ineffective unless she got other people on side. But politically engaged people repel her: she finds them abrasive, noisy, self-promoting, shallow, pragmatic, boring, angry, and arrogant in their conviction of their own rightness. She knows that with the help of her own guilt, they will drag her into protests, committee meetings, and door-to-door canvassing for signatures or votes—all the pointless paraphernalia of activism that make her tired of life. She recoils from the ugliness: the crowds and the constant jostling for power within and between political groups. The men—they usually are men—who lead radical reform or revolutionary movements tend to be made of the same cloth as their opponents: they are all magnetised by power. Brenda has no patience with men and their power games. They are pests sabotaging peace and harmony, like wasps at a picnic; they are like her brothers as boys: noisy, attention-seeking, boastful, and voracious for being in charge. Her only consolation is that, in their thirst for power, they are monomaniacal: as a result they lack inner fulfilment, freedom, and balance—though they ensure that *others* are made to suffer for this.

Carol Gilligan (1993) suggests that boys separate too early from mother, before the ego becomes fully established. What they need is to separate *to* father, but he is often absent, physically or emotionally. At the same time, the teaching profession is dominated by women, so boys lack male role models and discipline and are left rudderless in a void. A sociologist interviewed recently about gang culture claimed that the young men who had been in prison enjoyed the experience because it was their first exposure to the leadership and containment of older men. One way in which young boys contain their anxiety and lost-ness is to generate hierarchies and rules. This can be seen in the games of children: boys may appear rough and highly energised, but they also create abstract regulations for implementing justice and merit and negotiating the inherent conflict between these two principles; girls by contrast stay in constant empathic engagement with each other, moving between the poles of care and its shadow, rejection. Boys replace relationships with structures and thereby form the early beginnings of their political selves.

Thomas Merton (himself an anti-war activist in the USA) was aware of the dangers of activism to both the inner life and to the cause itself: "The frenzy of the activist neutralizes his work, because it kills the root of inner wisdom that makes work fruitful" (quoted in Andre, Foglio, & Brody, 2000, p. 91). This is why activism—while often aligned with moral integrity—is actually harmful to the integrity of the self. What happens is this: when you struggle with power blocks you are dragged from an internal to an external locus, where to succeed you must behave reactively and view the world from the other's ego perspective. However, this is a different process from empathy, where the self of the other is being entered into, only not for manipulative or strategic purposes. Staying ahead of the other's ego perspective, on the other hand, is a game of guessing the next move in the struggle for power *over* the other.

But is it ethical to simply cultivate the inner life or the private life without taking public stands? The Buddhist activists Macy and Brown (1998) assert that of all the dangers the planet faces, from environmental catastrophe to nuclear war, the greatest is widespread apathy—the deadening of heart and mind. To take an extreme example: in retrospect, it is clear that all should have taken a stand against the rise of the Nazis long before there was "no one left to speak out for me". But here is the problem: at the time we do not have the benefit of hindsight. If totalitarianism grows (in a country or an institution), we have three choices: we can remain silent; we can speak out rashly and be destroyed and ineffectual; or we can become skilful. Fighting injustice can feed rather than quench the flames of conflict. It must be done skilfully or not at all. However, the last option can be a corrupting one: as soon as you start thinking in such strategic ways, you endanger the very values you are trying to protect. You lose the "love-values" of empathy, ethics, and social responsibility and take on "power-over-values" whereby you instrumentalise others as tools or obstacles for the cause, with all the associated egocentricity and freedom to dominate. The will occludes the heart.

From her relatively unenlightened position, Brenda could see only these three alternatives, but she realises that true spiritual warriors can have their external lives stripped, yet maintain an inner power and fearlessness. From a more primitive, external perspective, they appear to choose the second option of speaking out and being destroyed, but the inner picture may be quite different if they no longer cling to worldly attachments. There are some religious such as the proponents of liberation theology in Latin America or Buddhist monks or laypeople in Tibet and Burma (Myanmar) who cultivate both the inner contemplative and the outer (non-violent) warrior. The Buddhist leader Aung San Suu Kyi exemplifies this balance. She sacrificed her private life and her liberty to maintain the spirit of opposition to the dictatorship in her country and has spent most of this time under house-arrest. She missed out on the childhood of her sons and even turned down the opportunity to visit her mortally ill English husband for one last time before he died because she knew she would not be readmitted to Burma. In her speech on freedom from fear, she says: "It is not power that corrupts, but fear. Fear of losing power corrupts those who wield it and fear of the scourge of power corrupts those who are subject to it" (www.cfwd. org.uk). She is an example of somebody who has cultivated contemplative discipline in the service of the political and has an inner practice of refusing to let fear dictate her actions. In her political leadership, she embodies the Buddhist values of courage, patience, tolerance, and non-violence. Aung San Suu Kyi and the Dalai Lama are examples of leaders who appear to have combined activism with integrity of the self. They may have sacrificed the possibility of a private (family) life, but they have actually strengthened rather than given up the inner (spiritual) life. However, it is debatable whether their activism has had much practical outcome beyond serving as a source of moral inspiration, and Brenda knows that in their position (but with her own limited awareness) she would wonder if the sacrifice had been worth it. Some remarkable individuals retain integrity hand-in-hand with activism, but what about ordinary mortals like Brenda whose inner life is fragile and would be easily blown away by "the frenzy of the activist"? What happens when a person acts out of duty, but entirely against their own abilities, wishes and personality type? To what extent are these traits malleable and subject to education, so that they can be formed in the process of activism? Did Brenda feel this pressure within her because she was resisting developing what Jung called the inferior function or was it because she intuited that she would be driving herself off her life path?

The curse of consciousness

Challenging situations and feelings are the subject of a CD by the Buddhist teacher, Tara Brach (2009). She tells the story of Houdini who travelled the world entertaining the public by escaping from a variety of captivities. In a small town in Ireland, he was tied into a straitjacket and placed in a cage. He managed to disentangle himself from the straitjacket but, try as he might, he couldn't undo the lock on the cage. Eventually, the public departed, disappointed, and Houdini asked his jailer to release him. He inquired what nature of new high-tech lock the jailer had used. The man replied: "it was the same lock as usual; I just didn't close it". I imagine the Irish jailer alternately as a trickster with a glint in his eye, or as a compassionate innocent who didn't believe in Houdini's "magic", but wanted to protect him against public humiliation. (Both are Irish archetypes.) The moral of the story seems to be that we only see what we expect to see. Our limited beliefs narrow our view as surely as the blinkers on the horses that could still be seen pulling coal and milk floats in 1960s Dublin. Could Brenda find another way to look at her moral dilemma? Jung observed that inner conflicts are never resolved, but they can be transcended (Stevens, 1990). Release from the conflict often lies in a dream.

In the midst of her inner struggle, Brenda had a dream in which her partner John had persuaded her that she could fly a passenger jet home, really that anybody could do it. She went ahead and the flying happened out of her awareness, on automatic pilot as it were, since she didn't actually *do* anything. Everything went well until she became aware that they were close to their destination. She realised that she had no idea how to land the plane, but was certain that it would not land itself. She called John but he didn't appear to know how to land either. Meantime, the plane was flying lower and lower and eventually between buildings, but miraculously not hitting them. By this time, she was a helpless spectator waiting to see what would happen. To her amazement and numbed gratitude the plane seemed to know what it was doing and landed safely in a crowded airport. There were some slightly cross though brief questions from the authorities, but she wasn't arrested and everyone appeared to move on and leave the incident behind. We can see that everything in the dream went well until Brenda became *conscious*—and then she felt a lot of anxiety that turned out to be unnecessary in the end. She was not nearly as responsible as she thought she was, the plane had an intrinsic wisdom that did not depend on her: she could trust life to carry her.

I am reminded of Thomas Hardy's poem "Before Life and After". Beginning with:

> A time there was …
>
> …
>
> Before the birth of consciousness
> When all went well.

the final verse goes:

> But the disease of feeling germed,
> And primal rightness took the tinct of wrong;
> Ere nescience shall be reaffirmed
> How long, how long?

(Collected Poems, 2001)

(This was later set to music by Benjamin Britten with a passion that brings new energy, the song ending with a repeating, entreating crescendo: "how long, how long, how *long*?".) This is the curse of Hamlet, "sicklied o'er with the pale cast of thought". He has far too much introspective awareness ever to make a decision and act. During his trial for corrupting the youth of Athens by encouraging them to challenge accepted beliefs, Socrates maintained that the unexamined life was not worth living. But, as we learn from Hamlet, the over-examined life isn't worth living either.

The thinker and the "natural" man

The tension between the outer life and the inner, between the actor/ doer and the thinker/feeler is a common theme in literature from the late nineteenth and early twentieth centuries. The protagonist is usually the neurasthenic thinker/feeler who is shown envying the ease and grace of "natural" man or beast. Thus Kafka contrasts the hunger artist who starves himself to death because he couldn't find the right nourishment with the panther who has no trouble getting the food he likes. The panther bursts with vitality: "the joy of life streamed with such ardent passion from his throat that for the onlookers it was not easy to stand the shock of it" (Kafka, 1978, p. 174). Likewise, in *Metamorphosis*, Kafka opposes the thoughtful, conscientious Gregor to his young blooming sister. Thomas Mann follows a similar theme when he portrays the sensitive agonies of Tonio Kröger alongside his unthinking friend, the good-looking, athletic Hans Hansen. In *Buddenbrooks*, Mann describes a family of practical businessmen who as the generations pass give way to more refined, cultured, self-tormenting—more *conscious*—types. Proust's Marcel is another example of a man who has travelled too far from his animal roots.

Interestingly, I can't think of any female parallels (perhaps Dorothea in *Middlemarch*?), whether as heroines or authors: however educated and cultivated, women don't seem to abandon the body and the instincts to the same extent as men. The tendency for thinking men to disembody is probably connected with the lack of intimate fathering which is necessary for boys once they become conscious of being different from mother. Nonetheless, there was clearly a peak of tormented self-doubt in young male intellectuals at the turn of the century, possibly linked to the luxury of affluence and the burden of the freedom to which this gave rise. Once a multigenerational family and class are secure in their material needs, leisure becomes available, and intellectual, aesthetic, and spiritual demands come to the surface. The ascent of the middle classes during the nineteenth century paved the way for a new crisis of male identity. The characters of Kafka, Mann, and Proust are shamed by their lack of confidence and vitality and undermined by their endless self-questioning. More than 400 years earlier, Hamlet emerges out of an entirely different historical imperative and yet appears to suffer a similar crisis of manhood. There is a difference in focus, however. Unlike the era of Freud, there isn't the same explicit contrast with unconscious man.

For Hamlet, the struggle is between doing and thinking/feeling, the doing being blocked by excessive thinking. The nineteenth-/twentieth-century characters are not required to take action; they have not been plunged into moral crisis. Hamlet arises out of the Reformation, where projections are beginning to be withdrawn and the conscience is becoming internalised; this is both cause and effect of greater self-awareness and greater paralysis of action.

Charles Taylor, who has written extensively about the historical phases of selfhood, describes the present era as "the Age of Authenticity". The expressive individualism which was the preserve of intellectual and artistic elites from the Romantic period of the late eighteenth century until about the 1960s has now spread to the masses. The 1960s and 1970s were a time of idealism, utopian vision, and revolt against the establishment. However, Taylor points out that these early utopian goals of self-expression, sensual release, equality, and social bonding can only be "united with difficulty, and for a time, in small communities at best" (2007, p. 477). In most cases, some elements must be sacrificed for others. This has led to the phenomenon of the "bourgeois bohemians" amongst the contemporary US upper class, where social equality and community have been eroded in support of self-cultivation. This fusion between capitalism and self-realisation is, I believe, giving rise more generally to the chameleon (or corporate) self: the flexible, unproblematically inauthentic self that is prepared to become anything that is required of it in this time of globalised capitalism (Dowds, 2008). Brenda, in her struggles with the company was trying to hang on to at least some 1970s ideals in the face of senior management's increasingly ruthless pursuit of profit.

The growth of individualism, the erosion of community, and new anti-union work practices (banning of unions, outsourcing of work, the growth in the part-time workforce) create considerable problems for political action. United action on the part of dissatisfied labour has fragmented: we have entered the era of the whistle-blower and individual cases taken to the labour courts. Darwinian social relations have rendered the term "injustice" quaint and outmoded. Nevertheless, when it hits us personally, we still feel angry: the cry "that's not fair" is one of the earliest expressions of social emotions in children. As discussed in the last chapter, we know in our bodies what's not fair, even though accusations of "injustice" or "disrespect" would be greeted with derision in most workplaces today, where human needs take second (or third or fourth) place to the instrumental concerns of profit, efficiency, and competitiveness. That this is also the case in many psychotherapy organisations is a shocking indictment of therapy's sell-out to business practices and values.

In the end, for Brenda, it came down to energy management, and escaping what Guignon (2004, p. 159) called betrayal—of self and others—by inauthenticity. So she had to take some action, however incompetently, just to complete the energy cycle. Her body over-whelmed her Hamletian introspective and insoluble worrying. She went over the heads of her immediate superiors and complained to the parent company in California. She consulted a solicitor who specialised in industrial relations and spoke to management in other companies.

Love and power in activism

The evolution of moral development throughout the lifespan has been described—and to some extent prescribed—by the developmental psy-chologist Lawrence Kohlberg (Sugarman, 2001; Finlayson, 2005). Using a combination of philosophical argument and empirical evidence from male responses to hypothetical moral dilemmas, he generated a scheme of moral development based on an ethic of justice or rights. The more primitive reflex stages of moral development are motivated by avoid-ance of punishment, shame, or guilt, whereas the more advanced stages are associated with more long-term ego-ideals. We now know that these are mediated by quite distinct parts of the brain: the amygdala (threat avoidance) and the prefrontal cortex (thinking and planning) respec-tively (McGonigal, 2013). The most advanced levels equate with the utilitarian view of the "greatest happiness for the greatest number" (stage five), superseded by the Kantian view that principle is more important than common good (stage six). Carol Gilligan has challenged the universality of Kohlberg's thesis (Gilligan, 1993; Sugarman, 2001). In researching people's responses to actual rather than hypothetical moral dilemmas, she found that relationships, responsibilities, and care determined moral choices for most women and some men. She found that women generally see the world in terms of connectedness, whereas men are more likely to view it in terms of autonomy. Therefore, for men, justice and equality tend to be key components of morality, whereas for women relationships and the ethic of care predominate. Here again, we meet the motivations of power and love, this time dressed in the regalia of morality. Crucially, Gilligan regards maturity as a *combination* of the male and female developmental routes which balances separation with attachment, justice with care. Gilligan's highest level of feminine morality—care for integrity—balances care for others with self-care, on the grounds that denying one's own needs ultimately harms others—as most therapists are forced to learn sooner or later. (See Chapter Nine for George Eliot's Dorothea as an example of this shift.) The most mature and effective form of activism must take account of the masculine principle of justice *and* the feminine principle of care for self and others. I have argued elsewhere (Dowds, 2011) that societies need both justice and care, and that the Irish score well on the personal ethic of care. However, we rate badly on the principle of justice, as is so strikingly obvious with the poor currently paying for the crimes of the rich following on from the bail-out of the banks and property developers. Brenda, with her avoidant attachment, has a somewhat masculine approach to morality. She is more concerned with justice than care, and was outraged at the cavalier treatment that was meted out to the staff in her old workplace.

Morality and consciousness co-evolved, but too much thinking can also have the outcome of avoiding moral responsibility. In the end, Hamlet's hesitation resulted in his death and that of all those close to him. What does our current world need—more thought or more action? The answer is of course to become skilful at both and allow them to interweave with each other. We need both Tonio and Hans, and the more they are integrated in all of us, the better. If we equate action with power, and thought/feeling with love, then we are back to the old duality.

Charles Johnston (1991, p. 76) engages with the subject of "Us and Them", me and my enemy. He lays bare the fallacies of both separation (freedom lies in individualism, competition, and a free market) and unity (we are all one; the way to peace is simply to love): in other words, neither power alone nor love alone will solve our global problems of war and poverty. But, maintaining that the way to peace is to find the middle ground is another fallacy, this time of compromise. The only solution is the Jungian concept of bridging: to integrate opposites and to find identity in both what we hold in common and what separates us. If we can identify the common fear that lies behind the desire to dominate and the need for autonomy (see below), opponents may be able to start talking. But this requires willingness to sit at the same table. Sometimes, the two sides trust each other so little, they must first have talks about talks. At other times, there is such a power discrepancy that the more powerful feel they have nothing to gain from talks; they simply want to continue to oppress. This is the situation of the populations of Tibet and Burma vis à vis their governments. The extreme suffering of the people has driven Buddhist monks out of their traditional non-political stance into extraordinarily courageous acts of resistance. Brenda, though well aware of the vast difference in the scale of suffering and the numbers affected, can nevertheless identify with the powerlessness of those who struggle against dictatorships. She seeks to learn how non-violent resistance movements operate without losing their integrity—and indeed whether retaining integrity is tantamount to tying your hands and legs together and losing the battle.

What happens when the forces for good meet the forces of evil? Even the way I have phrased this shows how the two sides can become split and polarised. And what happens in the minds of the oppressors? Brenda imagines them either laughing with contempt or snarling with irritation at these high-minded saints who deny their shadows in their pursuit of holiness. Do the forces of good sometimes deepen the split that makes the oppressor dig in his heels? The dictatorship remains wholly identified with power and the religious resistance solely identified with love. Placing herself in the skin of a soldier living at a coarser level of reality, surviving in a psychologically and physically brutalising environment, Brenda imagines herself irritated by the saintliness of pacifist Buddhist monks. She imagines the soldier projecting weakness and ineptitude onto the unarmed resistance, resenting being implicitly shamed by contrast with them. They might become even more brutal to block any melting towards empathy or compassion. In an extraordinary and disturbing short story, *The Renegade*, Camus does more than look into the face of evil: he inhabits it through the character of the missionary who seeks in his arrogance to convert the inhabitants of a desert citadel to Christianity. The priest is captured and tortured and comes to identify with his tormentors and worship the evil Fetish god. In a state of masochistic exaltation, he rages about another missionary sent to the town:

> The fellow who was to come would not have his tongue cut out,
> he would show off his insolent goodness without paying for it ...

The reign of evil would be postponed, there would be doubt again, again time would be wasted dreaming of the impossible good ...

(Camus, 1962, p. 45)

He lies in wait on the trail, hidden behind a pile of rocks, and murders the new priest:

I laugh, I laugh, the fellow is writhing in his detested habit ... How pleasant is the sound of a rifle butt on the face of goodness ...

(ibid., pp. 46–47)

Brenda feels a paralysing degree of admiration for those who participate in unarmed resistance. They appear to her to occupy a higher plane, with greater awareness, discipline, refinement, and, most of all, courage than she could ever muster. However, she wonders tentatively whether their advanced level of evolution behoves them to incorporate their power shadow. To add a new twist to an old phrase: "sagesse oblige". It is up to those with greater awareness to incorporate the opposite pole into their consciousness. There would then be less of a split between the two sides. It is more difficult to bridge the divide by bringing some love motivation into the forces of the totalitarian regime, since they are in a state of greater blindness than the monks. Joanna Macy's deep ecology philosophy arises out of the central doctrine of the Buddha, that of dependent co-arising, the dynamic interdependence of all phenomena (Macy & Brown, 1998). Presumably this also applies to the interdependence of oppressor and victim. However, as we will see later, a Buddhist understanding of power transcends the simple power/love duality that constitutes Brenda's current limited worldview.

She concedes that activist Buddhist monks may feel that they are achieving something that may be of much longer-term significance than overthrowing dictatorships: they are keeping alive alternative values of non-violence, courage, and compassion for their opponents. Joanna Macy recounts the story of Choegyal Rinpoche speaking of another atrocity committed by Chinese soldiers against Tibetan monks: he murmured with tears in his eyes, "Poor Chinese, they make such bad karma for themselves". In a teaching on Macy's website, *Touching the Earth for our Adversaries*, the practitioner learns to recognise and be thankful for what their opponents bring to them, e.g., showing me what I value, or giving me the opportunity to hone my strength or to release attachment to my belief that my understanding is the only one (www.joannamacy. net).

In order to bridge the polarity between oppressors—those who are addicted to power over others—and the oppressed—those who struggle for freedom and autonomy—we must find common ground between them. This is what Barack Obama achieved in his 2008 speech in Philadelphia. He spoke about the anxieties about their futures that were common to blacks and whites in the USA: "we may have different stories, but we hold common hopes". He saw that most white people did not see themselves as privileged oppressors: "They are anxious about their futures and see their dreams slipping away". He knew that "we cannot solve the problems of our time unless we solve them together—unless we perfect our union" (www.huffingtonpost.com). Of course, on the scale of a nation, it is extremely difficult to bridge polarities, but at the level of an individual or a small institution, it becomes more possible. To grasp how we can do this, we must examine the genesis of power and its balance with love in our early development.

The psychogenesis of love and power motivations in childhood

McAdams (1997), drawing on similar themes in the thinking of Freud, Levinson, and Bakan, asserts that the needs for power and love are the two central psychological motivations in human lives. Power equates with separation from others and the independent agency that separation confers; love equates with communion with others, empathy, and dependence, or in a more mature form, interdependence. This polarity originates in the early relationship between mother and child, in which the child is in symbiotic fusion with mother who meets all the infant's needs. This is the first love relationship, characterised by selfless giving on the part of the mother and (primary) narcissistic receiving on the part of the infant. But then, this blissful unity consciousness is broken, the primal split or basic fault (to use Balint's term) occurs, the baby is disillusioned out of its omnipotence (Winnicott, 1990; 1991) and begins to realise that mother is a separate psyche with thoughts, feelings, motivation, and agenda all of her own that do not always match those of the child. The ground is set for psychological separation—or psychological birth as Margaret Mahler called it (See Rayner, Joyce, Rose, Twman, & Clulow, 2005; Lopez, 1997, for summaries). The theory of mind that the child now develops is accompanied by an increasing division between self and other, or subject and object, that in an extreme form can lead to schizoid alienation in adolescence and adulthood.

The child may, like Proust's Marcel, continue to be besieged with longing to recover that primal unity with mother and the participative consciousness with his environment; and indeed Proust, in both his life and work, lived entirely for love and without engagement with power. More usually, however, some degree of separation is accepted and the child may discover significant benefits from it. Avoidantlyattached children whose mothers failed to meet their needs very well may appear to thrive on independence and not request or accept help from others. Older children in families whose mother's attention has moved on to younger siblings may be required to become more independent, and may also relish punishing or dominating the younger siblings in various ways. For these children, the competition for resources starts young and they are primed for power battles throughout their lives. Children at the receiving end of bullying may despise power, refuse to exercise it themselves, but also be unable to receive love, though they may be able to give love to those younger or weaker than themselves. Children with loving boundaried mothers who encourage the child's independence at an appropriate time and pace will have high levels of agency (power) and communion (love). Ultimately we all need both separation from (agency) and communion with others, but we each have a unique balance between the two, depending on the psychodynamics of our early years.

But power comes in two forms: power within (ego strength), and power over, which derives from an insecure ego. Power from within originates in a clean separation in a relationship of secure attachment whereby the developing individual becomes capable of mature interdependence. The drive towards power over others derives from incomplete separation, where the child retains some of the desire for omnipotence, which was not fully disappointed by mother at the appropriate developmental stage. Here the child is allowed to continue to treat mother like a servant, and goes on to perceive others in the same light. Such an individual is in a state of secondary narcissism, where the point of other people is to do his bidding. The more he was allowed to bully mother into obeying him—or the more he saw father bullying mother—the more he will be driven to exert power over others. There is a kind of greed in power—in trying to get more from the world than you are entitled to—and it is not surprising that oldest children, especially oldest sons (males are on average genetically more aggressive than females (Plomin, DeFries, McClearn, & McGuffin, 2008)), are more likely to rise to positions of power in the world (Conley, 2004). Such a person differs from the Marcels of the world in that mother was probably less than satisfactory at providing for his needs. Accordingly, he does not want to regress back to a state of dependence (like Marcel). But nor is he able to move forward to a stage where he lets mother go and becomes genuinely independent. He cannot leave the table for two reasons: because his appetite has not been satisfied, and because he wants to hang round to punish mother for failing to feed him properly. Instead, he retains the intermediate place of using (m)other to do his bidding.

I propose that the quality of *attunement*, which gives rise to varying degrees of the illusion of omnipotence and security of attachment, determines the degree of love, whereas the extent and particular dynamic of *separation* determines power. What are the power-hungry after? I think it is actually a state of love and union with mother. The exercise of power over others is only a substitute for the love not received, and it is therefore addictive. The power hunger can never be appeased because it is not the real need. On the other hand, the genuinely powerful (those with inner power) do not need to exercise power over others, though they may be potent and charismatic leaders who are capable of wielding power but are not addicted to it.

Brenda's position in relation to power and love is very much that of the individual who doesn't trust genuine love—that is, love directed at her true and blemished self—to be delivered or to last, though she is aware of a drive towards loving others, particularly those who are in touch with their playful inner child. She loathes anybody trying to exert power over her, but has no desire to control anybody else except in repelling others' attempts to exploit, control, or abuse her. This sounds pretty much as expected for a middle child with an emotionally abusive father and in a state of avoidant attachment with her mother.

The love side of the equation is more complex than at first sight. The needs to give and receive love are separate, and therapy has paid a lot more attention to the receiving polarity than the giving. In recent years, however, it has been argued that we have a greater need to *give* than to receive love (Brazier, 2009). Brenda didn't trust her mother to deliver the goods, but she still had a need to love and protect her, and as an adult she is most able to love the child-like. When it comes to receiving love, what feels like love is not just a general valuing and care; these must be directed at who she actually is. This requires that the giver is able and willing to see who she is and to engage dynamically with her as she changes or hesitatingly reveals more of herself. It requires the giver, not necessarily to love every part of her, but not to judge even the disliked bits, to accept them as inevitable parts of the package. And it requires responsibility, the "for richer, for-poorer, in-sickness and in health" commitment to stay with the relational process: a view of love not as an emotion, but as a decision to commit.

But receiving love is not easy for Brenda; she is mistrustful and defended. After all, how could she operate in this frightening world with a softened heart? The threat of humiliation is around every corner. Humiliation engenders a determination to enclose her heart in steel casing so this won't happen to her again. Greater humiliation pushes her over the edge into revenge against selected individuals (e.g., her boss), or in extreme cases, revenge at the human race. It is only the pragmatic need for assistance that causes the avenger to split the world into those he will punish and those who will be cultivated as allies. Of course, the mere pulse of a mood can convert the ally into an enemy, as the colleagues of Stalin, Hitler, and all dictators know to their cost. What about the ordinary soldiers carrying out the orders of these dictators? They are of course a great mix of the conscripted, the impoverished, the volunteers, the mentally well, and the mentally sick; but whether by dint of fear or of fervour, the humiliation-generated hatred of the leaders is passed down through the ranks. Male hierarchies, whether in armies, corporations, football leagues, or play groups, are based on shame: the very concept of hierarchy is shaming, but it is fear of shame that keeps the hierarchy in place; there is no escape. This shamed humiliation is what the non-violent activist is dealing with. They may recognise that the oppressor is more psychologically wounded and vulnerable than they themselves are. But the question is, what is the most effective response? How do you get through to the brutalised?

In a one-to-one engagement, therapy clients who have been humiliated may be very angry or have terrible self-esteem. Whether they internalise their feelings into depression and anxiety or externalise into antisocial behaviour and addictions is highly gender dependent, men having a much higher probability of externalising (Plomin, DeFries, McClearn, & McGuffin, 2008, p. 222). Most men and some women who have been humiliated are touchy and reactive, prone to explosions and annihilating rages, and very likely to walk out of psychotherapy. They are very difficult to work with because their only way of simulating self-esteem is to deny their vulnerability and project out their hurt in rage, often at another who mirrors their inner state. They do not take kindly to any kind of compassion or sympathy, which is experienced as patronising and shaming. They will feel safe from such a heart-based "attack" if the therapist joins them in angry criticism and contempt at all they perceive as wrong with the world. In this way, some kind of shaky alliance may be formed. Of course the therapist may feel very uncomfortable at attacking some of the targets, but could form a relationship out of a more socially sanctioned and benign form of splitting, e.g., supporting a common football team against its rivals. Dave Mearns (Mearns & Cooper, 2005) is a master at laying the foundations for therapy with this kind of male-male camaraderie. It is difficult for a woman to work with such a client, because he will fear being unmanned by the softening effect of a woman. So beware the humiliated male: he wreaks havoc in the world and is very difficult to heal, even at an individual level. At the level of a marauding, colonising army, the challenge is well-nigh insurmountable. In one boss in senior management who controlled and abused the workforce like a totalitarian tyrant, Brenda recognised a man who was even more shamed than she herself was. This realisation took many months, but brought with it compassion and forgiveness, and removed from her the burden of plotting revenge.

A way out of the impasse: power-with

Using systems theory, Macy and Brown (1998) distinguish between two forms of external power: power-over and power-with. They argue that the belief that power-over generates invulnerability and domination is false and dysfunctional: it stems from the view that the world is made up of isolated entities. However, in reality, it is through increasing connection, interaction, feedback, and flexibility that complex, resilient, self-organising living systems are generated. True power lies in connection—power-with. This is the power of the mammal contrasted with the dinosaur, or the responsive liberal democracy compared with the totalitarian regime. Ultimately the rigid, armoured system becomes extinct because it cannot respond or adapt. This may be what happened as "Communist elites in Eastern Europe awoke to the bankruptcy of the Communist model" (Ignatieff, 2012). The concept of power-with transcends psychotherapy's dichotomy between power and love. It recognises the differentiation on which therapy's view of power rests, while simultaneously taking account of the connectedness of love. We are neither isolated from, nor fused with the other: rather we are in an ongoing process of dynamic interconnection. Power-with is the political equivalent of the psychological concept of intersubjectivity (see Chapter Four).

Political change

Despite the immense difficulties facing any movement that challenges an unjust regime, societies do change, and dictators are toppled. How does this happen? Frequently, one tyrant displaces or replaces another and nothing substantive changes. Sometimes the dictator gets old and, after a lifetime of fearing power in the hands of another, finds that there is no successor strong enough to replace him. On these occasions, there may be an opportunity for a grass-roots movement to move in and generate a new democracy; the tyrannies seem to die through lack of oxygen from without, and energy from within. There is no shortage of examples of this process of collapse of totalitarian regimes from the Soviet Union and Eastern European states to the current regime collapses in Islamic countries in North Africa and the Middle East. The same process seems to apply to multinational corporations controlled by a single ruthless individual, as witnessed in the decay of the Murdoch empire as its octogenarian leader declines. Many protestors and particularly would-be protestors ask themselves whether protest and resistance speeds up the rate at which change occurs. Do imposed regimes wear out because the entire population is pulling against them, in whatever ways are safely open to them? This may simply take the form of a kind of nationwide depression or work-to-rule, where private initiative is stifled through bureaucratic frustration and communal initiative is stymied though mutual distrust. As the years pass and the dictator ages, I could imagine him finding the control of a compliant and silenced populace increasingly pointless. Rebel groups might be just the lifeline the dictator needs to energise him into counter-action and convince him there is some point to remaining in command. So where does this leave activism? Does it actually keep the dictator in his palace? Is its main point to keep self-respect alive in the hearts of the activists?

In the case of organisations smaller than the nation state, where there are external regulatory bodies which can step in, the situation is entirely different. Here, protest within the organisation may be frustrated, but whistle-blowing to professional, governmental, or legal bodies may effect some changes. However, the situation within the institution may have arisen in the first place and remained unchallenged because it reflects a culture that is widespread in the rest of society, albeit in a less extreme form. Thus it is wise to be modest about the extent of change that is possible or likely.

The deadening of our responses to catastrophe is, for Macy and Brown (1998), the greatest danger we face. They examine the psychological sources of this apathy in Western democracies, where there is no outside authority silencing us, and suggest a list of things we fear and avoid such as pain, despair, morbidity, and guilt. Nevertheless, they are positive about the many initiatives underway to defend the world's ecology, to create structural alternatives, and to alter perceptions and values. There is some evidence (e.g., the Occupy movement) that the public discourse about the economy is changing, challenging previous exclusive focus on deficit reduction with talk of inequality, and the result of our recent presidential election indicates that we Irish may have learned something about integrity. Brenda feels that her protest was more beneficial for her (she felt empowered—heard and respected by colleagues) than for the company. She managed to break out of her old frustrating self-inhibition and release her libido. She trod a wobbly path between care for her superiors, care for her own needs for employment and balancing her inner truths while bringing issues of justice and rights onto the agenda. However, she knew that a great deal more energy would have been required for any substantive change to take place. Having no interest in leadership, she didn't draw anybody else into the long-term struggle and monitoring that would have been necessary. Since she was sick of working in IT anyway, her ultimate response to the new working culture was to change careers. This is not a story about a heroine who turned round an abusive workplace. It is just the story of someone who spoke out a few times, did some whistle-blowing but was not met with any real interest or action. In the end, Brenda got tired and she compromised. She gave up her job and left IT. The company didn't improve much, but *she* felt more empowered.

She was caught in the net between guilt and frustration: guilt about giving up so soon and frustration at the ineffectiveness of her actions.

When she considered more action, she felt washed over by exhaustion and despair. She holds an absolute belief in the impossibility of changing the other. If this is true at an individual level, how much more is it true at an institutional level? But she wrestled with her conscience as she thought about the selfishness and comfort of her apathy. She compared herself very unfavourably to her heroes and heroines: the Dalai Lama, Aung San Suu Kyi, Nelson Mandela, Mary Robinson, and Barack Obama. But she self-servingly wondered how much any of them have actually achieved and feared probably not that much. After all, Tibet is still occupied; Burma is still in the hands of a dictatorship. Totalitarian regimes do end, it is true, but can that be attributed to the actions of resistance movements or because the regime crumbles from within? As we have seen, Macy and Brown view power in terms of systems theory: "To the social system, power-over is dysfunctional because it inhibits diversity and feedback; by obstructing self-organizing processes, it fosters entropy—systemic disintegration" (1998, p. 53). Thus authoritarian systems *must* ultimately fail because of their structural rigidity and isolation. Perhaps the role of charismatic leaders such as those Brenda admires is not to make changes directly, but rather to kindle an alternate set of values through which hope and inspiration can flower and be kept alive.

It is clear that political movements should not try to replace one kind of power-over with another, however morally superior it may be initially. First, the movement will lose its moral validity through the imposition of one will over another. Second, its rigidity will carry with it a built-in tendency towards self-destruction. How then do Macy and Brown view the role of the activist? Clearly not in pitting one will against another. While their systems model does contain the implication that authoritarian regimes carry the seeds of their own destruction, they do not believe (as Brenda had hoped!) that we should just throw our hands up in the air and do nothing. Systems depend on communication and feedback for their responsiveness and adaptability.

> It is part of our systemic responsibility to give feedback to our body politic, and unblock that feedback that has been suppressed ... This is not a struggle to "seize" power so much as to release it for efficient self-governance. Thus we act, not only for ourselves and our own group or party, but also on behalf of all the other "neurons in the net". (Macy & Brown, 1998, p. 54)

In searching for the sources of human sympathy, Ward (2013) comes from a Buddhist perspective and suggests that our common human vulnerability to suffering could motivate such cosmopolitan solidarity. For Brenda, the vision of herself as one amongst many comes as a surprising relief. She does not have to carry the entire responsibility herself "because nobody else will lift a finger". This means she has an argument for her old tormenting and punitive conscience which keeps telling her she must do what she has no inclination for. She does not have to frustrate her natural instincts and force herself to become someone she is not. Rather, she can use whatever gifts she has and make common cause with others using theirs.

Summary

When working in IT, Brenda faced a dilemma about whether to speak out about abusive practices in her workplace. Her conscience bade her speak, but activism felt false to other aspects of herself: her need to protect herself against the frustration and despair she feels at being ineffective and not being heard, her dislike of the emptiness of power struggles, and her introvert's exhaustion through communal activity. Both the individual cost as well as the effectiveness of activism must be evaluated. The tension between the outer and inner, the actor/doer and the thinker/feeler was resolved for Brenda when she followed the demands of her energy: she started the process of blowing the whistle, but later resigned from the job.

The psychogenesis of the love and power motivations helps us to understand the conflict between them. Activists can be corrupted by power; but, equally, remaining innocent of power deepens the love-power split between activist and oppressor, as shown in Camus' story *The Renegade*. Both of these problems rely on the dualistic assumption that there are two opposing sides. A solution to this impasse is found in Joanna Macy's Buddhist concept of "power-with". Using systems theory, she deconstructs the belief that power over others generates invulnerability; true strength comes from systems that are interactive, flexible, and responsive to change. Each of us plays our part by pooling our diverse gifts for the universal good. For Brenda, this means not forcing herself to become who she is not, but rather contributing her strengths to the common cause.

PART IV

BEYOND FRUSTRATION: TOWARDS INTEGRATION AND WELL-BEING

CHAPTER EIGHT

Reflecting and creating the self: the uses of narrative

Narrative and the self

Stories are important to Brenda. Yet when she looks back at her life, she can find neither narrative themes nor emotionally-suffused and detailed memories, what Siegel (2012, p. 125) calls "mental time travel". Her perception of her life story is "just one damned thing after another" in a disconnected jumble. Her memory is poor and undifferentiated: when she talks to former classmates at school reunions, their anecdotes awaken no buried memories, just an empty despair that she wasn't really there. Her attempt to "begin to live" by giving up her work in IT has led to further frustration: she gave up a good salary, but the reward, the goal of "having a life", has so far evaded her. She recently joined a life-writing class to see if she can at least put some order and shape on her life, and pin down the occasional sensory and emotional memories that hover like a mist when she is surprised by the pregnant scents of musty rooms, sacks of flour, the cut grass or sweet pea of summer, the dead leaves and open fires of autumn. As a compensation for her own inner emptiness, Brenda has read fiction voraciously all her life, starting with Beatrix Potter, Enid Blyton, Susan Coolidge and L. M. Montgomery in childhood. Then, in her teens and twenties, she moved on to the—mainly English, French, and Russian—nineteenth- and early twentieth-century classics, along with a period of intense Irish romanticism. Membership of a series of book clubs followed, and she has now turned her erstwhile refuge into a new career teaching contemporary literature. She was guiltily aware that her pre-career reading was escapist and addictive, and so often restricted it to a reward for real-life engagement with others. Notwithstanding this, the stories also taught her how to live and mirrored and reinforced her nascent identity. In this chapter, we will see how stories both express and create self and examine how different literary modes help us to understand the nature of the self.

Jung once said that Goethe did not create *Faust*; rather, *Faust* created Goethe. We create identity through the story—whether spoken or unspoken—we tell about ourselves and our world. The stories we tell our friends are substantially affected by the version of reality that pertained in our families as well as by what our particular social subculture is capable of understanding and willing to hear. Alternatively, we can tell our stories in therapy and question and reframe some of the beliefs that no longer work for us because parts of us are in conflict with each other. Finally, when novelists write fiction they are, at a greater or lesser distance, telling the reader something about themselves. Emma Donoghue, comparing herself to her fellow Irish writer Maeve Brennan said: "I'm in the Anthony Trollope school. You go to your desk every day, and write your books, and you enjoy it, and then you have your dinner. With the Maeve Brennan style of writer you feel the stories are being dredged up out of her subconscious, that wounds are being left behind" (Wallace, 2012). Some writers such as Kafka, Anita Brookner, or Iris Murdoch tackle the same themes again and again and appear quite directly to be attempting to resolve personal issues. Others, like Trollope and Donoghue are storytellers who are more distant from their material.

In the West, according to Berman (1990), only young children create with unrestrained immersion, without inner conflict or performance anxiety. For the classic neurotic artist, the process of creation is stressful and obsessive because the unconscious is erupting through repressive defences: the real object being created is nothing less than the self. This process is powerful, focused, and draining; it depends on high levels of tension and instability, as manifested in the paintings of Van Gogh or the poetry of Sylvia Plath. Rilke famously feared that if his devils were to be tampered with by psychoanalysis, his angels would be placed at risk (Eigen, 1986, p. 20): therapy would have deconstructed the neurosis on which his creativity rested. Likewise, spiritual fulfilment can damage the creative impulse. Thanks to her quest for silence and solitude, Sara Maitland (2008) has found her spiritual practice greatly enhanced, but her ability or desire to write fiction has been extinguished.

There is no such thing as a self: there is only a self-in-the-world. The early environment of the family shapes the self; all its subsequent environments will support and consolidate or pressure and transform, or even deform and disintegrate this self. This forming and transforming process is described, supremely, by the novel—most explicitly in the genre of the Bildungsroman or novel of formation, such as *David Copperfield* or *Great Expectations*. The hero's career is seen in developmental terms, not just as the collection of contingent picaresque adventures characteristic of the eighteenth-century novel, but as a necessary learning process that, in the hands of a nineteenth-century realist novelist such as Dickens, yields a more or less coherent lesson about life.

What do we mean by this self that is created, either through the unproblematic storytelling of young children or the later more conflicted, contradictory, and complex narrative of adults? Many therapy orientations distinguish between an authentic or true self and the adaptive or false self that has compromised to fit in with parental demands and social mores (see Rowan, 1998, p. 74 for a summary). Similarly there is a variation in the scale or scope of the self—egoic or trans-egoic. Jung and his followers focused on the trans-egoic: the Self (capital S to distinguish it from the egoic self—see below) which may be defined as "the teleological purposiveness of the organism" (Hollis, 1993, p. 27). The ego—which carries the personality—arises out of the Self during early development and has the task of mediating between the Self and the world (Stevens, 1990). Equally, the ego is an expression of the Self and perceives meaning and assesses value (ibid., p. 30). Hollis defines different axes or orientations throughout the lifespan: parent-child axis in childhood, during which the ego is formed; ego-world from puberty to midlife; ego-Self in second adulthood; and Self-God in old age. Thus the demands of the ego are dominant in the "outer arc" of the first half of life, while the Self holds sway during the "inner arc" after midlife. Hence throughout life, whether through the smaller ego or the larger Self, our goal is individuation. This is partly a matter of expressing a pre-existing self and partly a case of building a self from innate seeds of potential: in creating a narrative of our lives, we express, build, and shape who we are. There is an implication in Jungian thinking that the Self is the destination of development, the end-result of individuation. In this chapter, I will write about the less ambitious egoic self with a small "s", that is the vehicle of development as much as its only partially complete end-product. It is more like Alan Sroufe's definition of self as "an internally organised cluster of attitudes, expectations, meanings and feelings" (Siegel, 2012, p. 210). Inevitably, the evolution of self is neither complete nor a linear process. In therapy, as in art, we unmake in order to build. Simone Weil said you must "decreate" yourself in order to create the work—just as God did in creating the world (Berman, 1990, p. 337): a process that is an exact parallel of the unmaking of self required to find union with God.

Symbolism and the self

For Lacan "we state our problems on the symbolic level before proceeding to solve them" (Berman, 1990, p. 323). Reflecting on the origins of language, the neurobiologist Terrence Deacon (1997) argues that consciousness of self can only be represented via the virtual reference created by symbols. Mankind's earliest communication must have been mediated by non-verbal symbols (we see the same process in the development of children), and even after language evolved, our earliest lasting communication that did not depend on our presence was not writing, but painting and sculpting. Certainly, early cave paintings constitute "the first concrete evidence of the storage of ... symbolic information outside of a human brain" (ibid., p. 374). The pre-modern mind attributed creativity not to the self but to God. In Herzog's film, *The Cave of Forgotten Dreams* about the 30,000-year-old drawings in the Chauvet cave in France, one of the scientists refers to an aborigine who was touching up a cave painting in Australia in the 1970s. The artist denied any agency of his own, but proclaimed it was spirit which was at work: the will of the human creator had not yet barred the way for the hand of God. Conversely, modern man takes personal credit for his creations. Indeed, Deacon maintains that "Its virtual nature notwithstanding, it is the symbolic realm of consciousness that we most identify with and from which our sense of agency and self-control originate" (Deacon, 1997, p. 452). In the pre-modern mind, spirit used man to express itself; in the modern mind, the individual person expresses *himself*, sometimes with a little inspiration from the muse.

Symbol-making, including the creation of stories, requires the ability to conceptualise what is not there: to make images in the mind. This facilitates thinking outside the immediate location and time, so we can imagine other places, and the past and future as well as the present. We can begin to imagine the hypothetical as well as perceiving the actual. These processes clearly delivered great advantage in terms of planning for safety, hunting, and gathering of food and acquiring mates, as William Golding shows in his novel *The Inheritors*. Here he portrays the difficulty of imagining for the primitive brain, as he shows Neanderthals struggling to form pictures so that they could recall and talk about memories, envisage consequences, and communicate future possibilities. Ultimately, the Neanderthal group is wiped out by *Homo sapiens*, with his quicker, more imaginative, and flexible thinking. Symbol-making and the capacity to live outside the present moment inevitably allow us to move beyond the actual and the material into the realm of the imaginary. Thus is born creativity in storytelling—whether in pictures, words, dance, or music. Creativity and storytelling are inextricably linked—in the great literature and art of our culture, but also in how we recount our life stories, in the form, the content, and the way our stories change. Narrative is never only an ordering of snapshot memories into a video. Facts are selected, changed, and coloured with value, so that a symbolic myth is created.

Attachment and narrative

In keeping with her avoidant/dismissing attachment style, Brenda has difficulty with coherent narrative or coming up with any meaningful life story. She has generalised memories with few specific emotionally coloured details and, to avoid dwelling on the past, is highly future-focused. She compensates for the way she avoids experiencing the present moment or "remembering" her past with a fascination with old places and family history from before the time of her own birth. At the same time, she is saddened and frustrated by what she experiences as not having had a life. She gave up her alienating career in IT to "get a life", but inevitably this has not worked. She must face the fact that, to have a life, she must feel and experience.

Attachment theory has become bound up with narrative theory because of the research observation that narrative coherence (autobiographical competence) is associated with secure attachment. Mary

Main, who created a way of measuring attachment security in adults, found that emotional security correlated, not with a "happy childhood", but with "an internally coherent and consistent narrative" (Gerhardt, 2004, p. 53). The Adult Attachment Interview asks the subject both to search for memories and to engage in collaborative social discourse. The communication is assessed for (1) truth and the evidence for it; (2) succinctness, yet completeness; (3) relevance; (4) clarity and order.

Secure/autonomous adults have good recall of their childhoods and describe their experiences in a fluid and self-reflective manner (Siegel, 2012, p. 118), characterised by "congruity, unity and free-flowing connections" (quoted in Siegel, 2012, p. 352). On the other hand, the minds of insecure adults display "incongruity, fragmentation, and restricted flow of information" (ibid., p. 352) with an absence of emotional richness and depth (ibid., p. 121). The dismissing (avoidant) adult has poor specific recall and generalised, brief descriptions (ibid., p. 122); while the entangled (ambivalent) adult has unresolved (past emerging into the present) and incoherent stories (ibid., p. 130). In contrast with the meaningful descriptions of the secure individual, dismissing and entangled styles are respectively under- and over-saturated with meaning (Holmes, 2010, p. 49). A person may develop a different pattern with father, mother, and other attachment figures in childhood, so that several conflicting relational patterns become internalised. Therefore, developing a cohesive narrative depends on integrating these various experiences into a shape that has internal consistency (ibid., p. 100). The empathically attuned mother not only builds emotional security (secure attachment), but also generates within the child a capacity for reflection and the organisation of experience into coherent narrative. This depends on a dynamic interaction between the two hemispheres of the brain (see McGilchrist, 2009; Siegel, 2012, pp. 125, 371): the right side provides rich, emotionally-suffused, context-dependent images, while the left takes care of logical interpretation and verbal representation. Wilkinson (2010, p. 136) refers to clients with early relational trauma for whom words were distanced from meaning and who accessed their experiences through art, music, dance, or other non-verbal kinds of symbolisation. Since language is primarily a product of the conscious left brain and art a product of the unconscious and holistic right brain, it is likely that, for all of us, images are closer to our raw experience. By contrast, talking or writing are secondary forms of representation that rely, as described above, on both left and right hemispheres. Language is alienated if coming from an isolated left hemisphere and only represents our experience if there is good communication between the two hemispheres (McGilchrist, 2009). Visual imagery is characteristic of primary process, whereas language aids secondary process such as the development of reality orientation (Rayner, Joyce, Rose, Twyman, & Clulow, 2005, p. 82).

Jeremy Holmes views the work of a therapist as the pulling together of a "tentative and disjointed" story into "a more coherent and satisfying narrative" (1993, p. 158). More than that, he (ibid., p. 151) and Wilkinson (2006, p. 148) believe that narrative is not merely a consequence of security but, on the contrary, the royal road to secure attachment through the process of psychotherapy. On the other hand, Gerhardt (2004, p. 54) questions whether the story itself *creates* security, rather than being a *consequence* of a responsive relationship. Just because narrative style *correlates* with attachment status doesn't mean that you can reverse-engineer from cohesive narrative to secure attachment. In his 2010 book, Holmes elaborates his thinking about the connections between therapy, narrative, attachment, and meaning (pp. 49–50). It is the move from private to shared experience that helps the client to create meaning. This is done, not just by passive listening, but by the therapist eliciting detail and imagery that enables her to enter the client's world. Narrative that is neither under- nor over-saturated with meaning is generated by successful therapy and is characteristic of secure attachment. However, it is not clear that fluid, emotionally suffused, and meaningful narrative necessarily generates the safety that permits interdependence in relationships and exploration from a secure base. Safety is not a cognitive, but an organismic state, as neuroscience is currently demonstrating. This led Wilkinson later (2010, p. 138) to revise her thinking somewhat: it is narrative "in the context of an enabling relationship" that can change the inner world. Moreover Cozolino (2006) insists that: "The *simultaneous activation* of narratives and emotional experiences builds neural connection and coherence between easily dissociable networks of affect and cognition" (quoted in ibid., p. 138, emphasis added).

"Secure attachment facilitates integration in the developing child by allowing for different forms of interpersonal resonance to occur" (Siegel, 2012, p. 374): left hemisphere to left in the form of verbal communication; right hemisphere to right in the form of tone, gesture, and facial expression; and bilateral to bilateral integration of interpretation and feeling, detail, and big picture. Attachment disorders affect this process so that, for example, the avoidant-dismissing mother-child dyad share primarily left-hemisphere communication and therefore lack the mentalising property (ability to perceive and understand the mind of the other) of the right brain. Brenda, unlike her brothers, acquired some of the latter capacity from her compulsive compensatory novel-reading and by learning from other girls at school.

Memory and narrative

Memory is crucial to a valid personal narrative. The kinds of experiences recalled are those of moderate to high degrees of emotional intensity, while those of low or overwhelming intensity will be blocked (Siegel, 2012, pp. 71–72). But our memories differ enormously, partly because of great differences in perception. While doing an exercise in a Myers Briggs workshop, one acquaintance was found to be a strong sensing type. In response to an unanticipated challenge, she was able to close her eyes and describe every detail of furniture, décor, and clothing in the room—as well as how they had been in a previous week. Brenda could as soon do this as fly to the moon. With intuition as a superior function, her memories are more implicit and difficult to communicate—she remembers feelings, atmosphere, possibly discussions, but not the actual words used. Brenda's "poor memory" is connected with her attachment style. Like other avoidant/dismissing types, Brenda retains only generalised memories of childhood, and describes herself as "spaced out a lot of the time" or "communing with nature"—a state of participative consciousness. Siegel (2012, p. 123) warns against interpreting this lack of recall associated with avoidant/dismissing people as the blocked memory of early trauma. Research shows that other aspects of personal memory (e.g., childhood television programmes) are normal in avoidant/dismissing people. Siegel links the "low-affect environment" of emotionally distant and rejecting families with the dissociative symptoms found in avoidantly-attached children (p. 123). Brenda herself links her poor specific memory with "not taking things in in the first place": her unwillingness to be fully present and open to experience. When pushed, she will acknowledge that this is connected with the pain of contact with others. She tolerates only a narrow range of emotional intensity, and therefore doesn't take in things she considers "too boring" and, at the other end of the scale, whatever brings up the pain that she associates with contact: excruciating feelings of self-undermining, self-hatred, and embarrassment.

Siegel (2012, p. 125) categorises autobiographical memory into "general periods, general knowledge, and specific events". It is the details that dismissing adults lack, not the generalised picture, and it is this lack of sensory and emotional detail that gives their narrative such a dry and unnourished quality. Siegel distinguishes between autonoetic consciousness (from noesis, pertaining to the intellect) and autobiographical memory. Some recall is experienced only within noetic consciousness: "In other words, we may know that a past event occurred, but we do not have a sense of ourselves in the past. This factual knowledge of even personal past events is recalled as a semantic (factual) recollection, rather than as part of the episodic process of mental time travel" (p. 125). This is indicative of left rather than right-hemisphere recall and describes Brenda exactly, particularly since breaking all connection with her family and refusing to engage with her past. Some other dismissing adults have a complete lack of recall even for the facts of their childhood. It is probable that their families lacked the kind of reminiscing conversation where parents aid in the co-creation of the child's memory by integrating explanatory narratives, the subjective with the objective, as well as by making comparisons with other times and places. As Siegel (2012) puts it: "our relationships not only shape what we remember, but how we remember and the very sense of self that remembers" (p. 59).

While speaking at a memorial to her father, the writer Siri Hustvedt found herself shaking uncontrollably. She interpreted her convulsions as a conversion reaction (hysteria) due to unresolved grief about her father's death, and she went on a quest to try to understand buried memory through the lenses of psychoanalysis and neuroscience. She finds people with brain damage that created various neurological oddities, such as the boy who had amnesia when talking but not when writing (Hustvedt, 2010, p. 65), or the man who was unable to read what he had written (p. 68). Hustvedt wonders if she herself has such a systemic disconnection, which would explain the fact that she shakes but does not know why. At the other end of the scale, she describes a synesthetic man with a capacious memory as a result of his vivid visual associations with words and numbers (pp. 103–105). However, while he could easily remember a list of unrelated numbers or words, he had difficulty integrating the mass of pictures that overloaded his mind, and it was hard for him to follow stories or poems because of the confusion of competing images.

Thus, to make sense of ourselves and our lives, we need a good enough episodic memory, but not too good. For those of us with little recall, Hustvedt has a game that she plays with psychiatric patients to whom she teaches creative writing. Simply repeatedly writing the words "I remember" turns up unexpected and forgotten "nuggets from their mental gold mines" (p. 63) with all the joy and amazement of exploration and discovery. This is something Brenda has tried, and she found herself surprised by memory into vitality. She trusted enough to let go into it and discovered many more positive incidents than she had expected. However, they seemed like random balls thrown in the air, and more work needed to be done to integrate the memories into an expanded version of Brenda. Interestingly, dreaming has been found in some studies to be necessary to reformulate daytime experiences by condensation and symbolisation so that they can be stored in memory (Rayner, Joyce, Rose, Twman, & Clulow, 2005, p. 126); but other research indicates that REM sleep and dreaming are not necessary for memory consolidation (Siegel, 2012, p. 62). Brenda frequently wakes up exhausted and fretful after Kafkaesque dreams that are never resolved. This may be a sign of unsuccessful integration in dreaming and could play a role in her poor autobiographical memory.

Fragmentation of narrative and the self

Brenda's narrative is broken into pieces: a shattered mosaic that would need an archaeologist to piece it together—rather like Brian Dillon (2005) who has written a memoir, but remembers little and records no actual events other than the premature deaths of his parents. Brenda becomes bored and despairing when asked for a sequential narrative of her life-course. She wants a fresh perspective; she doesn't care about earliest memories, significant people, peak and nadir experiences, and turning points any more: this view feels stale and excessively personal. Therapy has left her with much greater awareness, but also with a fragmentation that is linked to the awareness: a sense both of the impossibility of putting it all together and a scepticism about whether it matters anyway. Her experience of therapy is that it has deconstructed her: ameliorating certain practical difficulties, but leaving her with *less* sense of self than she had before. She no longer has faith that she will ever develop a *felt sense* of having had a coherent life.

In the sixteenth century, Montaigne was able to observe: "I am unable to stabilize my subject: it staggers along with a natural drunkenness ... I am not portraying being but becoming ... I shall perhaps change soon, not accidentally but intentionally" (1993, pp. 907–908). How much more difficult is it in the twenty-first century to persuade oneself of having a life story that holds together. Rather, we sample here and there: we try out not just a dozen casual jobs, but multiple serious careers requiring lengthy training; we serially move and renovate houses; we have perhaps dozens of sexual partners and multiple serious long-term relationships. I have used the word "serious" several times, but really we know from a young age that everything is replaceable, temporary, and constantly exposed to a deconstructing gaze: is this partner, job, career, house, country, shampoo meeting my wishes and "needs", or is there some other partner, job, career, house, country, or shampoo that would do the job better because—"I'm worth it"? We are fragmented, "the centre cannot hold;/mere anarchy is loosed on the world" (Yeats, "The Second Coming", 1974).

A narrative exercise would have to take account of this; it would have to be a written mosaic—pieces assembled that have no continuity but represent multiple lives and subpersonalities which all happen to occupy what is recognised as one person, more like a hologram perhaps. Brenda may be recognised as one person, even though she doesn't actually *feel* like one. Her memories are thin, patchy, unreliable, and could as easily be the imaginings of a dream, film, or novel. She cannot identify with the photograph of a joyous perky toddler standing in reins in the pram in perhaps her second year, nor with the confident child in wellingtons in her grandmother's garden, or the wild-haired, fearful, lonely, and angry adolescent. She feels different from the tense and alienated IT manager worrying about being uncovered for the fraud she is, like a Special Operations agent dropped into wartime France. She pictures each as a specific photograph, and she has no memory of the first two occasions or the state of mind that is portrayed in them. She remembers the miserable adolescent and the stressed-out manager, but holds them at bay as undigested chunks of a past she wants to forget. As an adult at Mme de Saint-Loup's, Proust's Marcel finds that he leads, in the same place, a different life from that of childhood: it is "another sort of pleasure I take in going out only at night, in following by moonlight those lanes where I used to play in the sun" (2003, p. 11). Marcel is on a constant quest to reconcile the magical past of his childhood with his disenchanted adult life of love affairs and high society. How, indeed, can the child and the adult be the same person?

My whole bodymind, my thoughts, feelings, physiological states, change moment by moment when alone, and with others they are subject to invasion by the same dynamic process in the other. Likewise, I affect them and so on, so that an ever-changing field is created. When I sleep, I become a different exciting other and when waking (especially out of an afternoon nap) may feel quite disoriented and, not knowing the time of day or place, momentarily lose the context of my life, in particular what I have to do next. Very occasionally, the awakening brings a terrifying loss of self, as if one is caught in a void between the worlds of sleeping and waking. Aged twenty, in love for the first time with a man who was six years older than me and much more worldly-wise, I go wilderness camping with him beside a lake in the White Mountains of New Hampshire. There are no signs of other human beings, just the mountains, the lake, and our tent. I awake while it is still dark. For a few moments, which remain with me more than three decades later, I do not know who I am. But that statement does not come close to expressing what I experienced. I was all terror of absence without even knowing what presence might be. I didn't simply lack a name, I lacked personhood, and even the concept of what personhood might be. I lacked location, and even the concept of what place might be. It was an experience of complete nothingness, other than the panic that rushed in to fill the vacuum. It was an absence of consciousness, but an awareness of the full horror of the absence, such as I fear Alzheimer patients might feel at a certain stage of degeneration. Here is Proust writing of the loss and reassembly of self after sleep at the beginning of *In Search of Lost Time*: "I did not know where I was, I did not even understand in the first moment who I was; all I had, in its original simplicity, was the sense of existence as it may quiver in the depths of an animal; I was more bereft than a caveman" (2003, p. 9). As Marcel puts himself back together, he imagines he is waking as a child in his bedroom in his grandparents' house in Combray, but then realises that years have passed and he is, in reality, an adult staying at Mme de Saint-Loup's.

* * *

REFLECTING AND CREATING THE SELF   211

The term "centration" is used by Piaget to describe the cognition of pre-operational children (aged two to six) who cannot focus on more than one dimension of an object or situation at a time. Taking the perceptual dimension, the young child who resents the older sibling being given two biscuits compared to his one can be fooled by mother breaking his biscuit in two. The concept also includes egocentrism—the child's inability to see situations from other than a personal perspective: the child has seen keys being hidden and assumes that mother, who was not present at the time, must also know where they can be found. Five-year-old Jack in Emma Donoghue's novel *Room* cannot understand how his mother could be awake while he was asleep. Decentration around the age of six or seven allows the concrete-operational child to see another's perspective and to classify according to multiple dimensions (Sugarman, 2001).

This builds on an earlier developmental step when the child becomes aware of separation from the other. There has been a lot of controversy about whether the young baby experiences himself as a separate individual or is in a state of symbiosis with mother (Rayner, Joyce, Rose, Twman, & Clulow, 2005, p. 51). Balint's theory of the "basic fault" rests on the excessively abrupt shattering of such a symbiotic state. This results from a lack of attunement of the carer towards the baby or from more overt trauma; either way, the individual is left with a sense of brokenness that runs through their being and lasts for a lifetime (Gomez, 1997, p. 117). Whatever the degree of fusion or unity the baby experiences with its environment, changes in the baby's behaviour (interest in the purposes of the other, pointing, stranger-anxiety) in the second six months of life imply the beginning of a theory of mind. The baby begins to have a sense of having a mind of its own and that other people have separate minds that contain feelings, attitudes, and intentions (Rayner, Joyce, Rose, Twman, & Clulow, 2005, p. 62). This early experience that others have a different agenda from ourselves is supplemented at the age of six or seven by the ability to understand those agendas and predict from the other's perspective—in other words, decentration has been achieved.

I want to argue that decentration has a cost, that it creates a wound to centredness, that the steady fixed gaze becomes flickering and fragmented. Suddenly, we no longer inhabit just our own world but the world of everyone we encounter as well. This may be why "the best lack all conviction and the worst [those with arrested development] are full of passionate intensity". We may become so adept at seeing the world through the eyes of the other that we spend most of our time on their side of the fence and lose touch with our own perspective. The more people we have to deal with in a short space of time, the more confused we become—there are a lot of fences to jump over and a lot of views from which to see the world. How do we maintain the decentration that is essential to ordered and peaceful social living alongside the centredness that keeps us stable and self-directing? According to Boadella (1987, p. 77) centring involves recovering emotional equilibrium, with its associated harmonious breathing, by re-establishing the balance between the sympathetic and parasympathetic parts of the nervous system responsible for arousal and relaxation respectively. When anxiety disturbs the rhythm of the breath, we contract and lose our connection to our gravitational centre which is located at the hara, two inches below the navel. Loss of centre can be observed in a literal way when floating in water: in a relaxed state our weight is distributed around the hara, but in a state of rigid contraction the individual sinks. Loss of centre is associated with under-contained feeling (hysterical patterns) and with lack of contact with the in-breath and shallow thoracic breathing (Boadella, 1987, p. 79). Boadella implies that anxiety leads to loss of centre, but I maintain that loss of centre equally renders us vulnerable and anxious. In either case, the in-breath must be deepened to provide centre and containment, and the decentration must be countered with attention to boundaries. If I am always at others' beck and call, turn off the mobile phone; if I worry about losing all my friends, be aware of how damaging my current way of relating is. Which is worse: no friends or no self?

Child development studies by Susan Harter and colleagues suggest that our experience of a unitary, continuous self is an illusion: the child must take on different roles and adapt to different social contexts, thereby entering into multiple self-states which are sometimes in conflict with each other (Siegel, 2012, pp. 209, 211). What counters the constantly changing self is what Lacan called "the mirror phase", in which infants invent an illusion of "I": we are taken in by the apparent stable oneness of what we see in the mirror. But "the 'I' is tirelessly intent upon freezing a subjective process that cannot be frozen, introducing stagnation into the mobile field of human desire" (Bowie, 1991, p. 25). What other therapists conceive as a strong ego, Lacan regards as a disturbed psyche (Berman, 1990, p. 41). As adults, we continue to grapple with this chasm between our constantly changing thoughts and feelings and a cohesive visual image of ourselves. Thus, Douglas Harding can say "I, who am nothing here, place myself there [in the mirror] where I am a man" (quoted in Berman, 1990, p. 1), while Camus (1975, p. 21) writes of "the stranger who at certain seconds comes to meet us in a mirror, the familiar and yet alarming brother we encounter in our own photographs". Of course the mirroring we receive from others—at its most basic their ability to consistently recognise us—constantly reinforces this mirage of unity and one-selfness.

Continuous vs. discontinuous narrative

Psychotherapists generally regard cohesive and consistent narratives as a good thing, a sign of a stable and secure sense of self. However, in the worlds of philosophy and literary theory, there are some opposing views. The philosopher Galen Strawson (2008) has suggested that there are two ways of experiencing life: as a continuous narrative flow or in discontinuous episodes. He argues that reviewing your life in the latter episodic way has nothing to do with poor memory, and he illustrates the point with the example of John Updike who had a prodigious memory and also a persistent sensation of just beginning. The continuous and discontinuous narrative positions are the stances of the realist and the modernist writer respectively, though some of the discontinuous writers predate the first half of the twentieth century, which is technically the age of modernism. Strawson cites Balzac, Dostoyevsky, Fitzgerald, Graham Greene, and Evelyn Waugh as falling into the continuous narrative group, and classifies Laurence Sterne, Proust, Virginia Woolf, Borges, and Iris Murdoch as writers who portray the episodic experience of life.

Proust above all others is aware of how time and intervening events change our orientation towards the past. To take a crude example, a good memory of an event with a spouse will be revised to some degree when a subsequent event such as divorce from that spouse muddies the original feelings. Strawson challenges two narrative theses, which claim that ordinary humans experience their lives as a continuous narrative or that they *should* do so if they are to have rich and unified lives. Most contemporary advocates of narrative such as Paul Ricoeur and Charles Taylor believe in both these propositions. But Strawson (whose episodic nature Brenda shares) argues that such views narrow our thinking and distress those who do not fit the model, and moreover that repeated retelling of our life story puts us at risk of losing touch with the truth of our being. We need to be aware that any account of ourselves is simply a snapshot of a particular moment, taken from a particular angle. It is not some grand statement of objective, comprehensive, and unchanging reality. From a different perspective, Buddhists, too, warn against the danger of becoming trapped by our stories which can perpetuate our suffering by cementing the "small self" in place, thus blocking spiritual growth.

Brenda shares Strawson's experience: "I do not experience my childhood as belonging to *me* as I now apprehend myself to be when apprehending myself specifically as a self" (Strawson, 2008, Chapter Seven). She looks back over her life as a mosaic of episodes whose chronology is uncertain and jumbled; her view of the past is ever-changing, and events feel separate and unrelated. Sometimes her memory of the same event becomes split: for example when recalling her first reading of D. M. Thomas's *The White Hotel*, she characterised the book by its early Freudian erotic fantasies and other free-associative musings of the unconscious. On other occasions, she had vague intrusions into consciousness of a nightmarish scene of a woman being bayonetted through the genitals in a concentration camp mass grave. She imagined that this came from another book that she didn't otherwise remember. It was only on the second reading that she realised this event took place in the penultimate section of *The White Hotel*, which she had mentally deleted from the book. Her splitting off of the shocking and unexpected ending of the novel from the sensuous enchantment of the earlier sections may go some way towards explaining episodic reviewing of life. Likewise, Brenda has difficulty remembering map routes. She remembers sections, but fails to link them together or connect them to the destination. These may be small examples of a more general difficulty with digesting and integrating experience—a difficulty that underpins the lack of narrative coherence in the insecurely attached. The problem with integration is managed on a larger scale by splitting into subpersonalities, each of which handles different kinds of relationship or life events.

Unlike Strawson, despite being largely episodic in her experience and memory, Brenda is not anti-narrative. Indeed, she is greatly comforted by the grounded and chronologically ordered worlds portrayed in realist fiction, because they complement her own fragmentation.

However, she recognises that such narrative would not be true to her way of looking back on her life. Thus, I want to argue for a position in between the anti-narrative stance of Strawson and any-narrative-even-at-the-expense-of- truth stance of Ricoeur. I propose that episodics would benefit from assembling their lives into a loose structure, without sacrificing embodied truth. Rather than relying on strict chronology, such a narrative would—like that of Proust's Marcel—assemble incidents of similar feeling tone, atmosphere, or place. This idea is close to Grof's concept of a system of condensed experience (COEX), which he defines as "a dynamic constellation of memories (and associated fantasy material) from different periods of the individual's life, with the common denominator of a strong emotional charge of the same quality, intense physical sensation of the same kind, or the fact that they share some other important elements" (Grof, 1985, p. 97). In such a model, exemplified by Proust, linear chronology would be supplemented with narrative COEX; and, similarly, linear *causality* would be replaced by matrices of interrelated themes. Thus, the Freudian mechanistic view of psychological process—that the past determines the future—would be supplemented by the Jungian teleological view (Stevens, 1991) that we are led on, through our purpose, meaning, and values by (ideas about) the future. In other words, we are pulled by the future, not just pushed by the past. Add into the past and future the present moment where the people I am talking to, the food I am digesting, the economic position of the country, the weather, and thousands of other small and large factors, many of them contingent, determine who I am at this moment, and some of which, to varying degrees, will affect who I will be in the future.

Literary modes reflect changes not just in how we perceive and represent the self, but also how the self is constituted. Realist fiction (e.g., the works of Dickens) has been supplemented—though never superseded—by the modernist novel, whose depiction of character comes a lot closer to the episodic and incohesive way in which Brenda experiences her life. So, what can the novel tell us about the creation of self through narrative?

Narrative of the fragmented self in the modernist novel

Within literature, the experiences of the ego as alternately a solid entity or a dynamic process are most vividly illustrated in the differences between the realist novel of the nineteenth century and the modernist novel of the twentieth century. Kern (2011), in contrasting the two forms, shows how character presence was subverted by absence; substance by concrete nothingness; structure by blurring and fragmentation; and stability by volatile egos.

The impossibility of pinning down self or other comes up again and again in the novels of Woolf, Joyce, Musil, Sartre, Faulkner, and others. In *As I Lay Dying*, Faulkner makes explicit the link between excessive consciousness and blowing of existential circuits, when Darl says "I don't know if I am or not. Jewel knows he is, because he does not know that he does not know whether he is or not" (Faulkner, 2009, p. 80). Likewise, Woolf writes of Mrs. Dalloway that "she would not say of any one in the world now that they were this or were that" (Woolf, 1996, p. 10). Whatever one might say could be immediately contradicted. We are multiple in the moment and multiple sequentially as exemplified by the thirteen time frames, each told from three self-perspectives (I, you, and he), shuffled like cards in Fuentes' *The Death of Artemio Cruz*. The realist *vs.* modernist novel's portrayal of self is analogous to the dichotomy in quantum physics, where subatomic elementary particles can be equally well described as particles or as waves. We are both fragmentary (or perhaps really more like waves) and we have and need the illusion of having solid particulate egos. Virginia Woolf entitled perhaps her most difficult work *The Waves*. This novel goes considerably further than *Mrs. Dalloway* in not merely refusing to pin down the nature of an individual, but also in blurring the boundaries between separate characters who "merge repeatedly in waves of experience that flow through one another" (Kern, 2011, p. 27). Something similar is seen in the films of Terrence Malick where the inner musings of the characters are played over unrelated action, weaving in and out in unattributed ways, so that without a script it is often unclear who is speaking. Leopold Bloom in Joyce's *Ulysses*, in a state of acute empathy with the sentient world, imagines a cattle market as if he is the cattle, the butcher, the shopper, and the observer. The fragmentation of the individual is portrayed in Hesse's *Steppenwolf*, where the protagonist aspires to cultivate as many selves as possible, or in Gertrude Stein's *The Making of Americans*. Similar to Picasso's cubist portraits in which the face is viewed from multiple perspectives within the one painting, "Stein offered multiple images of persons sequentially from slightly different perspectives in slightly varied sentences" (Kern, 2011, p. 29). Borges writes of the two parts of him: the writer and the private person: "Things happen to him, the other one, to Borges" and "Little by little, I yield him ground, the whole terrain, though I am quite aware of his perverse habit of magnifying and falsifying" (1972, p. 171).

In line with the indefinability and fragmentation of self and our blurring with others, it can be expected that characters in the modernist novel lack stability even in the absence of external pressures. The consequent disorientation is explored particularly by Kafka. In *Metamorphosis*, Gregor wakes up one morning to find that he has become a beetle: the German word Kafka uses implies that he is contaminated vermin, covered in shame to pay off the "debt/guilt" of his parents. Here the disorientation emerges from Gregor's internal psychodynamics, but it can also be provoked by an unfathomable sociopolitical world, as in *The Trial* with its famous opening line: "Someone must have been telling lies about Joseph K., for without having done anything wrong he was arrested one fine morning".

Peter Labanyi has characterised the aims of three stages of the novel as portraying: self in the world (realist, e.g., Balzac and George Eliot); the world in the self (modernist, e.g., Proust and Kafka); and the self alone (the extreme late end of modernism as exemplified in the late works of Beckett). We may wonder which model of the person as portrayed in the realist, modernist, or the late modernist novel is more valid. Charles Taylor (1992) has shown how the self has mutated and developed in accordance with the historical and social conditions it inhabits and, in his more recent work (2007), in relation to the scientific or religious models with which we understand the world. The self is not separate from the world or even in the world: rather it is "thrown" into a world not of its own making, it is in a state of "being-in-the world", as Heidegger put it. Darwin's mortal blow to our creation myth and our anthropocentrism, increased urbanisation, reactions to the horrors of war, genocide and colonialism, Freud's exploration of the unconscious; improved human rights for women, non-white ethnic groups and the working class, and many other factors—all played a role in questioning and disrupting society, and hence the way in which the self was experienced. Out of this maelstrom emerged the modernist novel. Likewise, specific socio-economic and technological changes have led to the social and cultural development known as postmodernism.

The non-self of postmodernism

The shift from modernist to postmodernist fiction is associated with a transition from "epistemological uncertainty" to "ontological plurality or instability" (McHale quoted in Sim, 2002, pp. 201–202). Postmodernism is less a theory of narrative—how to represent who we are—than an ontological theory of who we are, or rather, who we are not. "While modernism dissolved form and narrative to meet the challenge of conveying, as a 'higher realism', the quality of twentieth-century experience and the nature of the twentieth-century subject, postmodernism, by contrast, dissolved *belief*, not just in realism, narrative, and history, but even in experience and the subject (self)" (Peter Labanyi). Like the modernist, the postmodernist identity is incoherent and continuously unfolding, but it differs by its nihilism and abandonment of the pursuit of meaning and by a disbelief in the existence of the self (Frosh, 1991, p. 21).

This dissolution of identity is portrayed in Paul Auster's *The New York Trilogy*, though the coherence of the narrative discourse brings it into the realm of neo-realist fiction. The first of the trilogy, *The City of Glass*, explores layers of identity and confused reality, in which "even the truth would be an invention, a mask to hide behind and keep him safe" (1990, p. 89). In the second novel, *Ghosts*, a character named Blue investigates a man named Black for a heavily disguised client called White. Eventually, it becomes apparent that Black and White are the same person who by forcing Blue to investigate them/him have effectively imprisoned Blue. Blue loses himself in trying to enter into Black's mind. When he starts to reciprocate every movement of Black's, "it is as though Blue were looking into a mirror, and instead of watching another, he finds that he is also watching himself" (ibid., p. 172). An example of a schizoid, fragmented, nihilistic, and alienated *character* is found in the teenage mass murderer Kevin in the otherwise non-postmodernist novel, *We Need to Talk About Kevin*. Kevin's school papers display a postmodernist rejection of (psychological incapacity for?) linear narrative and all aspiration to meaning: "Abraham Lincoln was president. Abraham Lincoln had a beard. Abraham Lincoln freed the African-American slaves", etc. The narrator/mother notes Kevin's lack of affect, his "intuitive appreciation for the arbitrary, for the numbing powers of repetition, and for the absurdist possibilities of the *non sequitur*" (p. 276). She might also have added his lack of any value judgements in equating the possession of a beard and the freeing of slaves.

Postmodernist theory originated in Lyotard's scepticism about "grand narratives": overarching theories that modelled the world into a coherent order (Sim, 2002). Grand narratives like Marxism, Darwinism, Freudianism or the isms of science or religion are rejected in favour of multiple micro-narratives, in a perspectivist approach first advocated by Nietzsche. As Frosh (1991) puts it: "large scale theorising is replaced by detailed analysis of the separate moment in time and space, and of the specificity of the position from which that analysis arises" (p. 23); there is no past and no authenticity because there is no foundation for it (p. 29). Equally, postmodernism does not believe in the possibility of representation; thus art becomes a form of playing, as exemplified in magic realism or in Almodóvar's films. The writer/director is thereby absolved from being held ethically or politically accountable: it's only a game after all. This makes it impossible for the reader/viewer to sink into the work and experience it at a feeling or visceral level; all that is left is superficial, disembodied, head-level entertainment. Participatory empathic engagement with characters' struggles and joys is replaced by alienated voyeurism; stories, characters, life experience, and context are reduced to mere text.

My partner Peter and I go for a four hour woodland walk and he helpfully writes notes of our conversation in tiny red writing in a ring-bound pocket notebook. He is much exercised by his outrage at postmodernism and stops to scrawl: "French theory believes that all structure is top-down and therefore oppressive ...". We walk into one of the few non-sprawled hilltop towns in Ireland, imagining it as the work-seeking heroes in a Hardy novel might perceive it: the distant church steeple with houses tightly clustered round reached after a full day's walk. We have lunch at an outdoor café and Peter writes his highly specific order on the same piece of paper for me to deliver to the waitress while he visits the Gents: "baguette, mayonnaise, cheese, coleslaw, tomatoes, hot water, and two glasses of tap water". At home, later, he crosses out his remarks on French theory with a "rubbish" comment in black pen, but circles the lunch order along with the helpful suggestion: "would go well in Chapter Eight!" *This* is a (postmodern) joke told against postmodernism.

Taking their cue from Lacan, a cohesive self is portrayed by some postmodern theorists as a source of tyranny, of repression of the free play of libido frolicking amid the polymorphously perverse. In Milan

Kundera's novel, *The Unbearable Lightness of Being*, Tomas bounces like a buoy on the contingency of an arbitrary, floating, groundless life. He takes nothing seriously; he commits to nothing, but, as Newman (quoted in Frosh, 1991 p. 27) says: "if everything is permitted then it makes no difference what we do and nothing is worth anything". Such fragmentation and meaninglessness ends up, not as liberation but psychosis, where there is conflict between what the social order is offering and the intrinsic human need for the establishment of a stable and secure self (Frosh, 1991, pp. 146–147). Likewise, Deleuze and Guattari speak of "a subjectless machine" and "impersonalised flows of schizoid desire" so that they can perversely reframe schizophrenia as heroic "transgression" (Elliott, 2002, p. 158). A borderline client of mine, who struggles desperately with holding together what fragments of self he has, loathes what he perceives as the gloating sneers of postmodernist poseurs, smugly secure in their all-too-solid identities. He views them as "psychosis tourists", just like privileged Westerners holidaying in war zones or spending a few weeks "assisting" the poor in the Third World.

As for Brenda, she is inevitably repelled by the alienation of postmodernism, as she struggles in the *opposite* direction—*towards* meaning to escape the pit of depression: "I have more than enough alienation myself, thanks, without going swimming in that poisoned pond". In her reading, she vastly prefers realist fiction, though she will occasionally challenge herself with modernist works. She finds that the latter represent the reality of who she is; but it is the former which carry the healing—the containment and nourishment—she needs for her fragmentation.

Brenda may hate technology; she may love old places, a pastoral environment, and Romantic poetry. But despite all this, her favouring (in everyday life) of head over heart, her avoidance of commitment, her fleeing from the past and her weaving round any unpleasant current difficulties by creating an ever-changing future—this all makes her a quintessentially postmodern character. She makes a virtue of freedom and authenticity, but in refusing to adapt to the ethos and rules of institutions, she does not take on the responsibilities appropriate to her age. Our current late capitalist society makes it both possible and desirable—because it rewards adaptability—for her to remain trapped in her pathology. She is a pragmatic survivor, but she starves emotionally. It is difficult for her to make progress in therapy because her culture fixes her in her alienated thinking and contact–avoidance patterns.

Polkinghorne (1992, cited in Burr and Butt, 2003) identifies four interrelated themes that characterise postmodern psychology. (1) Foundationlessness: there is no objective world, no universal human nature; language is a tool, not for *describing* an objective world but for *constituting* a personal world. (2) Fragmentariness: we are plural beings, each of us having multiple attitudes and feelings about a given topic; e.g., I am happy in *and* limited by my job. (3) Constructivism: we construct our worlds, but there are some objective limits, so we also encounter the world. (4) Pragmatism: our constructions are judged, not in terms of truth, but of usefulness.

Polkinghorne's summary of postmodern thought, while it inches closer to the truth of how we make sense of our world than the old positivist model, nevertheless has a very ungrounding effect even on somebody reading about it, much less living in this awareness. To adapt T. S. Eliot: humankind cannot bear too much unreality. We need some solid ground to walk on and some objective truths to rely on. Brenda fits all the categories, though she is grounded and embodied enough to know that experience is not just a matter of "discourse": for her words *describe* much more than they *construct*. She insists on the distinction between primary process (the world, the body, experience) and secondary process (language and other forms of mediation).

Postmodern psychology has an impact on whether and how we can knit together narratives of our lives. Musil's man without qualities, Ulrich, observes that public life "no longer follows a thread, but instead spreads out as an infinitely interwoven surface" (1995, p. 709). Stefan Jonsson (2000), examining the impact on identity, maintains that the condition of late modernity "is inimical to narration" (p. 137). But we need storytelling to "stabilise subjectivity"; with the weakening of narrative, the links between events are lost and identity fails to cohere. All sense of destiny or purpose evaporates and we feel as aimless as corks bobbing on water. Is there any help for Brenda in narrative therapy? Will developing a cohesive narrative help her to heal her anxious attachment?

Narrative and integration

The way in which we tell stories, whether in literature or in life, reflects the nature of the self, though not in a straightforward way. The individual may express who they are directly, as when a fragmented identity is revealed in a discontinuous narrative, or a secure and stable sense of self in a cohesive story. Or they may compensate: as when a solid individual plays with postmodern forms, or a dangerously shattered self is pulled together into a rigidly-structured story which may classify as realist, but is not real or true to life. Brenda is unable to form a cohesive narrative of her own life and resonates with the modernist way of recounting her story, even if this is not what she would choose for her leisure reading.

Cozolino (2010) proposes that language and narrative are crucial for neural integration, including top-down and left-right coordination within the brain. The need to tell stories stems from the left hemisphere as a means of making sense of information from the right hemisphere (Hart, 2008, p. 259). Siegel (2012) asserts that "the central, coherence-creating, narrative process has a unifying quality that links otherwise disparate aspects of memory within the individual" (pp. 87–88). Our unconscious models of life reveal themselves in our narrative themes and styles, and these lend us narrative continuity over time. Thus, story-making helps make sense of the minds of others and of our own lives, aids in memory formation, problem solving, goal attainment, affect regulation, self-creation, and self-maintenance. Storytelling enables the members of a community or tribe to inhabit each other's perspective, to cooperate, coordinate, share common history and goals, and transmit culture. In psychotherapy, Cozolino notes three levels of conversation: one is the clichéd maintenance of social bonds; a second is the internal dialogue; and the third is the language of self-reflection. He believes that the last reflects a higher level of integration where thoughts and feelings work in tandem. Cozolino's levels contrast with Perls' five layers of neurosis, which he defined in terms of contact with self and other. Perls conceived of the therapy process as working through these layers, from superficial clichés and games and roles, to the impasse and implosive layers, followed finally by the explosive layer where the individual is capable of experiencing and expressing his genuine emotions such as grief, anger, joy, or sexual release (Perls, 1969, pp. 59–60). Such changes in contact capacity are what deepen our awareness and thus underpin changes in a person's narrative form.

One way of conceiving therapy is as a process of outlining and changing life stories. Narrative theorists of the life course focus on reinterpreting the past to develop narrative coherence (Sugarman, 2001, p. 169). Dan McAdams proposes that a new narrative element arises at different stages in the lifespan: narrative tone is laid down in infancy, then personal imagery in the pre-school years, followed by themes, ideologies, characters, generativity scripts, and finally, in old age, narrative evaluation (Sugarman, 2001, pp. 101–108). Narrative themes derive from unconscious implicit memory and reflect the generation of coherence within the narrative process. They link disparate aspects of memory within the subjective sense of self (Siegel, 2012, p. 87). In telling our own stories, whatever the context, we give ourselves an identity, and we understand our lives in terms of the narrative we subsequently live out. But our stories are meaningless if they are restricted to facts: they must be coloured with emotion and charged with values. Well-being is dependent on responding to the draw of goodness (Vernon, 2008, p. 124): to make sense of our lives, "we need an orientation to the good, … [and] this sense of the good has to be woven into my understanding of my life as an unfolding story" (Taylor, 1992, p. 47).

The dangers of alienated narrative are revealed in two fictional passages which appear at face value to display opposing views. The first is from Musil's *Man Without Qualities*:

> Terrible things may have happened to him, he may have writhed in pain, but as soon as he can tell what happened in chronological order, he feels as contented as if the sun were warming his belly. … Most people relate to themselves as storytellers. … they love the orderly sequence of facts because it has the look of necessity, and the impression that their life has a "course" is somehow their refuge from chaos. (Musil, 1995, p. 709)

Though Musil acknowledges that there is a real human need here, in the context of the novel this passage is ironic. In Thomas Mann's eponymous novella, Tonio Kröger is scathingly bitter about the right or capacity of writing to capture feelings or contain life, via charges that could just as well have been made with psychoanalysis in mind.

> As for "words", I wonder if they really redeem our passions: is it not rather that they refrigerate them and put them in cold storage? … What does one do when one's heart is too full, when some sweet or sublime experience has moved one too deeply? The answer is simple! Apply to a writer … He will analyse it all for you, formulate it, name it, express it and make it articulate, and so far as you are

concerned the entire affair will be eliminated once and for all. ...
Don't you see, what the literary artist basically fails to grasp is that
life goes on, that it is not ashamed to go on living, even after it has
been expressed and "eliminated". (Mann, 1998, pp. 163–164)

Throughout his work, Mann returns repeatedly to his conflict between
the Apollonian life of the mind and the Dionysian life of the body:
he reminds us that however much we talk or write (or therapise ourselves?), life will go on happening. But we should not forget that story-
making—as a necessary fiction—can actually help. As Paul Ricoeur
(quoted in Jonsson, 2000, p. 308) stresses: "It is in telling our own stories
that we give ourselves an identity".

The difference between integrating storytelling and alienated verbalising depends on the degree to which we are in touch with our primary
process. This is the form of right-brain thinking directly linked to bodily and emotional experience, which, as in visual imagery or dreaming, condenses meaning into symbols (Rayner, Joyce, Rose, Twman, &
Clulow, 2005, p. 82; McGilchrist, 2009). Secondary process, on the other
hand, is a form of left-brain logical thinking that includes the formula-
tion of thought into language. Yeats was aware of this difference when
he wrote:

> God guard me from those thoughts men think
> In their mind alone;
> He that sings a lasting song
> Thinks in the marrow bone.
>
> ("A Prayer for Old Age", 1974)

The facility of a great writer with language must inevitably—at times—
generate a distrust of their slickness, knowing they can make words do
anything. For storytelling to be meaningful, it must represent our bodily truth, and accessing that truth depends on the manner in which the
story emerges in the context of relationship. This is why I disagree with
what Ricoeur goes on to say: "It makes very little difference whether
these stories are true or false, fiction as well as verifiable history provides us with an identity" (quoted in Jonsson, 2000, p. 38). While any
story and any identity may be better than none, the lie, however unin-
tended, can never be as grounded, sustainable, or nourishing as the
truth. The dangers of inauthenticity are discussed below.

Authentic self?

How do we cope in the face of dislocation, fragmentation, loss, and alienation, together with the awareness of our lack of stable solidity? Most of the time, most of us, whatever our awareness of the cracks in our experience, nevertheless persuade ourselves of an intrinsic cohesive authenticity, which seems contrary to the wave-like, field-like insubstantiality portrayed in modernist novels, and even more contrary to the wilfully transgressive, nihilistic self of postmodernism or the commodified, self-branding identities of late capitalism. Sartre's awareness of the contingency of life's events did not stop him insisting on our freedom to respond authentically to circumstances—an authenticity that depends, however, on our having no fixed essence. He expressed contempt for those who behaved in bad faith (i.e., inauthentically), like the waiter playing the part of a waiter just that bit too well. Nowadays, "performing the self" is regarded as simply a description of reality in some intellectual circles, and indeed is a requirement to survive in the corporate world of multinational conglomerates and television reality and "talent" shows (Dowds, 2008).

Psychotherapy, notwithstanding all the posturings of postmodernism, continues to regard the possession of a stable cohesive self to be a *sine qua non* of psychological health (e.g., Frosh, 1991). Winnicott (1990) believed in a true self and Perls, Hefferline, and Goodman (1973) in an authentic identity that could be excavated from all the accretions of a false or socially adapted self. Sartre argued that a self emerges when our centre of consciousness coincides with what we do in the world (Sartre in Van Deurzen, 1998, p. 37). However, if we behave as if solidly constituted as an *object*, we live in bad faith, so he regarded *a* self as undesirable. Likewise, the existential therapist Emmy Van Deurzen (1998, pp. 38–39) regards self as process rather than essence. In body therapy terms, I would suggest that a solidified identity correlates with muscular (character) armouring and therefore cannot be authentic. Conversely, an identity that is pure process is disembodied and ungrounded. A healthy and authentic sense of self is embodied without being over-defended, and thus lies somewhere on the continuum between a solid essence and a perpetually changing process.

The self is not just our own creation or even that of our social environment: it entails both nature and nurture. The significant role of genetics in personality (genetics accounts for twenty to fifty per cent of our variance in extraversion, neuroticism, agreeableness, conscientiousness and openness to experience) (Plomin, DeFries, McClearn, & McGuffin, 2008, p. 243) and the anecdotal evidence of parents that babies are born with individual personalities strongly implies that there is a core self that is peculiar to each of us. However, the rest of the package is constituted by our upbringing and early and later experiences, along with a dynamic interaction between the nature and nurture components of our being. The existence of such a core self implies that the self is partially an emergent rather than solely a constructed phenomenon, as so many sociologists and philosophers claim (e.g., Baggini, 2011). No less crucial are the implications of this core self: it provides a grounding for (1) the notion of the *continuity* of the self over time; and (2) the concept of an organismically based *authenticity* to the self. Contemporary psychodynamic theorists (Frosh, 1991; Elliott, 2002) and narrativist philosophers and psychologists (Guignon, 2004, pp. 126, 139) know that a self is essential, but that it needs to be worked at—the core self is just a potential, as Winnicott recognised. Hence, psychotherapy must entail, not just deconstruction, but also active building—or rather birthing—of a self and, if it is to incorporate and integrate the mind, body, emotions, and spirit, must be holistic.

In Lionel Shriver's novel *We Need to Talk About Kevin*, the narrator and mother of Kevin says: "Now my perspective is European: I am a bundle of other people's histories, a creature of circumstance. It is Kevin who has taken on this aggressive, optimistic Yankee task of making himself up" (2003, p. 197). Shriver is pointing out the difference between self-determination and determination by others, individualism and the collective. "It takes a village to create a child" is the usual wisdom, but the omnipotently deluded American male grandiosely arrogates to his individual ego the power to create himself into whomsoever he wills: whether a schoolboy mass murderer or a Wall Street hedge fund manager. (This is exemplified by the outrage felt by Republican supporters when President Obama ventured to point out, contradicting Thatcher's notorious quip, that business cannot be built without the support of a societal infrastructure.) This raises the important point about who or what level of self is doing the creating and what are the limits to that creation. It is crucial to let go of the fantasy that, starting now, we can become anything we want—which usually means what our particular subculture tells us we should envy. What we *can* do is start from the blend of our genetics and experiences up to this point and embark on a process of centering and reinforcing boundaries to pull together the fragments of self and protect them against the invasions of others. This constitutes the more modest task of strengthening what we *have* to generate more cohesion and stability.

The philosopher Charles Guignon (2004) raises this point of who exactly is doing the self-making. He cites Sartre's example of the gambler who resolves to give up his habit. However, the gambler has enough self-awareness to know that he has made good resolutions before, but given in to temptation within weeks. Sartre referred to this third-person stance as the self of "facticity" (quoted in Guignon, 2004, p. 144): something "finite, vulnerable and unsteady" (ibid., p. 144). Thus "my own self-making activity lacks the force to determine what I *am* in an absolute sense. ... The promise here of wholeness, continuity, coherence, constancy, purposiveness and responsibility for self—qualities definitive of this new conception of an authentic existence" begin to look a bit of a hoax (ibid., p. 145). Sartre uses this example to point to a bifurcated self: the transcendent self of the first-person stance towards the self and the third-person self of facticity. In therapy terms (Stone & Winkleman, 1989), there are at least three different selves here: the gambler, the non-gambler, and the aware ego. Humanistic therapists such as John Rowan (1990) and the person-centred therapists Mearns and Thorne (2000) accept a multiplicity of selves and don't judge which are more "true" than others. Some are apparently "for growth" subpersonalities that lead to a more realised self, whereas "not for growth" subpersonalities are regarded as important for fitting into the social order and maintaining psychic stability.

In humanistic psychotherapy, in line with the current foregrounding of relationship and intersubjectivity, the self-realising monadic self of Rogers or Maslow in the 1960s has, in the late twentieth and early twenty-first centuries, been replaced by a more *social* concept of self (Mearns & Thorne, 2000). The shift from thinking of authenticity as a solely personal matter to a socially determined state is explored by Guignon (2004). He critiques Rousseau's belief that while self-revelation uncovers passing and conflicting moods and attitudes, in the end the true self will become apparent to the other. He opposes this with Bernard Williams' assertion that our inner life can be steadied only through interactions with others, via subtle social pressures that nudge us into stable patterns (pp. 152–154). Williams views this transition from chaotic transient responses to stable identities as a process of maturing.

Charles Taylor (1992) makes a related point—but emerging out of an explicitly ethical viewpoint—that our life stories must be embedded in the public sphere in order to generate a full identity. In his view, this is a self with responsibilities and commitments to community: "[my identity] is the horizon within which I am capable of making a stand" (Taylor, 1992, p. 27). Guignon (2004, p. 159) suggests that the inauthentic person not only betrays herself, but lets us all down. A free and democratic society rests on a populace willing to discover and uphold the truth through the unrestricted exchange of ideas and to be vigilant and active politically. With this argument, it becomes clear that authenticity is not just personally desirable but is a public virtue.

Creating a healthy narrative

A psychologically healthy narrative is one that is cohesive, authentic, flexible, and emotionally-coloured. So here is the challenge: how to use narrative in a therapeutic context to authentically create and nourish self and organise meaning rather than to create a falsehood, or a rigid and restricted partial truth, or to deconstruct, desecrate, or otherwise destroy. Don't imagine that words alone can create a self; they may actually un-make one and leave the individual more fragmented and alienated than ever. This can happen by alienation from our primary process and the creation of a verbal surrogate self (the bane of the person with writing facility, but little contact with his body and feelings); or by relentless self-disassembly or undermining (e.g., masochistic filleting of one's motivations as a defence against the other getting the knife in first). Here is the novelist Tim Parks:

> I think that Teach Us to Sit Still [his book on meditation] ended up being a criticism of narrative. It was saying that one's constant engagement with narrative—the presentation of one's own life to oneself as an ongoing trajectory—is what feeds the frenetic voice in your head. I don't think of myself as a Buddhist, in spite of all the meditation, but I'm attracted to some of the common sense of Buddhism. And one idea is that maybe it's possible to live without that sort of self-narrative.

> (Crown, 2012)

It is crucial to stay in touch with the embodied experience and not get carried away by art for art's sake, or by theory for the sake of a quick and easy explanation. Does our narrative arise out of our felt sense of who we are? Unfortunately, our felt sense is more mercurial than the weather and we must question whether the body does indeed hold the ultimate truth, or is it only the jelly shaped by the mould of our past and current stories? Our body responses help us to know the truth in this moment, but a longer-term integration of subpersonalities needs resolution of inner conflicts. The assembly and ordering of our entire life story requires memory, both explicit and implicit, and a willingness to honour the messy truth of our experience. Brenda has an incoherent and discontinuous narrative. Her current best chance at integration is to attempt to represent her story in that form. As time goes by, she sees the gradual emergence of a story that is more nuanced, complex, and less contradictory. There is a movement away from either/or telling to both/and recounting of experience.

Stories, whether in childhood or in therapy with adults, are co-created within a relationship. Accordingly, their truth, usefulness, and power to reinforce the self depend on the engagement and empathic responsiveness of the other(s). Do we privilege subjective or objective reality; do we co-construct a narrative out of the transference and countertransference in the therapy or do we delve back into the client's past to attempt to retrieve lost experience? Is the function of narrative to reframe our habitual stories into something more acceptable, something more whole or aware, or is it about integrating split-off parts of ourselves and our relationships?

Burr and Butt (2003) deal with some of these questions about the role of stories in our confusing, ungrounded, constructivist age: "Within narrative theory, mental illness becomes a framework in which to interpret experience, rather than surface expression of real underlying disease entities" (p. 89). Narrative, like memory, is not a fixed and comprehensive photograph, but a highly selective, fluid, and ongoing process: we edit and re-edit our stories to make sense of what we are currently confronting. Our stories are embedded in the time and social context, not of when the recounted events happened, but when they are told. The flavour of events and how they are judged depend on the listener who encourages and mirrors, as well as on the social milieu, its labels, and what it judges to be valid. A story told in 1950s Ireland of a child being beaten by an adult was a story of a "bold" child; the same story told sixty years later is a tale of child abuse. In a non-mirroring environment, some stories are not possible, not only because of retribution if the story is told but, more fundamentally, because the theme is not recognised in the absence of prior naming. A decade or two ago, groups of angry or single women met every complaint about husband or male partner as evidence that the relationship was not working and that the partner should be left by the wayside. On the other hand, such complaints are seen as opportunities for personal development in environments where spiritual work or coupledom are valued, where gender differences are accepted, where projections are restrained, and where the imperfection and shifting nature of all relationships is recognised. These differences in context don't just affect the responses or advice given, but they reflect how you conceive and mould the story, knowing in advance or as you go along what is acceptable, what curries favour, what offers tacit support, what will be understood. Do I use scientific, therapeutic, poetic, or political language, concepts, and justifications; am I comprehensive, conclusive, or open-ended; do I speak with a broad or limited range of feeling? Do I blame myself or others or recount without blame?

The issue for constructivists is not so much the truth (did this event actually happen?) as the manner of narration, and what it says about the interpretation of experience. Do the stories do justice to and make sense of a person's experience; do they help them to live their lives? I am reminded of a client who couldn't leave the least tiny detail of a story out, and who was burdened with the need to be scrupulously true in her rendition. There were endless divergences, irrelevancies, and red herrings coupled with disputations with herself about the exact sequence and nature of events. Her monologues were painful to listen to and— I imagine—excruciating to live with. She was bound in steel cables by her superego's conscientiousness, and quite unable to move forward in her therapy or in her life. Choosing and decision-making were torments to her, duty precluded self-nourishment, and her therapy was motivated, not by concern for herself, but by her guilt at the impact of her depression on her daughters. This was a client in whom the manner of her narrative revealed everything about her world view—or her psychopathology.

If the manner of narrative is accurately mirrored, and if it is allied with the integration of memories, relationships, and recurring themes, then we slowly begin to build a self. In the process of telling a story about ourselves, we build boundaries between self and other. Most of the work of counselling and psychotherapy focuses on relationship problems, depression, anxiety, loss, trauma, abuse, illness, and death. I have found that when clients—and some friends—run out of themes of pain and difficulty, we often don't know how to engage with each other. Much as Tolstoy had little to say about happy families (who according to him are all the same—despite Levin and Kitty in *Anna Karenina* having to "work at" their happiness), we therapists fall short when we run out of the endless varieties of unhappiness. We are much better at the process of deconstruction than the process of forming and nurturing. Deconstruction was useful when Freud was developing the talking cure in a society all too smug and solid in its convictions, when repression of the id by an overwhelming superego was the dominant issue for clients. Nowadays, we live in an age of fragmentation, lability, alienation from ourselves and others, and id acting-out—to counter which the self needs to become more solid and integrated, and more embedded in society. Whether engaging with a client or in our own lives, we need to keep this process of building, strengthening, and integration in the foreground, alongside finding a way of developing a narrative that is positive yet authentic, of allowing the light to shine in our darkness and reveal some structure in the chaos.

Summary

Brenda's autobiographical memory and stories of her life are fragmented, arid, and lacking in sensory and emotional detail. She fills her inner emptiness by compulsive reading of novels. This raises the question of the relationship between life narrative and the creation and maintenance of self, here examined through the lenses of psychotherapy, literature, and philosophy. Symbolisation (including story-making) plays a central role in developing awareness of the self and imagination, visualising future possibilities and solving problems. Brenda's fragmented narrative is characteristic of her avoidant/dismissing attachment style and emerges from her inability to deeply experience her life and reflect on it long enough to lay it down in long-term memory. This leads to an account of the relationships between fragmentation of self, decentration, and loss of centre with examples of continuous and discontinuous narrative in literature. Brenda is representative of the discontinuous and alienated kind of identity portrayed in modernist and, to a lesser extent, postmodernist novels. While the fragmented self of modernist fiction most accurately represents the way Brenda experiences life, she prefers to read realist fiction for compensatory comfort. It is argued that post-modernism, rather than being a path to liberation, is actually the road to ungrounded, meaningless alienation and, in extremis, to psychosis.

The emergence and creation of an authentic self are discussed in relation to nature and nurture: the self is not personally determined; rather it is both emergent from our genetic legacy, and also created by our social environment. What is the role of narrative in integrating the self? For narrative to be healthy and life-enhancing it must involve not only the verbal left hemisphere of the brain but also the right hemisphere which mediates primary emotional process. A way of narrating a discontinuous story is suggested that is based less on linear chronology and causality and more on a spatial matrix of themes of related emotional tone.

CHAPTER NINE

Integration: perspectives from complexity theory and neuroscience

So far, we have gained some insight into Brenda's attachment style and how this manifests in the way in which she manages her energy, so that her inner charge is constantly fighting with her muscular armouring. The blockage in her energy flow impacts on her capacity to cathect—or alternatively, to be bored. Her over-focused attention and energy affects her receptiveness to experience, which leads to her craving more soulful living, along with more time, space, and silence. Brenda's anxious attachment also generates poor self-esteem, which causes her to obsess about competitiveness and power and her place in the pecking order. Her avoidant style means that she is understandably resistant to feeling her hurt and humiliation. She keeps the world at bay and takes in little. Consequently, Brenda has a poor "memory"—though in reality she hasn't taken in things in the first place—and her life narrative is patchy and lacks cohesion. When she experiences judgement or disrespect from another, she simply cuts them out of her life, while she keeps people she loves at arm's length to protect her fragile boundaries. She is resistant to digesting her past, but is driven by dreams of a better future. As a result, she changes career, partner, and home at regular intervals, and refuses—indeed panics in the face of—commitment to anyone or anything. All of this change and distancing from others and from herself adds to the episodic texture of her life as well as to her failure to experience it.

The question is, what are the prospects for Brenda? Is the only solution to start feeling what she avoids? Must she face the past, where what she remembers are the sneers and jeers from father and brothers, and from mother the assumption that her daughter had second-class status. Her mother's meek acceptance of—indeed insistence on—her own inferiority rendered Brenda incandescent with fury. To this day she cannot look at a burka-clad woman without hatred, because there she sees the same betrayal of their own sex. What made all this particularly excruciating was that none of it was explicitly named. Her mother would not argue, but disappeared in the face of her daughter's rage, while the others denied anything beneath the surface of the words used: feeling and tone could not be "proved", therefore they did not exist. The first years of Brenda's therapy were filled with a desperate need to be heard accurately, behind so great a fear of being seen—with its accompanying potential humiliation—that she was barely able to access and speak what she needed to say. Even now, with all the therapy she has done, she is in constant danger of falling into depression and despair. Even if she were not too proud to show her feelings, it is difficult to see how rubbing her nose in being despised could help her. However, without facing her feelings, she is constantly running from the past and any reminders of it, which includes all the members of her family. As she gets older, Brenda increasingly feels she has not had a life. She blames this on her poor memory, though she is beginning to admit that the problem is not her memory but her avoidance.

It is clear that Brenda has the makings of a self—in fragments. She has leaky boundaries, is uncertain about relationships and how much she is willing to risk them. She has a poor memory, a fragmented life story, a libido that comes and goes, and a general lack of creativity. She is like a broken pot from an archaeological dig: most of the pieces are there and the pot can be reconstructed, though she imagines that it will always be a patchwork. She knows that she cannot continue with a self so fragmented. But, what would integration mean for Brenda?

Siegel views the integrative function as reflective. It derives from the ability to mentalise (what he calls mindsight), which creates mental maps of self and other. He hypothesises that "the mind may be capable of dis-associating component modules by impairing the integrative function of essential associative neural pathways" (2012, p. 261).

He proposes that we can adaptively impair mindsight during our development when communications are emotionally empty—as in the relationships that lead to avoidant attachment. This might depend on blockage of the corpus callosum and of interconnections within the right hemisphere of the brain.

Integration—what is it and should we bother?

Integration is the means of achieving a healthy mind and healthy relationships. It is a state of vitality and harmony, where the whole is more than the sum of the parts (Siegel, 2012, pp. 9–10). Indeed, Ogawa and colleagues, with a view of the self as an end-product of development, have stated: "Integration is not a function of the self, it is what the self is" (quoted in Siegel, 2012, p. 355). In the absence of an integrated self, we ignore, repress, or split- off parts of ourselves. When this happens we lack the characteristics of flow: being flexible, adaptive, coherent, energised, and stable (ibid., p. 336). According to systems theory, in an integrated system the parts must be both differentiated and linked. If the parts are fused, the system becomes rigid: e.g., the repressed individual or the avoidantly attached infant who, in the absence of a responsive caregiver, relies on imposing internal constraints for self-regulation. If the parts are differentiated but disconnected, the system tends towards chaos—e.g., the intrusions and hyperarousal characteristic of PTSD, or the fragmentation of disorganised attachment. Optimum integration is a dynamic process of movement between the poles of sameness and novelty, rigidity and chaos (ibid., p. 361). In biology, tissue differentiation relies on structural segregation and functional specialisation. It is clear what this means in terms of group psychology, but what could it mean in terms of the mental and emotional integration of the individual self? As the mind develops, a more limited, but more specialised, range of states becomes possible; this greater differentiation enables greater complexity, through varying connections between the parts (ibid., pp. 201–202). Relationships both create this self-organisation and interact with it to generate complexity: "Secure attachment involves both the differentiation of child from parent and the empathic and attuned communication between the two" (ibid., p. 354). Anxious attachment affects both differentiation and connections, and the avoidant/dismissing individual is both created substantially alone and acts alone, and therefore has reduced complexity (ibid., pp. 204–205).

Barbara Fredrickson has proposed that positive emotions both arise from and support complexity (ibid., pp. 337–339). They broaden an individual's "thought-action repertoire", stimulating the urge to play, explore, and savour (i.e., integrate), whereas negative emotions provoke narrowed mindsets, for example, fear triggering the reflex of fight, flight, or freeze. Positive emotions promote resilience, well-being, complexity, and integration. Siegel claims that "emotion is inherently an integrative function that links internal processes and individuals together" (ibid., p. 345), and that it is a "fundamental process reflecting shifts in integration" (ibid., p. 356).

There are as many ways of conceiving of integration as there are models of the self. We could speak of integrating the ego, id, and superego, or the true but separated self with the adaptive but social self, or—in relational terms—the Kleinian split-off good and bad other. Here I will use two fundamental models of integration that can incorporate all of the other splits within us. The concept of integration can be applied to a given time (synchronic) or across time (diachronic).

Diachronic integration

Integration across time may be viewed as the primary, conscious work of all forms of psychotherapy. It involves assimilating experience that has not yet been digested and accepting parts of ourselves we have hitherto rejected. It is a process of catching up with our past and bringing its imprint into the present so that we cease trying to avoid or repress or otherwise defend against what is painful or unacceptable. It crucially revolves round a paradoxical theory of change: that we change when we become aware of who we *are*, not when we try to become what we are not.

When we are truly integrated across time, we recognise ourselves in our earlier being because we have learned to experience our essence, the part of us that is unchanging throughout our lives. This is what Proust's Marcel accomplished as he moved back and forth repeatedly between past and present. The critical feature of his time- travelling was the way he worked with his memories to catch the transient associations and deeply experience his past in the present moment. He achieved that ability to be fully present in the moment that advanced meditators have mastered; but in Marcel's case, it is the past as much as the present that he is presencing. In learning to experience his timeless essence, Marcel transcends time. He has moments of living in what T. S. Eliot (1974) called "the still point of the turning world".

Of course time flows seamlessly, so it is difficult to differentiate between integration in one moment and integration across time. But as Siegel (2012, p. 351) says, the brain's "capacity for abrupt shifts in state ... more clearly define the neural edges of time". Let us first look at some of those abrupt state transitions, and then at what synchronic integration might mean.

Integration of subpersonalities

The switch from one integrated state to another across time depends on new linkages forming between differentiated areas of neural circuitry (Siegel, 2012, p. 205). Emotion is fundamental to these shifts in states of mind, and of course to maintaining stuck patterns in the first place. In typical development, there are many selves whose expression depends on relationship context. Apart from the true and false selves of Winnicott and others (Winnicott, 1990; Rowan, 1998), there are selves corresponding to our different needs and relational states, such as survival-orientation or friendship, sexual, status-seeking, caring, intellectual, and soulful selves, and an infinity of others. These self-states correspond to what John Rowan calls subpersonalities (Rowan, 1990), or Mearns and Thorne (2000) call "configurations". They define a configuration as a "construct denoting a coherent pattern of feelings, thoughts and preferred behavioural responses symbolised or pre-symbolised by the person as reflective of a dimension of existence within the Self" (Mearns & Thorne, 2000, p. 102).

These distinctive self-states have specialised ways of processing information which may or may not work well together. Some of them conflict with each other and may hold quite different beliefs and values. Montaigne clearly knew about the deep divisions between subpersonalities when he wrote: "I may happen to contradict myself but, as Demades said, I never contradict truth". He goes on: "If my soul could only find a footing I would not be assaying myself but resolving myself" (1993, p. 908). Here we find Montaigne longing for the creativity that would enable him to integrate, implying that the best he could manage was to *attempt* it in his essays (from the French "essayer"). Subpersonalities are frequently found in pairs, and in fiction may be represented as character doubles, such as Jekyll and Hyde or Hermann Hesse's Sinclair and Demian or Narcissus and Goldmund. Such pairs represent Jung's law of opposites (Jung, 1986): for every characteristic that describes us, we also possess its opposite to the same degree. The resolution of conflicts between opposing self-states contributes to emotional resilience. This depends not on "unifying continuity, but [on] how the mind integrates a sense of coherence—of effective functioning—across self-states through time" (Siegel, 2012, p. 211).

Mearns and Thorne categorise conflicting configurations into "growthful" and "not for growth" types, which may speak in the voice of the true self and the socially-adaptive self respectively. Siegel (2012) has another explanation: he suggests that these "multiple self-states" may have arisen out of an experience of different, possibly conflicting, relationships to early attachment figures. While each self-state functions cohesively, there is an "inherent incompatibility of mental models, drives and modes of emotional regulation" across states (p. 348). As an adolescent, Brenda felt repeatedly humiliated by her parents. A number of years ago, she encountered somebody in an IT training group who literally screamed abuse at her, who twisted her every action and word into wrongdoing and blamed her for an incident she wasn't even aware of. Externally, she thinks she revealed little apart from the colour draining from her face; internally she fell apart. Returning to the group felt about as safe as entering the cage of a wounded lion. She left the group. The self-state that needed affiliation and acceptance from others was in direct opposition to the self-state that needed respect and safety.

Whatever the origins of the multiple states, there are frequent clashes between them and no amount of Gestalt chair-work will persuade one to give way to the other. Another perspective on working with them comes from Jung's theory of the transcendent function. He argued that the tension between these opposites within the personality cannot be resolved by choosing one over the other, or by compromise, but only by our unconscious transcendent function coming to our aid (Stevens, 1990). This may come in the form of a dream, in which we rise to another level at which the inner conflict becomes outdated because an underlying need has been met. In Brenda's case, the struggle between her rational, practical, egoic self—that was proud of her successful career in IT—conflicted with her dreamy, soulful self that was stifled by the job. The dreamer wanted to wander in the woods or lie on the couch and read novels. The career woman wanted to work, achieve, and be successful and respected. The two parts of her didn't acknowledge the existence of the other and they clicked in at different times. However, outside of Brenda's awareness, each subpersonality was competing to occupy more and more of Brenda's attention and time. As she became increasingly aware of this struggle between them, a decision had to be made; but she had no basis for making it. Her unconscious came to her rescue, not through a dream, but through her body giving way under the stress. Her sickness forced a resolution, and was sufficiently lengthy and unpleasant for the earlier struggle to seem irrelevant. Her mind calmed as her body sickened.

Greater flexibility and flow between self-states can be generated through psychotherapy. One borderline (with disorganised attachment) client's intense need for contact was balanced by an equal, split-off fear of contact. What made these states subpersonalities was that they were equipped with different needs and values, so that when stuck in one state, he was unable voluntarily to move into its opposite. He began to integrate these parts when he learned how to easily move back and forth between the two. Brenda, likewise, had contact and non-contact dimensions whose acute separation became clear in therapy. In her case, her contact-self communicated a superficial and socially-acceptable part of her identity. In therapy she connected with a place of greater depth which was so vulnerable she wasn't able or refused to speak. She would then become so embarrassed by her silence that she fell into one of her double-binds where speech and silence both felt dangerous because either would draw attention to her. On one occasion early in therapy, she remained in silence for the entire therapy hour before slinking out of the room. On another occasion, with a different therapist, she was able to speak about the pit she had dug for herself and was able to describe it as like the pit that held John the Baptist in the film *The Life of Brian*. She wasn't able to climb out of the hole, but managed to communicate from it. With such small advances, these two attachment types took baby steps towards integrating two fundamental subpersonalities on which depended their future relationships and therefore their developmental growth.

Synchronic integration

At a given time, we must integrate thinking (including current attention along with memories of past experiences linked to the same mental model), feelings, physiological processes, and behaviour. Examples of non-integrated states include a highly repressed person who is out of touch with their feelings and body sensations, or a hysterical individual who at certain times has difficulty utilising rational thought. In terms of neuroscience, both of these have top-down and left-right imbalances (see below). The consequences of such lack of connection can be envisaged by imagining Brenda in situations of threat and safety. When she senses the danger of being humiliated, her mind shuts down so she becomes unable to defend herself. In her everyday life her emotions are switched off so that she becomes undernourished and life seems meaningless; just a business of getting through her "to-do" list. So in non-threatening states, she is limited to mere survival; in threatening states, she cannot even manage that.

A state of mind is a pattern of activation of perceptual bias, emotional tone and regulation, memory processes, mental models, and behavioural responses (Siegel, 2012, p. 189). Siegel proposes that emotion coordinates states of mind mediated by convergence zones in the brain, such as the prefrontal cortex. His model suggests that states of mind behave according to the non-linear dynamics of complex systems, having the characteristics of: (1) self-organisation; (2) non-linearity; and (3) emergent patterns (ibid., pp. 195–202). (1) Certain patterns that become stable in specific contexts are called attractor states. States of mind are highly sensitive to external, particularly social, conditions. Our history determines the particular states of mind we easily fall into. Thus for Brenda, if she senses the slightest doubt in her partner about a plan of action, she is thrown into a state of despair where all her enthusiasm and motivation drain away. Early frustration of her relational libido is all too easily reactivated into this familiar attractor state of despair. (2) Non-linearity refers to how a small change in input leads to large and unpredictable changes in outcome. Psychotherapy could be perceived as the art of finding the kind of relational input that leads to the client getting out of the rut of engrained, restrictive, and rigid attractor states, "including bad habits, intrusive memories or isolation of information processing" (ibid., p. 200). I will return in the last chapter to the kind of input that jolts Brenda out of her isolated and inflexible patterns. (3) The organism develops repeating patterns of more specialised states, which may appear to restrict the system's flow. In reality, though, "such a differentiated system actually enables states of activation to achieve more complexity" (ibid., p. 202). This happens through differentiated elements interlinking with each other to increase complexity. This is what is meant by integration.

This attainment of maximum complexity depends on the balance between flexibility and continuity, or novelty and familiarity (Siegel,

2012, pp. 216–217). Avoidantly attached individuals have rigid states of mind where input from others is blocked. Because of their parents' lack of attunement they are intolerant of disequilibrium (ibid., p. 217); thus they have learned to rely on *self*-regulation of their emotions (p. 203). Such rigid patterns are mediated by disassociating the information processing of the right and left hemispheres (p. 217), which leads to the consequences discussed in earlier chapters. Connecting the right side of the brain to the left and developing right-hemisphere—to-right-hemisphere relating between therapist and client is, according to Allan Schore (2010), the only way in which attachment issues can be healed. Some of these right-hemisphere approaches include working creatively through visualisation, body therapy, artwork, drama, journal writing, or dream work.

Functional family systems are, according to Murray Bowen, charac-terised by both differentiation and connection between family members (Weeks & Treat, 2001; Nichols, 2013). We can understand this by exam-ining the communication patterns within the mother-child dyad (Siegel, 2012, p. 204). In avoidantly attached pairs, each member behaves as if the other wasn't heard. At the opposite end of the spectrum, ambiva-lent dyads are excessively well matched. Conversely, securely attached pairs fall in the middle, where they attune to each other but are also free to introduce independent responses: thus the secure base facilitates autonomy and creativity. Siegel proposes that "the midrange response in communicative contingency is the pattern allowing maximal com-plexity to be achieved" (ibid., p. 204). Insecure attachment damages one or other of these elements: the avoidantly attached person is differenti-ated but acts alone, while the ambivalently attached is over-sensitive to the other and in a state of undifferentiated clinging and fusion with them. Self-organisation does not just occur within a single individual, but is also a function of the interaction with other people (ibid., p. 206).

Neuroscience and integration

Cozolino's model

Cozolino (2010) argues for four pathways of integration in the affec-tive parts of the brain. Two of these, the left-right and top-down path-ways, depend on Allan Schore's hierarchical model of affect regulation in which the left cortex connects with the right, which in turn interacts with the subcortical (limbic) part of the brain, which in turn regulates body physiology via the autonomic nervous system (2003b, 2010). In a psychologically healthy individual, these connections run in both directions so that the right brain regulates the emotions, but body signals are also received by the brain which processes this information into awareness.

The right hemisphere is specialised for dealing with the whole in context rather than parts in abstraction and is also more connected with the body than the left (McGilchrist, 2009; Schore, 2010). Schore (2003b, 2010) has proposed that the right brain is the locus of the unconscious mind, and his model of affect regulation proposes that repression depends on top-down (cortex-subcortex-body) and left-right inhibition. Thus, becoming aware of their body process through Gendlin's focusing or Gestalt or other body psychotherapy exercises can assist the client to experience their feelings and access the unconscious (Carroll, 2005a; Afford, 2012). Brenda has come a long way in listening to the information coming from her body (gut feeling, shallow breathing, tight stomach etc.) and experiencing, expressing, and acting on her feelings.

Part of top-down integration depends on balancing activity in the subcortical and cortical parts of the brain, particularly the amygdala and orbitomedial prefrontal cortex (OMPFC) respectively. The amygdala mounts an immediate reflexive response to threat, including social stress, whereas the OMPFC updates information so that we can alter our behaviour beyond old conditioned reflexes. Thus Brenda picked up a terror of public speaking passively from her socially-reclusive parents and actively in response to her critical and annihilating family. However, she was able to overcome her panic attacks—over several years—by switching her attention from what she feared the audience were thinking about her (amygdala response) to the material of her IT presentation (thinking process engaged after finding that the audience were not in fact hostile or contemptuous). Interestingly, much of what is conceived as conscience-driven behaviour is in reality mediated by the amygdala. Guilt and shame lead us to make short-term reflexive choices to avoid pain, whereas a more mature ideal self with long-term goals is mediated by the prefrontal cortex (McGonigal, 2013).

Integration also occurs within the prefrontal cortex which is divided into four regions that engage in two pairs of coordinated activity: the orbital and medial areas together (OMPFC) and the dorsal and lateral zones together (DLPFC) (Cozolino, 2010). The OMPFC regulates emotional tasks in response to impulses, drives, and emotions, whereas the DLPFC controls cognitive functions according to "higher order rules" such as context and prediction. When these two loci are optimally balanced, we can achieve cognitive-emotional integration. This generates greater affect tolerance, ego strength, and resilience to stress.

A fourth major balancing act within the therapeutic process concerns the amygdala (in conjunction with the OMPFC) and hippocampus (along with the DLPFC). At moderate levels of arousal, the amygdala tags emotional experience so that the hippocampus knows what is important to learn, while the hippocampus aids in cognitive evaluation of situations and signals the amygdala to scale up or down its emotional reaction. At high levels of arousal, these two parts of the brain dissociate, so that visceral-emotional and declarative-conscious processing become disconnected. Brenda has spent a large part of her life in therapy bringing her reflex danger response under the control of her rational mind. I should emphasise that this was not possible during a panic attack or while experiencing intense anxiety. Rather, it is in the moments of calmness that she was able to think about how to avoid, defuse, or distract from terrifying situations. Taking better care of herself and living at a less stressful pace played a considerable part in calming her autonomic nervous system, so that she became more resilient to occasional stress.

Dorothea as an example of integration

In George Eliot's great novel *Middlemarch*, we see an example of left-right and top-down integration in the central character of Dorothea. Despite her "ardent nature", Dorothea is firmly ruled by her super-ego, for instance: "Riding was an indulgence that she allowed herself in spite of conscientious qualms; she felt that she enjoyed it in a pagan sensuous way, and always looked forward to renouncing it" (1997, p. 9). Because "all Dorothea's passion was transfused through a mind struggling towards an ideal life" (ibid., p. 40), she marries the desiccated pedant Mr. Casaubon in order to dedicate herself to helping him in what she believes is his great work. Many pages later, she has painfully withdrawn her projections about the greatness of his intellect (the work is limited and out-of-date) and his spirit (the malign and dishonouring codicil to his will). In the early and middle stages of the novel, Dorothea represses her own bodily (id) needs as described above–her left hemisphere controls her right, thereby keeping the body in its place as a servant of the will (see Carroll, 2005a, p. 26 for model for repression). Later, after Casaubon's death, she unexpectedly meets Will Ladislaw again, but mistakenly believes she has now lost him to Rosamond. Her defences crack in her dark night of the soul: "the limit of resistance was reached, and she had sunk back helpless within the clutch of inescapable anguish. ... 'Oh, I did love him!'", she moaned, as "waves of suffering shook her too thoroughly to leave any power of thought" (Eliot, 1997, p. 703). Her brain is finally listening to her body (her heart) and the right hemisphere overwhelms the left. Some further obstacles to fulfilment are overcome, but it is only the strength of her feeling and impulse that finally bring her and Will together. Dorothea ultimately reaches more of an equilibrium between the needs of others and her own needs (Gilligan's most mature stage of moral development—see Chapter Seven); between left-brain idealism and right-brain attention to her body to create a self that is now based on embodied lived experience as much as on ego ideals. Her previous top-down repression has been replaced by a two-way communication: brain to body and body to brain.

Siegel's model

Siegel (2012) has proposed a more extensive neuroscience model of integration, relying on "nine domains of integration" (p. 380). As well as bilateral, vertical, and memory integration, which equate to three of Cozolino's loci, he includes six additional axes of information and energy flow. These are: integration of consciousness, narrative, state, interpersonal, temporal, and transpirational integration. State and temporal integration have already been discussed in this chapter under synchronic and diachronic headings respectively, while narrative integration is the subject of Chapter Eight and interpersonal integration suffuses the entire book. Integration of consciousness refers to differentiation of objects of awareness and is related to the subject of Chapter Four. Finally, transpirational integration brings all the domains together and allows the individual to feel part of a greater whole—a movement into the transpersonal realm.

Synthesis vs. integration

Integration—in whatever model—means the bringing together of two or more separate parts of the self. If we take integration of the right and left hemispheres of the brain as an example, this implies that both sides of the brain are used when appropriate, and that the two hemispheres communicate with each other. The question is, do we inhabit the two sides alternately or simultaneously? And, as we shall see, is integration identical with synthesis? In McGilchrist's model (2009) we oscillate between the two sides: knowing and experiencing through the right hemisphere, then analysing with the left, and finally synthesising the two ways of knowing through the right (see Chapter Three). The Oxford theologian and psychologist Peter Hampson (in a lecture in NUI Maynooth, 22 April 2013) has put forward an alternative to this oscillatory process, inspired by the philosopher William Desmond's reflections on the nature of being (1995). Hegel transcended Kant's subject-object split by bringing together the components through a dialectical process into a greater subject-object unity. However, Desmond suggests, this dialectical synthesis fails to account for the complexity and depth of being because the other is *incorporated* into the self. Desmond proposes an alternative negotiation between opposites, what he calls the metaxological—the between space—which has affinities with the intersubjective space in psychotherapy. If we take males and females as an example of the two opposites, we can understand the difference between the dialectical and metaxological. In the former type of relating, the sexes orient towards each other because of a lack that can be filled by the other. Mark Grear Mann asserts that in metaxu, by contrast, "the between is selves given in otherness because of the overflowing, agapeic fullness of being" (www.bu.edu/). This is the basis for the plurality of between-states, the ground for what Desmond calls "agapeic astonishment". Such non-erotic love enables us to appreciate the sheer wonder of the other—and also, by reverse mirroring, of our own self. Hampson has proposed this metaxological between-state of being as an alternative to McGilchrist's oscillatory relationship between the two hemispheres of the brain. In Hampson's model of the between, there is no synthesis: we inhabit the two sides simultaneously in an interactive field. To come to the crucial point: this is what I take integration to mean, whether we are talking about left-right, top-down, front-back neurological models, or indeed a past-present temporal model. We don't simply alternate between the two states. Nor do we synthesise, to use an analogy, the distinct beings of red and white into some pink compromise. On the contrary, we live in a constant, simultaneous, multi-perspective *process* in which both (or all) are engaged in dynamic interaction and the distinctness of both aspects is honoured. This is true integration.

Integration and the usual measures of success in therapy

Some of the dominant themes we have explored concern balancing and integrating thinking and feeling, the whole with the part, and the conscious with the unconscious. After taking a break from therapy and later returning, it was clear that Brenda had regressed to some of her old patterns. As several chapters have shown, Brenda has a poor memory and is quite undernourished: she spends too much time in her left cortex, thinking and analysing: she still tries to solve her problems by thinking about them, and has a defensive stance in avoiding feelings and exposure to others. As a consequence, Brenda's creativity is quite blocked. Brenda's rigid and obsessive need to deal with one thing at a time—her horror of multitasking, her inability to take a whole view of her life—would be greatly assisted if she could allow her right brain to come to her aid. The main barrier to all forward movement for Brenda, as for many clients, is to face the feelings she is *avoiding*. Her therapist can help her through the relationship, through bringing her attention to her body, and by attending to her narrative—though, as the previous chapter showed, as much to its (affective and cathectical) style as to its content. Cozolino (2010) views storytelling as the path towards integration of neural networks. But while Siegel concurs, his more differentiated model proposes that narrative is not the sole integrative factor:

> the associational areas of the neocortex, such as the prefrontal regions (including the orbitofrontal cortex) that link various widely distributed representational processes together, are fundamental to narrative *and form dynamic global maps or complex representations* in order to establish a sensorimotor integration of the self *across space and time*.

> (Siegel, 2012, p. 371, italics added)

What Siegel seems to imply here is that therapy needs to work not with narrative alone but, at a deeper level, with the client's underlying and implicit maps and representations (e.g., of relationship dynamics): integration must therefore be synchronic as well as diachronic. In any case, as we have already seen, it is crucial that the storytelling take place in the context of an empathic, attuned relationship that is not just the container, but also the material for therapeutic work.

All forms of therapy have explicit or implicit goals, or at least wayside markers that light up when progress is being made. Some of the outcomes clients look for are relief of symptoms (amelioration of extreme feelings such as anxiety, sadness, pain, anger, poor self-esteem, or lack of confidence) alongside an improved capacity to engage in rewarding relationship with others. Therapists aim to foster catch-up of developmental deficits: this includes greater ability to self-regulate, followed by flexibility/trust in process, authenticity, aliveness, and expansion or growth. Freud modestly aimed to replace neurosis with ordinary unhappiness and to gain more regulation of the emotions: "where id was there ego shall be". Rogers (1967, pp. 115–123) enumerated the characteristics of the client who has successfully engaged in therapy as: being open to experience; trusting in their organism; having an internal locus of evaluation; and being open to process. Humanistic, Jungian, and transpersonal therapists all aim towards expansion of the self, using a variety of overlapping terms such as self-actualisation, individuation, or spiritual development. Whatever the therapy model and the stages along the way, the ultimate desire of the client is for greater well-being or happiness. How do such outcomes relate to the more abstract aims of integration? An integrated state is one in which there is free but coherent flow of information and energy between the different parts of the psyche and between the individual and their human and non-human environment. In this way, the individual is neither rigid nor chaotic, but flexible and regulated. This enables the person to engage with life with an outlook of trust and spontaneity. Rather than behaving defensively, they can explore and expand outwards and upwards. This must surely form the ground of well-being, which is the subject of the last chapter.

Summary

This chapter begins with a summary of Brenda's issues. It then moves on to describe integration within a given time and across time according to two different models. Daniel Siegel proposes that states of mind behave according to the non-linear dynamics of complex systems. Thus we are vulnerable to: (1) falling into patterns determined by our past history; but (2) small inputs can lead to large and unpredictable change; and (3) differentiation leads to emergent patterns of increased complexity, i.e. integration.

Taking a neuroscience model, integration is shown to comprise better communication between key elements of the nervous system such as better top-down interaction and improved communication between right and left hemispheres. Integration is linked to the client's and therapist's view of desirable outcomes of the therapeutic process.

CHAPTER TEN

Achieving well-being: play and spiritual practice as transformational hubs

Empty are the words of that philosopher who offers no therapy for human suffering.

—Epicurus, in Long & Sedley, 1987

Primary needs and transformation

Brenda is frustrated in her quest for happiness and well-being largely because, as a consequence of her avoidant/dismissing attachment, she lives too much in the narrow, arid, impersonal, unnourished, and sticky left hemisphere of the brain. In the last chapter we saw how complex systems are non-linear: a small input leads to a disproportionate effect. In Brenda's case, what kind of input could help her emerge from her rigid and frustrating states of mind? What we are looking for is, as it were, Brenda's psychic hub—more specifically, for what Bollas called a transformational object that would trigger this hub. According to him, mother is first experienced as a source of alteration in self states. This experience is retained unconsciously in the adult, "who relives it through his adamant quest for a transformational object: a new partner,

249

a different form of work, a new material acquisition, an ideology or a belief" (Bollas, 1979). Therapy would then be a matter of being attentive to the arising of early need states (whether manifesting as bodily or mental needs) so that they can be satisfied by the therapist (Hedges, 1994, p. 156). Transformational hubs are a way of reframing the inner maps and representations referred to in Chapter Nine. The experience of benign transformational objects results not just in change, but in the belief that change is possible, and thus in reorienting the psyche in a more positive direction.

Brenda's frustrations derive, as we have seen, from a mother who was unavailable for contact and relationship. This blocked her intrinsic desire to reach out to others, and also had knock-on effects with respect to developmental tasks that rely on attuned relationship: affect and energy regulation, self-formation, and resilience against environmental impingement. In all of these ways, she developed self-frustrating patterns that replicated the primal frustrating relationship. The outcomes of these patterns have been examined in previous chapters. Now I want to explore how change has come about for Brenda and what her prospects are for the future.

Underlying many of Brenda's issues—incomplete cathexis, boredom, addiction, over-focused attention, poor boundaries, and vulnerability to impingement—is her need for energy regulation: to be soothed when overcharged—anxious, or angry; or to be aroused when undercharged—withdrawn or depressed. Energy availability is a product of both charge and boundedness: the charge is triggered by stimulus and boundedness is the manifestation of regulation. Such affect regulation must first be provided from the outside—by mother or therapist—and then internalised so that self-regulation can be achieved (Schore, 2003a; Gerhardt, 2004). For Brenda, this would mean being able to access energy when needed and to calm herself when anxious or raging, and, crucially, to move with ease back and forth between the poles. Having lived in her youth with high levels of anxiety, culminating in a breakdown in her early thirties, she became very conscious of and fearful about overstimulation. In consequence she avoids stimulating situations and keeps her arousal level dampened down, almost depressed. In other words, Brenda responded to the bodily conflict between her high level of charge and her overboundedness by lowering her libido and excitement. Optimal regulation for her would involve decreasing her defensive boundedness. This overboundedness is the product of avoidant attachment, where the child was expected to be seen but not heard but where the parents did not provide the regulation that would have made this possible without accompanying neurosis. Thus, Brenda substituted her own muscular armouring for parentally-provided and later-internalised intra-psychic regulation. When reacting to stress or shock (e.g., an angry voice), the armoured individual has an amygdala response and experiences high levels of alarm despite not revealing it in their behaviour. In contrast, the regulated individual is immediately able to calm the reflexive amygdala response by means of the neocortex. This enables them to evaluate the alarm, and usually find that the situation is not life-threatening (Cozolino, 2010, p. 243). It is this slower flow of stimulus to the amygdala via the cerebral cortex that is deficient in Brenda and other insecurely attached individuals. Since her anxiety is largely social, her behaviourally-derived management of stimulus is achieved through avoidance of people. One could play devil's advocate and argue that Brenda's introversion and neuroticism are genetically determined. However, while genetic make-up does predispose some people to these personality traits (Plomin, DeFries, McClearn, & McGuffin, 2008, p. 243), the environment plays a crucial, though neglected, role in gene expression (Spector, 2012; McGowan et al., 2009; Zhang & Meaney, 2010), so there is no reason not to believe that Brenda can become more capable of self-regulation when exposed to social arousal.

A second and related focal issue for Brenda is the need to be seen, heard, and understood: in other words, a need for attunement. This is related to energy regulation because her particular sensitivity to misattunement makes her vulnerable to over-arousal of the sympathetic nervous system as described above. A previous four-year therapy relationship went a long way towards healing this particular deficit. However, a part of her ongoing tendency to avoid people and relationships is motivated by the desire to escape the dangers of misattunement and its accompanying dysregulation of the arousal of her autonomic nervous system. With friends she is often over-adapted to them, leading to exhaustion or boredom and frustration of her own libido. If misunderstood or judged, she can let rip her anger to a degree that is destructive of friendship. She is fearful of many people and feels vulnerable to humiliation and the rage and self-hatred this evokes. In formal work situations such as meetings, where feelings aren't allowed, she feels caught between the negative impact of both engagement and disengagement. When she becomes over-involved, she suffers from the speediness of trapped excitement (overcharged, overbounded) with the accompanying racing heart, red face, overheated body, shaking hands and voice, and acute social embarrassment. Conversely, if she restrains her enthusiasm in meetings, she spaces out, or becomes bored and frustrated when she fails to absent herself in this way. She is most comfortable with her partner but still often feels impinged upon.

Overall, a very large part of Brenda's attention is used in diplomatically avoiding exposure to people in order to manage her charge and emotions: she is using behavioural evasion as a substitute for intrapsychic regulation. Why then does she bother to connect with people outside of the bare minimum required for survival? The answer of course is that people matter deeply to her: it is because they matter that they are so difficult for her. She looks forward to escaping for long periods but becomes depressed and empty when alone. She has difficulty regulating her emotions, whether in response to the under-stimulus of being alone or the over-stimulus in company with others. When she hears that relationship and contact are central to therapeutic change, Brenda feels despair. She is comfortable with a learning-type relationship, such as one with a TCM practitioner who was a role model and spiritual mentor to her. Counselling relationships have, in contrast, tended to end up with the therapist sensitively respecting her boundaries so that the distance is maintained—not always productively—or, conversely, the therapist pursuing her for contact while she withdraws in alarm. With friends, she feels like the child who has to accept whatever the adults offer or require of her.

But one way she can be enticed out of her tower is by being thrown a toy: like a cat pouncing on a mouse pulled by a cord, Brenda will gleefully take chase. She looks back with love and delight on people who have played with her or whose lives are lived out through play. All playmates, whether aged six or sixty, are transformational objects for Brenda. The affectionate tease, the outrageous observation, eccentric innocence, and daring spontaneity—all hook her in. One artist friend's idea of packing—everything thrown into a towel and rolled up like a Swissroll—sent Brenda falling off her train seat with laughter as socks, knickers, banknotes, and paintbrushes fell to the floor while her friend searched for her passport at an international checkpoint. She adores her partner with his unselfconscious ways (the Stetson hats teamed with feminine pink scarves, the sugar-free chocolate bought in bulk in case he runs out, always in the front row at concerts, the back of his head as recognisable as his face), oblivious to the eccentric figure he creates; as one acquaintance said with a smile: "he's himself". Or to be taken by surprise: startled by the unmentioned present under the pillow, the cool wink across a crowded room, the cushion thrown as an invitation. The large man who teasingly wouldn't move out of the women's group but, unembarrassed, allowed two members to carry him away still seated on his chair, like a king on his throne. The visiting cat who strides past, "things to do" written over his body language, with a quick miaow in passing. All of these people (and the cat) model self-love and very cool, almost imperceptible contact: a delicate and unobtrusive dance into which Brenda is invited without announcement or pressure.

Play

Similarly, the elements of play are unselfconscious: spontaneity, surprise, the absence of planned outcome, doing things just to see what will happen. But experimentation or exploration may or may not be play: there must be a lightness of touch, an absence of expectation. Children have two developmental stages of play: solitary sensory exploration of objects and, later, symbolic social play where interpersonal dramas are enacted. It is the latter kind of play that kindles the light in Brenda—but only the pre-ego form of it, where competitiveness and power games have no part: just a delicate opening to contact where fun is the only agenda. Here, Brenda experiences not only the attuned entrainment that she missed as an infant, but also the play that, because of a lack of holding, is inhibited in the insecurely attached child. She is left with the freedom to be authentic, spontaneous, and creative; there is neither impingement nor demand, just an invitation which can be freely accepted or ignored. Here we have Yeats's prescription for happiness "when for everything inside us, there is a corresponding something outside us" (quoted in Wilbur, 1999, p. 134)—an acknowledgement, a meeting, a sharing of joy.

Evolutionary biologists note that play is costly and risky and that the most playful animals are those who are most intelligent and longer-lived (Konner, 2010, pp. 500–501). Play must therefore have a considerable selective advantage, which they believe is the development of adult skills and competencies, including social learning. The psychodramatist Kellermann (1992, p. 117) lists the functions of play as: learning social skills, mastering anxiety, satisfying needs vicariously, learning empathy, and tolerating waiting (turn-taking), as well as developing vocabulary and a variety of other skills. Dramatic symbolisation or make-believe play (Rayner, Joyce, Rose, Twman, & Clulow, 2005, pp. 115–118) kicks in at the age of two to three years and is used to create meaning from what would otherwise be experienced as a collection of random events. It depends on some capacity to generalise so that one thing—a stuffed toy—can stand for another—an animal in the zoo. The child must also have a rudimentary sense of being a separate self in order to pretend he is somebody other than himself—the zoo keeper. The ability to discriminate and generalise are what makes play possible, but what is its value to the child or adult? One is wish-fulfilment—playing at being stronger or more competent. A second, according to Angela Joyce, is about actively enacting what has been experienced only passively: being fed, being scolded, and being taught are turned into acts where the child himself feeds, scolds, or teaches. She claims that play is "a triumphant assertion of aliveness over deadness" or depression (ibid., p. 117). In this interpretation she points to our fundamental need to give and to do, not just receive.

Daniel Stern observed the play between mothers and three-month-old infants and found that the babies' response depended on optimal arousal: that is, intermediate between low stimulus—eliciting boredom and excessively high stimulus—provoking distress. He distinguished between satisfaction, where a need is being met, and joy, where satisfying calm alternates with a desired level of arousal (Konner, 2010, p. 505). This latter state of optimal arousal is the zone of play, so it is not surprising that Brenda, given her difficulty with energy regulation, so unhesitatingly throws middle-aged dignity to the wind when play is in the air.

For adults, the central function of play lies in fostering creativity, whether in work or in life. According to Winnicott (1991), it is only in playing that the child or adult is able to be creative, and it is only through creativity that we discover the self and that life is worth living. In therapy, play can provide a balanced perspective and hope, "a hand to those who feel bullied and overworked, and who may find themselves stifling below deck" (Nolan, 2012, p. 68). Nolan notes the range of ways of playing, which include teasing irony, daring, mock shock, fantasy challenge, mimicry, and seduction as defence. There are two fundamental psychodynamics going on here: teasing and fantasy, both of which are important to Brenda. Teasing includes an element of surprise, a kind of ambush in which some of one's least loved attributes may be laid bare, but wrapped in affectionate acceptance. If done with a light touch and without aggression, it draws Brenda into no-strings, non-threatening contact. Fantasy is an imaginative exploration of the unconscious realm and can be mediated verbally or through imagery, creative visualisation, artwork, or drama. Together, these two kinds of play draw Brenda out of her grim industry, her anxious avoidance or compensatory ego-driven conflicts, her Sisyphean chores, her sense of life as one damned thing after another.

The two thinkers who have contributed most to the use of play in therapy are Jacob Moreno and Carl Jung. Both had, unlike Freud, a positive view of the unconscious, seeing it not just as a sink for repressed memories and desires, but also as a source of wisdom and creativity. They and their followers use creative methods in their therapy practice: psychodrama in the case of Moreno, and active imagination, artwork, and sandplay in the case of the Jungian school.

Explicitly based on the dramatic enactments of childhood, socio-drama generates a collective story which reveals each individual's life experience and patterns of relating. It is the therapeutic equivalent of childhood play where all members of the group co-create a drama whose symbolic meaning may unfold only gradually over a long period (Carlson-Sabelli, Sabelli, & Hale, 1994). In psychodrama, on the other hand, there is a single protagonist and other members of the "cast" play the roles of other figures in her life or psyche. Psychodrama enables the protagonist to experience emotionally how things were and are or how things might be. It can return you to the sandpit and paddling pool of childhood, or it can be used to dramatise adult dynamics in the family or the workplace. Equally, it can be used to explore dreams or other intrapsychic material, such as struggles between subpersonalities. The protagonist can play him/herself, but can also ask another member of the group to play him, so that they can take the position of observer of the drama. Seeing their own behaviour laid out in front of them can shock the protagonist into embodied awareness. Brenda lives her life with hard-nosed realism, without delusion, wishful thinking, or the consolation of any form of "opium of the masses". For her, psychodrama is an enormous relief: it loosens all that grim adult responsibility; it breaks through rigidity and frustration; and yet it is not ungrounding or phoney because it stems from psychological truth. But the great shifting of Brenda's life burden comes from the realm of make-believe because, as Blatner (1996, p. 148) says about play, it is "a special frame of mind where actions don't generate ultimate consequences". In other words, Brenda can avoid the traps of real life for which she is so vigilant and thereby hold on to her freedom. In psychodrama she was given permission to be spontaneous, which according to Moreno is the best way to foster creativity (Blatner, 1996, p. 153).

Participating in a psychodrama group gives the individual the chance to play roles in other people's dramas and this, as much as being the protagonist themselves, can expand their role repertoire and lend creativity and flexibility to their interactions in "real" life. Playing the role of another builds the "internalising processes" of "imitation, mirroring, identification, modelling, introjection and assimilation" (Kellermann, 1992, p. 117). Brenda came from a background where only a very limited and unchanging version of self was considered acceptable and authentic and where her energy boundaries were far too tight: she took to psychodrama with relish, like a prisoner released from a cage. She played a wide range of roles—the carefree child, the attuned mother, the abusive man—the combination of which gave her energetic expansion, freedom, and power.

Moreno claimed that "roles do not emerge from the self, but the self can emerge from the roles" (quoted in Kellermann, 1992, p. 118), rather as Jung asserted that fictional characters can help create their author (Faust creating Goethe), or Sartre's proposition that "existence precedes essence". When we play a role initially, it has a provisional "as-if" quality; but if we play it often enough, we begin to identify with it and the role becomes incorporated into our sense of self. Thus when Brenda began her new career as literature lecturer, she was self-conscious and felt like a phoney, but with time, the job stopped being a role she was playing on stage and became incorporated into an expanded sense of who she really was: we become what we do, as neuroscience has verified.

Integration

To summarise, play—both in life and in therapy through psychodrama—has had the effect of pulling Brenda into relationship, providing her with mirroring and empathy, and developing her creativity and spontaneity. It has decreased her social anxiety, regulated her charge and boundedness, and exercised a major role in softening her rigid, controlling, and frustrating patterns. Play alone would not have been sufficient, and part of the change—acquiring the sense of existing through accurate mirroring—has come about with a deeply attuned one-to-one therapist. The sense of being valued has come to a large extent from the love of her partner.

In her twenties and thirties, her greatest terror used to be abandonment—though she was too proud to admit this to anyone. At that time in her life, she had no real friends and no intimacy with anyone, while her family was a source of attack rather than comfort. She believed—perhaps correctly—that she would literally go mad if her partner left her. Indeed, she experienced the edges of this on one occasion with a previous boyfriend when they had a row and the relationship appeared to have ended for about two days. For Brenda, madness meant falling into a void of no orientation where self evaporated. It was like floating around in outer space, with no direction and no feedback for who she was, so that in the absence of the atmospheric pressure provided by other people her self would actually explode in the vacuum. She found herself searching frantically for anything that would tell her that she existed, but was met with nothing but her own disintegration.

Her sense of self has strengthened enough that she no longer feels annihilated by the abandonment, anger, or dislike of another. Until recently, she could only envisage being the *victim* of contact, but she is learning the transformational lesson that she can take charge in relationships. She is discovering that she is better off if a friend drops her than if she always accedes to their wishes, that losing one friend is not losing all her friends. The price of Brenda's former autonomy was disconnection from society. In the absence of such supports, her own self became a problem for her. She is now learning how to reconnect from a place of authenticity, so that she no longer has to choose between self and other. In other words, she is moving from self-versus-the-world to self-in-the-world. She has grown quite tough in work situations where assertive negotiation is required. She has a continued desire for solitude that is, however, more a desire to make time for her own personal projects, which are increasingly satisfying, rather than a fleeing from people. Increasingly, she feels able to take the risk of being assertive in relationship.

Having a stronger sense of self protects her against that old terror of madness, but this would not be enough without open relationships with others. We go on having a lifelong need for what Kohut called mirroring self-objects (Lessem, 2005), and without intimate relationship Brenda knows she still wouldn't survive the death of her partner. She has made the monumental discovery that it is not holding on to friends that matters, but knowing how to *be* a friend, how to be in contact. She is learning how to be *open*! She feels strong enough now to reveal her vulnerability, and she knows that this is what warms her to other people. She trusts herself to recognise who it is safe to be open with, but also that if she makes a mistake she will not fall into self-loathing. In short, she is maturing into a tough old bird. What she needs at this stage is further slowing down, so that she can experience feelings through body sensations. She is finally taking on board that feelings are not dangerous and she will survive them. At this stage in her development, this just requires a shift in cognitive patterning. This way she is achieving the very things she needed but feared—more time, space, and silence, more digestion of her experiences, less overbounded armouring against them, more openness to others, more receptivity to the soul and to spiritual experience.

As she does just this, Brenda is occasionally surprised by joy—through the body rhythm of a swaying, bouncing walk that expresses all her strength, vitality, confidence, and good health; through the smell of an autumn breeze or the ozone off the sea, or the soporific hum of a wood pigeon in the calm of twilight.

To pursue what we love integrates the psyche. It channels the processes of perception and absorption, feeling, thought, and action into coherent patterns. Thus, the self that is inspired by meaning becomes an attractor for centripetal integration, and it is this that we will explore in the next section.

Meaning

It is the things that give meaning to our lives that constitute transformational objects for all of us. Meaning may be derived from a project invented to distract ourselves from grief or emptiness. But, as the philosopher Mark Vernon (2008, p. 32) points out, this sense of meaning is utilitarian and different from meaning that is inherent. Similarly, Irvin Yalom argued that "any compelling human activity can be so cathected that it serves as a caricature of meaning. [But] when the activity has no intrinsic goodness or rightness, then it sooner or later will fail the individual" (1980, p. 452). Sartre believed that we have to invent our own meaning in a world that has no inherent meaning, but existential therapists Yalom and Emmy Van Deurzen maintain that ideals and beliefs are always present, though they are often out of awareness (Dowds, 2003). Likewise, Vernon (2008) suggests that the activities that appear to provide meaning actually *reveal* meaning. Even the person taking his own life but leaving a suicide note is showing where meaning resides for him—in being understood or forgiven by the people he loves (Yalom, 1980). In *The Outsider* (Camus, 1983) Meursault's authenticity rests on his refusal to play the game of society, but even he has a source of meaning in his defiance: as he willingly goes to his execution, he hopes that the spectators will greet him with cries of hatred and thereby mirror his authenticity back to him. Even an outsider needs an other. Indeed, the most fundamental meaning for all of us is contact, even for those like Meursault taking themselves out of the world. Contact is fundamental in validating our sense of existing and, equally, it legitimates our life as worthwhile.

Meaning refers to what we live for and believe in: it represents our deepest values. In modernity, our quest for meaning is driven by our uprootedness from the earth and from community. We have lost touch with what matters. For our ancestors and for traditional tribal groupings, meaning comes from stewardship of the earth, maintaining tradition, and being part of a community and an ecosystem. In contrast, the isolated urban monad becomes the inevitably narcissistic focus for his or her life. But as Iris Murdoch said: "Man is not the measure of all things, we don't just invent our values, we live by a higher law, yet we can't fully explain how that is so" (Murdoch, 1998, p. 525). In this light, the individual is merely a surface manifestation of something whose roots are transpersonal and, perhaps, ultimately mystical. The question is, how do we discover the nature of that higher law, which is inherent, not arbitrarily invented according to the will or the ego? Meaning is inseparable from cathexis: the things that matter to us are charged. To the degree that I pursue the things I love and value, to that degree will my life have meaning and value.

Allport categorises people into six types according to their source of values and motivation: the theoretical (living to seek knowledge, insight, and truth); economic (orientation towards utility); the aesthetic; the social (love for others is the highest value); the political (interested in power); and the religious. Jacobsen (2005) points out that Allport makes no value judgement in his system, but it is clear that morally, and probably developmentally, there is a hierarchy here. We cannot view making money (economic type) or exercising power over others (political type) as morally equivalent to loving others (social type) or seeking spiritual fulfilment, as is argued by a range of moral philosophers (Neiman, 2008; Kleinberg-Levin, 2005; Vernon, 2008). Using Allport's classification, we can see that Brenda is primarily motivated by the theoretical, the aesthetic, and the religious. She has a strong drive towards exploration in the service of making connections and building understanding. This is most primally true for her in exploring paths across the land in the hills and woodlands of Ireland and elsewhere. Here she combines her love of nature, beauty, and exploring: the basis, for Berman (2000), of a non-theistic nomadic spirituality.

Van Deurzen-Smith suggests that each of our existential dimensions—the physical, social, psychological, and spiritual—is associated with its own meaning. On the physical dimension, we find meaning through a sense of efficacy; on the social through establishing values and relationships with others; and on the psychological through a sense of self-worth and identity (1997, pp. 100–101). But it is on the spiritual plane that we find ultimate meaning: through discovering our sense of purpose from our deepest strivings and most intimate longings (ibid., pp. 123–128). These qualities may be understood as a developmental sequence, and many theorists claim that later developmental stages cannot be accomplished until earlier steps have been completed (see Sugarman, 2001). However, in reality, for many of us, we develop in jigsaw fashion, taking some steps in spiritual development, for example, despite deficits at earlier stages. The parts of us lacking a firm footing may then be revisited repeatedly to build or re-build the foundations. Brenda's primary difficulties lay on the social and psychological dimensions, and therefore much of this book has been taken up with her frustrations and the progress she has made with relationships and self-formation. These blocks haven't stopped her from deriving meaning on the spiritual plane. However, she is aware that her draw to the spiritual has been partially motivated by the desire to escape from the pain of relationships and poor self-worth. Working through these issues may be essential for her further spiritual development.

Vernon cautions that "too instrumental an approach to well-being, as in the advice to go for flow, has an unfortunate side-effect: it nurtures self-centredness" (2008, p. 38). Meaning does not reside in narcissism, which may instead result in melancholia (p. 118). So we must allow meaning to emerge and reveal itself rather than patching something arbitrary together in the utilitarian hope that we will feel happier. Vernon concludes his treatise on well-being by saying that it is not about how you live, but about what you *love* (p. 103)—which, as we have seen, is a factor in integration. Love in relationships works best when it is not selfish or limited, but shared with others and focused outside the couple. But our deepest meaning is derived from the desire to inhabit more than the personal and egoic realm, from our longing for the transcendent. Vernon asserts that the "desire for what we lack, supremely so in the case of the transcendent, powers the drive to reach out. It is precisely this dimension of the human condition that allows us to love, that makes us lovers" (ibid., p. 122).

Brenda has behind her a lifetime of longing to transcend her small self and to merge with the natural world or the transpersonal realm, though she wouldn't presume to use that word. Until recent years that longing has been contaminated by a fear of the social world and a fleeing from the quotidian. Having made considerable strides in strengthening her ego and assembling a self, she can now breathe a sigh of relief. She feels safe in taking a break from the small self without fearing that she will develop an agoraphobic fear of returning to everyday engagement with others. Brenda is what Vernon calls a "religiously inclined agnostic" (Vernon, 2008, p. 123), and has difficulty accepting any theology or rigidly prescribed path, even that least theistic of traditions, Buddhism. She must find her own way, but it is not an entirely solipsistic path. Her partner and those of her friends engaged on the same quest for meaning share with her the landmarks along the way.

Vernon views love as the path to the good. However, Brenda associates such a striving for the good with all the old moralising restraints of her upbringing, which placed principles before the self, ideals before humanity. A view of pleasure as immoral was implicit in her mother's religiosity, and this must take some of the blame for Brenda's frustrations. Some of the good may indeed have transcended the self. But she has early personal experience of two distortions of the moral stance: one the ego-bound and the other the pre-ego. The dynamic is Victorian in its Dickensian polarity between active and passive types, authoritarian-patriarchal and meek and "suffering" feminine. The former, such as Brenda's elder brother, are over-attached to their self-perceived "goodness", triumphantly wrong-footing the other by their bullying self-righteousness and judgementalism. The latter, by contrast, have an undeveloped ego: Brenda's mother. Having grown up with such a model of—literally—self-lessness, Brenda has a vehement loathing of saints and martyrs. She sees the selfless as refusing the responsibility of being honestly present in the world. For Brenda, pursuit of the good is far too bound up with putting the other first and suppressing—and eventually killing—healthy libido. She sees nothing admirable or good for the world in being there for others when there is nobody there to be there. Those who attempt to be good simply by an absence of self bring back Brenda's frustrated rage at trying to making contact with a mother who was not there.

Brenda is with Nietzsche (see Sedgwick, 2009; Van Deurzen-Smith, 1997; Howard, 2000) in her visceral and exasperated repulsion towards Christian guilt and shame and the accompanying exaltation of the humble and meek. Mary Oliver's challenge ("Wild Geese", 1992) to Puritan self-abnegation might have been penned as an exhortation to her mother: you do not have to spend your life repenting for the "sin" of being human. Brenda snarls when her partner, whose family was a dog-eat-dog jungle, starts talking about the wonders of discovering moral philosophy. But what she is really rejecting so strongly is the anti-life stance, the massacre of the energies of the id—and, potentially, of all pleasure and passion—by the superego. She has deep ambivalence about Iris Murdoch (whose novels she teaches) and her Platonic concept of the good and is incapable of being rational about them. If she were, she would see that the pursuit of the good does not need to entail the suppression of self and its energies. But she has yet to get beyond the point where the entire might of her psychic immune system is mobilised against the word "good" and its attendant frustration and guilt. For the moment, we must accept that while meaning may not reside in selfishness, Brenda needs to experience the narrowness and fatigue of selfishness herself before she can go beyond it. She will not give up the self that she has fought so hard to build merely at the behest of another. When she does get sick of the small self, she will transcend it; but moral exhortation will simply cause her to dig her heels in—she will not tolerate anything that induces guilt.

Where she is going, with her most urgent and unstoppable drive, is towards freedom from her anxiety, frustration, guilt, and shame, and towards fearless expansion: like Mary Oliver ("The Journey", 1992) saving the only life she has it in her power to save. Until now, she has been driving with the brakes on, applied by her inner censors of fear and shame, and with a back-seat driver giving the orders—what Carl Rogers calls an external locus of evaluation. Having rejected Platonic perfectionism, she can begin to forgive herself for being human. Now she can enter wholeheartedly into the world with her authenticity grounded in her body's sensitivity and responsiveness. In choosing what to love she will apply neither to religion or moral ideals but to her body. She knows what *feels* good: a relaxation in muscular tension, a release and deepening in her breathing, a sense of softening, expansion, the brakes coming off. This is how she feels when held by an inspiring novel, when in nature, in the presence of beauty, of innocence, or the open heart. Or, as she sets off to explore a path over the mountains or an idea with a class, she feels a focusing and orientation for her energy that is balanced by the relaxation of joy—in smooth succession like the pulsing of the heart. She follows what she loves for her own selfish reasons, but the knock-on effects for all around her are incalculable. The softening of muscular armouring is leading to an openness to others and a compassion for them that is different from her previous overwhelmed and paralysing horror at the suffering of the world.

But how do we distinguish between the lower pleasures of overeating, drinking, malicious gossip, winning the match, and so on and the higher loves? The former hungers belong to the addictive id. However, as Reich and subsequent body psychotherapists and neuroscientists argue, the id does not have to be insatiable (Carroll, 2005a; Schore, 2003a). In the securely attached, our id hungers become self-regulated and enough is enough. But even in such relatively rare non-addictive people, the lower pleasures are empty of meaning. The higher loves yield long-term satisfaction and constitute part of an ongoing process of development. But sometimes a higher love, whether spiritual development or the love of the earth or of other people, can become infected or taken over by destructive parts of the self. Vigilance is required to prevent loving turning into a chore of the superego or a demand of the competitive ego. Genuine loving transcends the id, ego, and superego, and is not controlled by any of them. It brings peace, joy, and sometimes pain, but not the unquenchable demand, shame, guilt, resentment, or the competitive urge to outdo the other. With love there is no ulterior motive: it is sufficient onto itself.

Brenda, with Nietzsche in this, is highly reactive to the hypocrisy and phoniness of what so often passes for "goodness" because of the dampening effect it has on libido. But libido alone is not sufficient for meaning. On its own, the unregulated id can degenerate into addiction. Nietzsche made development of authenticity, freedom, and inner power—the creation of the *Übermensch* (the "over man" who had overcome himself, i.e., his moral conditioning)—the cornerstone of his philosophy. But Brenda already intuits that this is not enough, that a world centred round herself feels narrow, pointless, sickening, and boring—in fact the opposite of meaningful. Meaning requires not just gratification but contact: interest in and exchange with the rich and complex world about her. And moving beyond self-sick narcissism and its frustrations is a matter of giving as much as receiving. It is this contact with the world that can transmute addictive pleasure into satisfying well-being. We need to back the self and be authentic (internal locus of evaluation), but also to go beyond it, to transcend (towards an external locus of worship). This well-being that extends beyond the self (self-in-the-world) must be counterbalanced by appropriate retreat into the self-alone. Contact and withdrawal are the two poles of the dialectic of life.

Brenda is beginning to know that it is the target and the quality of *attention*—attention to what we love—that matter most in the process of our lives. She feels drawn to a spiritual practice, but in a particular way. John Cottingham (2003) maintains that what is central in religion and spirituality is not the beliefs or doctrines, which he acknowledges are impossible for many people to espouse, but the spiritual practices, whether of meditation, prayer, or self-purification. Brenda, of all people, cannot go along with what St Paul called the "circumcision of the mind" (ibid., p. 89), the restriction in the freedom to pursue her own truth that has been central to the established religions. She also suspects that Buddhist practice may be too ascetic and life-denying for her needs. Cottingham suggests that the elements of a spiritual praxis that provide meaning are: viewing life as a precious gift; taking responsibility as a moral agent; adopting traditions and rituals of worship; and loving of a self-giving kind (ibid., pp. 90–91). When we observe rites of passage and rhythms of living through collective and aware gratitude, this will persistently remind us of both the gifts and the responsibilities of life. As philosophers, psychotherapists, and neuroscientists have shown, we become what we do. Through the *act* of authentic worship, which engages our love, we become lovers and reach out towards the world, reconnect with life.

Summary

Brenda's central needs are for energy regulation and attunement. Her transformational hubs—constituted by the small inputs that have led to large and unpredictable change—have been play and attention to what is meaningful for her. This chapter asks, first, what constitutes play and examines its role for children and adults; for Brenda, it is about fun, creativity, and spontaneity. The theory and practice of play in therapy is viewed particularly through the lens of psychodrama. The second part of the chapter shows that pursuing meaning leads to well-being and psychic integration. Meaning must be revealed not constructed, and arises from immersion in what we love. We look at different levels of meaning and the centrality of love to meaning. The lower pleasures are distinguished from the higher loves. Brenda, with Nietzsche, loathes the hypocrisy and phoniness of what passes for goodness; yet, she is what Mark Vernon has called a "religiously inclined agnostic". What might be involved in such a path is explored with the help of John Cottingham's argument that what is central to religion is spiritual practices, not beliefs and doctrines. The book concludes by stressing that we become what we do: by attending to what we love, we become lovers of life.

REFERENCES

Abram, D. (1997). *The Spell of the Sensuous: Perception and Language in a More-Than-Human World*. New York: Vintage.

Afford, P. (2012). Engaging the body changes the brain. *Eisteach*, 12 (2): 8–12.

Allen, B. (1992). *Mad White Giant: A Journey to the Heart of the Amazon Jungle*. London: Flamingo.

Allport, G. (1961). *Pattern and Growth in Personality*. New York: Holt, Rinehart and Winston.

Andre, J., Foglio, J., & Brody, H. (2000). Moral growth, spirituality, and activism: the humanities in medical education. In: D. Wear & J. Bickel (Eds.), *Educating for Professionalism: Creating a culture of Humanism in Medical Education* (pp. 81–94). Iowa City: University of Iowa Press.

Armstrong, K. (2009). *The Case for God: What Religion Really Means*. London: Bodley Head.

Auster, P. (1990). *The New York Trilogy*. New York: Penguin.

Baggini, J. (2011). *The Ego Trick: What Does it Mean to Be You?* London: Granta.

Bakewell, S. (2010). *How to Live: A Life of Montaigne in One Question and Twenty Attempts at an Answer*. London: Chatto and Windus.

Banks, L. R. (1998). *Fair Exchange*. London: Piatkus.

266

Barrows, A. (1995). The ecopsychology of child development. In: T. Roszak, M. Gomes, & A. Kanner (Eds.), *Ecopsychology: Restoring the Earth, Healing the Mind* (pp. 101–110). San Francisco: Sierra Club Books.

Bate, J. (2001). *The Song of the Earth*. London: Picador.

Becker, E. (1973). *The Denial of Death*. New York: Free Press.

Beckett, S. (1979). *The Beckett Trilogy: Molloy, Malone Dies, The Unnamable*. London: Picador.

Benjamin, J. (1990). *The Bonds of Love: Psychoanalysis, Feminism, and the Problem of Domination*. London: Virago.

Berman, M. (1984). *The Reenchantment of the World*. Toronto: Bantam.

Berman, M. (1990). *Coming to Our Senses: Body and Spirit in the Hidden History of the West*. London: Unwin.

Berman, M. (2000). *Wandering God: A Study in Nomadic Spirituality*. Albany, NY: SUNY.

Bienenfeld, D. (2006). *Psychodynamic Theory for Clinicians*. Philadelphia: Lippincott Williams & Wilkins.

Blackstone, J. (2012). *Belonging Here: A Guide for the Spiritually Sensitive Person*. Boulder, CO: Sounds True.

Blatner, A. (1996). *Acting-In: Practical Applications of Psychodramatic Methods* (3rd edn). New York: Springer Publishing Company.

Boadella, D. (1987). *Lifestreams: An Introduction to Biosynthesis*. London: Routledge & Kegan Paul.

Bollas, C. (1979). The transformational object. *International Journal of Psychoanalysis, 60* (1): 97–107.

Boorstein, S. (1997). *Clinical Studies in Transpersonal Psychotherapy*. Albany, NY: SUNY.

Borges, J. L. (1972). *A Personal Anthology*. London: Picador.

Bowie, M. (1991). *Lacan*. London: Fontana.

Bowlby, J. (1971). *Attachment and Loss, Volume 1: Attachment*. Harmondsworth, UK: Pelican.

Bowlby, J. (1973). *Attachment and Loss, Volume 2: Separation*. New York: Basic Books.

Bowlby, J. (1988). *A Secure Base: Clinical Applications of Attachment Theory*. London: Routledge.

Brach, T. (2000). *Radical Self-Acceptance* (Audio CD). Boulder, CO: Sounds True.

Brach, T. (2003). *Radical Acceptance: Embracing Your Life with the Heart of a Buddha*. New York: Bantam.

Brach, T. (2009). *Meditations for Emotional Healing: Finding Freedom in the Face of Difficulty* (Audio CD). Boulder, CO: Sounds True.

Brazier, D. (2009). *Love and its Disappointment: The Meaning of Life, Therapy and Art*. Winchester, UK: O-Books.

Burr, V., & Butt, T. (2003). Psychological distress and postmodern thought. In: Y. Bates & R. House (Eds.), *Ethically Challenged Professions: Enabling Innovation and Diversity in Psychotherapy and Counselling* (pp. 75–93). Ross-on-Wye, UK: PCCS Books.

Calhoun, J. B. (1962). Population density and social pathology. *Scientific American, 206* (2): 139–148.

Camus, A. (1962). *Exile and the Kingdom.* J. O'Brien (Trans.). London: Penguin.

Camus, A. (1975). *The Myth of Sisyphus.* J. O'Brien (Trans.). Harmondsworth, UK: Penguin.

Camus, A. (1983). *The Outsider.* J. Laredo (Trans.). London: Penguin.

Caplan, M. (2001). *The Way of Failure: Winning Through Losing.* Prescott, AZ: Hohm Press.

Carlson-Sabelli, L., Sabelli, H., & Hale, A. (1994). Sociometry and socio-dynamics. In: P. Holmes, M. Karp, & M. Watson (Eds.), *Psychodrama Since Moreno: Innovations in Theory and Practice* (pp. 147–185). London: Routledge.

Carroll, R. (2005a). Neuroscience and the 'law of the self': the autonomic nervous system updated, re-mapped and in relationship. In: N. Totton (Ed.), *New Dimensions in Body Psychotherapy* (pp. 13–29). Maidenhead, UK: Open University Press.

Carroll, R. (2005b). Rhythm, reorientation, reversal: deep reorganization of the self in psychotherapy. In: J. Ryan (Ed.), *How Does Psychotherapy Work?* (pp. 85–112). London: Karnac.

Carter, R. (2009). *The Brain Book: an Illustrated Guide to its Structure, Function and Disorders.* London: Dorling Kindersley.

Chatwin, B. (1988). *The Songlines.* London: Picador.

Clarkson, P. (1989). *Gestalt Counselling in Action.* London: SAGE.

Conley, D. (2004). *The Pecking Order: Which Siblings Succeed and Why.* New York: Pantheon.

Cooper, M. (2008). *Essential Research Findings in Counselling and Psychotherapy: the Facts are Friendly.* London: SAGE.

Cooper, M., & Adams, M. (2005). Death. In: E. Van Deurzen & C. Arnold-Baker (Eds.), *Existential Perspectives on Human Issues* (pp. 78–85). Houndmills, UK: Palgrave Macmillan.

Cortright, B. (1997). *Psychotherapy and Spirit: Theory and practice in transpersonal psychotherapy.* Albany, NY: SUNY.

Cottingham, J. (2003). *On the Meaning of Life.* London: Routledge.

Cottingham, J. (2012). C. Stephen Evans, Natural Signs and Knowledge of God, and Paul Moser, The Evidence for God: a review. *Times Literary Supplement*, 27 January, pp. 28–29. Available at: www.the-tls.co.uk/tls/.

Coyne, J. C. (Ed.) (1985). *Essential Papers on Depression*. New York: New York University Press.

Cozolino, L. (2010). *The Neuroscience of Psychotherapy: Healing the Social Brain* (2nd edn). New York: W. W. Norton.

Critchley, S. (1997). *Very Little … Almost Nothing: Death, Philosophy, Literature*. London: Routledge.

Crown, S. (2012). A Life in Writing: Tim Parks. *Guardian*, 28 July. Available at: www.guardian.co.uk.

Deacon, T. (1997). *The Symbolic Species: The Co-Evolution of Language and the Human Brain*. London: Penguin.

Deatherage, O. (1996). Mindfulness meditation as psychotherapy. In: S. Boorstein (Ed.), *Transpersonal Psychotherapy* (2nd edn). Albany, NY: SUNY.

Desai, K., & Desai, A. (2011). In conversation: Kiran Desai meets Anita Desai. *Guardian*, 12 November, Review, p. 12. Available at: www.guardian.co.uk.

Desmond, W. (1995). *Being and Between*. Albany, NY: SUNY.

De Waal, F. (2005). *Our Inner Ape*. London: Granta.

Dillon, B. (2005). *In the Dark Room: A Journey in Memory*. London: Penguin.

Donoghue, E. (2011). *Room*. London: Picador.

Dowds, B. (2003). Working existentially with the inescapable. *The British Journal of Psychodrama, 18* (1): 3–22.

Dowds, B. (2008). The chameleon self: over-adaptation and the death of feeling. *Eisteach, 8* (4): 9–14.

Dowds, B. (2010). The evolution of human consciousness and spirituality. *Inside Out, 61*: 20–29.

Dowds, B. (2011). Are we mature enough for shame?—learning from the economic crisis. *Eisteach, 11* (1): 23–26.

Eigen, M. (1986). *The Psychotic Core*. Northvale, NJ: Jason Aronson.

Eliot, G. (1997). *Middlemarch*. London: Everyman.

Eliot, T. S. (1974). *Collected Poems 1909–1962*. London: Faber and Faber.

Elliott, A. (2002). *Psychoanalytic Theory: An introduction* (2nd edn). Durham: Duke University Press.

Faulkner, W. (2009). *As I Lay Dying*. New York: W. W. Norton.

Faulkner, W. (2012). *The Sound and the Fury*. New York: Random House.

Feltham, C. (2012). *Failure*. Durham, UK: Acumen.

Finlayson, J. G. (2005). *Habermas: A Very Short Introduction*. Oxford: Oxford University Press.

Fisher, A. (2002). *Radical Ecopsychology: Psychology in the Service of Life*. Albany, NY: SUNY.

Fogarty, T. F. (1979). The distancer and the pursuer. *The Family, 7* (1): 11–16.

Foley, M. (2011). *The Age of Absurdity: Why Modern Life Makes it Hard to be Happy*. London: Simon & Schuster.

Frankel, R. (1998). *The Adolescent Psyche: Jungian and Winnicottian Perspectives*. Hove, UK: Brunner-Routledge.

Frazer, J. G. (1963). *The Golden Bough: A Study in Magic and Religion*. New York: Macmillan.

Frosh, S. (1991). *Identity Crisis: Modernity, Psychoanalysis and the Self*. London: Macmillan.

Gerhardt, S. (2004). *Why Love Matters: How Affection Shapes a Baby's Brain*. Hove, UK: Brunner-Routledge.

Gerhardt, S. (2011). *The Selfish Society*. London: Simon & Schuster.

Gilligan, C. (1993). *In a Different Voice: Psychological Theory and Women's Development*. Cambridge, Mass.: Harvard University Press.

Gomez, L. (1997). *An Introduction to Object Relations*. London: Free Association Books.

Gray, J. (2002). *Straw Dogs*. London: Granta.

Grof, S. (1985). *Beyond the Brain: Birth, Death and Transcendence in Psychotherapy*. Albany, NY: SUNY.

Guignon, C. (2004). *On Being Authentic*. London: Routledge.

Guntrip, H. (1992). *Schizoid Phenomena, Object Relations and the Self*. London: Karnac.

Hall, M. (1981). *The Bowen Family Theory and its Uses*. Northvale, NJ: Jason Aronson.

Hamburger, M. (1969). *The Truth of Poetry*. Harmondsworth, UK: Pelican.

Hardy, T. (2001). *The Complete Poems*. Houndmills, UK: Palgrave Macmillan.

Hart, S. (2008). *Brain, Attachment, Personality: An Introduction to Neuroaffective Development*. London: Karnac.

Hay, D. (2006). *Something There: the Biology of the Human Spirit*. London: Darton, Longman and Todd.

Hedges, L. (1994). *Working the Organizing Experience: Transforming Psychotic, Schizoid, and Autistic States*. Northvale, NJ: Jason Aronson.

Hoffman, E. (2009). *Time*. London: Profile Books.

Hollis, J. (1993). *The Middle Passage: From Misery to Meaning in Midlife*. Toronto: Inner City Books.

Holmes, J. (1993). *John Bowlby and Attachment Theory*. London: Routledge.

Holmes, J. (2010). *Exploring In Security: Towards an Attachment-Informed Psychoanalytic Psychotherapy*. London: Routledge.

Howard, A. (2000). *Philosophy for Counselling and Psychotherapy: Pythagoras to Postmodernism*. Houndmills, UK: Palgrave Macmillan.

Howe, D. (2011). *Attachment Across the Lifecourse*. Houndmills, UK: Palgrave Macmillan.

Hughes, L. (1994). *Collected Poems* (Eds., A. Rampersad & D. Roessel). New York: Random House.

Hustvedt, S. (2010). *The Shaking Woman or A History of My Nerves*. London: Sceptre.

Ibsen, H. (1994). *Peer Gynt* (Trans. M. Meyer). London: Methuen Drama.

Ignatieff, M. (2012). The man who shaped history: review of The International Human Rights Movement: a history by Aryeh Neier. *New York Review of Books*, 11 October. Available at: www.nybooks.com.

Jacobsen, B. (2005). Values and beliefs. In: E. Van Deurzen & C. Arnold-Baker (Eds.), *Existential Perspectives on Human Issues*. Houndmills, UK: Palgrave Macmillan.

Jacobson, H. (2011). They may be criminals, but we're the ones who have created them. *Independent*, 13 August. Available at: www.independent.co.uk.

James, O. (2008). *The Selfish Capitalist*. London: Vermilion.

Johnston, C. M. (1991). *Necessary Wisdom: Meeting the Challenge of a New Cultural Maturity*. Seattle: ICD Press.

Jong, E. (1973). *Fear of Flying*. New York: Holt, Rinehart and Winston.

Jonsson, S. (2000). *Subject Without Nation: Robert Musil and the History of Modern Identity*. Durham and London: Duke University Press.

Joyce, J. (1968). *Ulysses*. Harmondsworth, UK: Penguin.

Jung, C. G. (1983). *Memories, Dreams and Reflections*. London: Flamingo.

Jung, C. G. (1986). *Psychological Reflections: An Anthology of His Writings 1905–1961* (Ed., J. Jacobi). London: ARK.

Kafka, F. (1978). *Wedding Preparations in the Country and Other Stories* (Trans. W. & E. Muir). London: Penguin.

Kavanagh, P. (1996). *Selected Poems* (Ed., A. Quinn). London: Penguin.

Kegan, R. (1982). *The Evolving Self: Problem and Process in Human Development*. Cambridge, MA: Harvard University Press.

Keleman, S. (1981). The foundations of emotional biology. *The Journal of Somatic Experience* 4 (1): 8–21.

Kellermann, P. (1992). *Focus on Psychodrama: The Therapeutic Aspects of Psychodrama*. London: Jessica Kingsley.

Kern, S. (2011). *The Modernist Novel: A Critical Introduction*. Cambridge, UK: Cambridge University Press.

Kleinberg-Levin, D. M. (2005). *Gestures of Ethical Life: Reading Hölderlin's Question of Measure after Heidegger*. Stanford, CA: Stanford University Press.

Konner, M. (2010). *The Evolution of Childhood*. Cambridge, MA: Belknap Press.

Kornfield, J. (1994). *A Path with Heart*. London: Random House.

Krznaric, R. (2012). Stop the clock! In: *Making the Most of Your Time* (pp. 5–7). Guide published by the Guardian in association with The School of Life. Available at: www.guardian.co.uk/make-time.

Labanyi, P. (2008). The emotional costs of globalization. *Eisteach, 8* (4): 26–29.

Lally, C. (2012). Crime Statistics Ireland. *Irish Times*, 18 August, Weekend Review pp. 1–2. Available at: www.irishtimes.com.

Leader, D. (2002). *Stealing the Mona Lisa: When Art Stops Us From Seeing*. London: Faber.

Leader, D. (2008). *The New Black: Mourning, Melancholia and Depression*. London: Penguin.

Lee, H. (2012). Portrait of a novel: Henry James and the making of an American masterpiece by Michael Gorra—review. *Guardian*, 8 September, Review, p. 9. Available at: www.guardian.co.uk.

Lessem, P. A. (2005). *Self Psychology*. Lanham, MD: Jason Aronson.

Levin, D. M. (1988). *The Opening of Vision: Nihilism and the Postmodern Situation*. New York: Routledge.

Long, A. A., & Sedley, D. N. (1987). *The Hellenistic Philosophers (Volume 1): Translations of the Principle Sources, with Philosophical Commentary*. Cambridge, UK: Cambridge University Press.

Lourenco, S. F., Longo, M. R., & Pathman, T. (2011). Near space and its relation to claustrophobic fear. *Cognition, 119*: 448–453.

Macy, J., & Brown, M. Y. (1998). *Coming Back to Life: Practices to Reconnect Our Lives, Our World*. Canada: New Society Publishers.

Maitland, S. (2008). *A Book of Silence*. London: Granta.

Mann, T. (1960). *The Magic Mountain* (Trans. H. T. Lowe-Porter). London: Penguin.

Mann, T. (1998). *Death in Venice and Other Stories* (Trans. D. Luke). London: Vintage.

Maslow, A. (1970). *Motivation and Personality* (3rd edn). New York: Harper Collins.

McAdams, D. P. (1997). *Stories We Live By: Personal Myths and the Making of the Self*. New York: Guilford Press.

McGilchrist, I. (2009). *The Master and His Emissary: The Divided Brain and the Making of the Western World*. New Haven: Yale University Press.

McGonigal, K. (2013). The neurobiology of willpower. New Brain Science Teleseminar series, *The National Institute for the Clinical Application of Behavioural Medicine*, 30 January. Available at: www.nicabm.com.

McGowan, P., Sasaki, A., D'Alessio, A., Dymov, S., Labonte, B., Szyf, M., Turecki, G., & Meaney, M. (2009). Epigenetic regulation of the glucocorticoid receptor in human brain associates with childhood abuse. *Nature Neuroscience, 12* (3): 342–348.

Mearns, D., & Cooper, M. (2005). *Working at Relational Depth in Counselling and Psychotherapy*. London: SAGE.

Mearns, D., & Thorne, B. (2000). *Person Centred Therapy Today: New Frontiers in Theory and Practice*. London: SAGE.

Miller, G. (2007). A surprising connection between memory and imagination. *Science, 315* (5810): 312.

Montaigne, M. de (1993). *The Complete Essays* (Trans. M. A. Screech). London: Penguin Classics.

Moore, T. (1992). *Care of the Soul: How to Add Depth and Meaning to Your Everyday Life*. London: Piatkus.

Moreno, J. (1987). *The Essential Moreno* (Ed., J. Fox). New York: Springer.

Murdoch, I. (1998). *Existentialists and Mystics: Writings on Philosophy and Literature*. New York: Allen Lane.

Musil, R. (1995). *The Man Without Qualities* (Trans. S. Wilkins). London: Picador.

Needleman, J. (2009). *What is God?* New York: Penguin.

Neiman, S. (2008). *Moral Clarity: A Guide for Grown-up Idealists*. Orlando, FL: Harcourt.

Nichols, M. (2013). *Family Therapy: Concepts and Methods* (10th edn). Boston, MA: Pearson.

Nolan, P. (2012). *Therapist and Client: A Relational Approach to Psychotherapy*. Chichester, UK: Wiley-Blackwell.

O'Donohue, J. (2003). *Divine Beauty: The Invisible Embrace*. London: Bantam.

Ogden, P., Minton, K. and Pain, C. (2006). *Trauma and the Body: a Sensorimotor Approach to Psychotherapy*. New York: W. W. Norton.

Oliver, M. (1992). *New and Selected Poems*. Boston, MA: Beacon Press.

Panksepp, J. (2006). The core emotional systems of the mammalian brain: the fundamental substrates of human emotions. In: J. Corrigall, H. Payne, & H. Wilkinson (Eds.), *About a Body: Working with the Embodied Mind in Psychotherapy* (pp. 14–32). Hove, UK: Routledge.

Pearmain, R. (2001). *The Heart of Listening: Attentional Qualities in Psychotherapy*. London: Continuum.

Perls, F. (1969). *Gestalt Therapy Verbatim*. New York: Bantam Books.

Perls, F., Hefferline, R., & Goodman, P. (1972). *Gestalt Therapy: Excitement and Growth in the Human Personality*. London: Souvenir Press.

Pink, D. (2011). *Drive: The Surprising Truth About What Motivates Us*. Edinburgh: Canongate Books.

Plath, S. (1965). *Ariel*. London: Faber & Faber.

Plomin, R., DeFries, J. C., McClearn, G. E., & McGuffin, P. (2008). *Behavioural Genetics* (5th edn). New York: Worth.

Pollard, J. (2005). The value of attachment theory in understanding how psychotherapy works. In: J. Ryan (Ed.), *How Does Psychotherapy Work?* (pp. 187–211). London: Karnac.

Polster, E., & Polster, M. (1974). *Gestalt Therapy Integrated*. New York: Vintage.

Proust, M. (1996). *In Search of Lost Time, Vol VI: Time Regained* (Trans. A. Mayor and T. Kilmartin). London: Vintage.

Proust, M. (2003). *In Search of Lost Time, Vol I: The Way by Swann's* (Trans. L. Davis). London: Penguin.

Ramsden, E., & Adams, J. (2009). Escaping the laboratory: the rodent experiments of John B. Calhoun and their cultural influence. *Journal of Social History, 42* (3): 761–192.

Rayner, E., Joyce, A., Rose, J., Twyman, M., & Clulow, C. (2005). *Human Development: An introduction to the Psychodynamics of Growth, Maturity and Ageing* (4th edn). London: Routledge.

Rilke, R. M. (1964). *Selected Poems* (Trans. J. B. Leishman). Harmondsworth, UK: Penguin.

Rogers, C. (1967). *On Becoming a Person: A Therapist's View of Psychotherapy*. London: Constable.

Roszak, T. (1993). *The Voice of the Earth: An Exploration of Ecopsychology*. New York: Touchstone.

Rowan, J. (1990). *Subpersonalities*. London: Routledge.

Rowan, J. (1998). *The Reality Game: A guide to Humanistic Counselling and Psychotherapy* (2nd edn). New York: Routledge.

Rowlands, M. (2008). *Fame*. Stocksfield, UK: Acumen.

Rowson, M. (2011). Cartoon. *Guardian*, 13 August, p. 39. Available at: www.guardian.co.uk.

Rustin, M., & Rustin, M. (2009). States of narcissism. In: E. McGinley & A. Varchevker (Eds.), *Mourning, Depression, and Narcissism through the Life Cycle* (pp. 209–234). London: Karnac.

Sabor, R. (1989). *The Real Wagner*. London: Sphere Books.

Sartre, J. P. (1948). *Existentialism and Humanism* (Trans. P. Mairet). London: Methuen.

Sartre, J. P. (1957). *Being and Nothingness* (Trans. H. Barnes). London: Methuen.

Satir, V. (1978). *Peoplemaking*. London: Souvenir Press.

Schore, A. (2003a). *Affect Dysregulation and Disorders of the Self*. New York: W. W. Norton.

Schore, A. (2003b). *Affect Regulation and the Repair of the Self*. New York: W. W. Norton.

Schore, A. (2010). The right brain implicit self: a central mechanism of the psychotherapy change process. In: J. Petrucelli (Ed.), *Knowing, Not-Knowing and Sort-of-Knowing: Psychoanalysis and the Experience of Uncertainty* (pp. 177–202). London: Karnac.

Searles, H. (1960). *The Nonhuman Environment in Normal Development and in Schizophrenia*. New York: International Universities Press.

Sedgwick, P. (2009). *Nietzsche: the Key Concepts*. London: Routledge.

Seligman, M. (2011). *Flourish: a New Understanding of Happiness and Well-Being and How to Achieve Them*. London: Nicholas Brealey.

Sheldrake, N. (1995). *Seven Experiments That Could Change the World*. 1: Fourth Estate.

Shriver, L. (2003). *We Need to Talk About Kevin*. London: Serpent's Tail.

Siegel, D. (2012). *The Developing Mind: How relationships and the Brain Interact to Shape Who We Are*. (2nd edn). New York: Guilford Press.

Sim, S. (2002). *Irony and Crisis: A Critical History of Postmodern Culture*. Cambridge: Icon Books.

Skolimowski, H. (1994). *The Participatory Mind: A New Theory of Knowledge and of the Universe*. London: Arkana.

Sloman, L. (2000). The Syndrome of Rejection Sensitivity. In: P. Gilbert & K. Bailey (Eds.), *Genes on the Couch* (pp. 257–275). Hove, UK: Brunner-Routledge.

Smith, E. W. L. (1985). *The Body in Psychotherapy*. Jefferson, NC: McFarland.

Spector, T. (2012). *Identically Different: Why You Can Change Your Genes*. London: Weidenfeld and Nicolson.

Starhawk. (1990). *Dreaming the Dark: Magic, Sex and Politics*. London: Unwin Paperbacks.

Staunton, T. (2002). Sexuality and body psychotherapy. In: T. Staunton (Ed.), *Body Psychotherapy*, (pp. 56–77). Hove, UK: Brunner-Routledge.

Staunton, T. (2008). Psychotherapy in a time of Narcissism. *Eisteach, 8* (4): 15–18.

Stevens, A. (1991). *On Jung*. London: Penguin.

Stevens, W. (2006). *Collected Poems*. London: Faber & Faber.

Stone, H. & Winkelman, S. (1989). *Embracing Our Selves: The Voice Dialogue Manual*. San Rafael, CA: New World Library.

Storr, A. (1989). *Solitude*. London: Flamingo.

Strawson, G. (2008). Against narrativity. In: *Real Materialism and Other Essays* (pp. 189–208). Oxford: Oxford University Press.

Sugarman, L. (2001). *Life-Span Development: Frameworks, Accounts and Strategies*. Hove, UK: Psychology Press.

Tallis, R. (2008). *Hunger*. Stocksfield, UK: Acumen.

Tallis, R. (2011). *Aping Mankind*. Stocksfield, UK: Acumen.

Taylor, C. (1992). *Sources of the Self: The Makings of the Modern Identity*. Cambridge, UK: Cambridge University Press.

Taylor, C. (2007). *A Secular Age*. Cambridge, MA: Harvard University Press.

Tolle, E. (2005). *The Power of Now*. London: Hodder and Stoughton.

Totton, N. (2005). Embodied-Relational Therapy. In: N. Totton (Ed.), *New Dimensions in Body Psychotherapy* (pp. 168–181). Maidenhead, UK: Open University Press.

Van Deurzen, E. (1998). *Paradox and Passion in Psychotherapy: An Existential Approach to Therapy and Counselling*. Chichester, UK: Wiley.

Van Deurzen-Smith, E. (1997). *Everyday Mysteries: Existential Dimensions of Psychotherapy*. London: Routledge.

Van Honk, J., Schutter, D., Bos, P., Kruijt, A. W., Lentjes, E., & Baron-Cohen, S. (2011). Testosterone administration impairs cognitive empathy in women depending on second-to-fourth digit ratio. *Proceedings of the National Academy of Sciences USA, 108* (8): 3448–3452.

Vernon, M. (2008). *Wellbeing*. Stocksfield, UK: Acumen.

Wallace, A. (2012). Room with a different view: Emma Donoghue interviewed by Arminta Wallace. *Irish Times*, 15 September. Available at: www.irishtimes.com.

Ward, E. (2013). Human suffering and the quest for cosmopolitan solidarity: a Buddhist perspective. *Journal of International Political Theory, 9* (2): 136–154.

Weeks, G., & Treat, S. (2001). *Couples in Treatment: Techniques and Approaches for Effective Practice*. Philadelphia: Brunner-Routledge.

Weixel-Dixon, K., & Strasser, F. (2005). Time and purpose. In: E. Van Deurzen & C. Arnold-Baker (Eds.), *Existential Perspectives on Human Issues* (pp. 227–235). Houndmills, UK: Palgrave Macmillan.

Whyte, D. (1996). *The House of Belonging*. Washington: Many Rivers Company.

Whyte, D. (2002). *Clear Mind Wild Heart* (Audio CD). Boulder, CO: Sounds True.

Wilber, K. (1985). *No Boundary: Eastern and Western Approaches to Personal Growth*. Boston, MA: Shambhala.

Wilber, K. (2000). *Integral Psychology: Consciousness, Spirit, Psychology, Therapy*. Boston, MA: Shambhala.

Wilbur, R. (1999). *Responses: Prose Pieces, 1953–1976*. Brownesville, OR: Story Line Press.

Wilkinson, M. (2006). *Coming Into Mind. The Mind-Brain Relationship: a Jungian Clinical Perspective*. London: Routledge.

Wilkinson, M. (2010). *Changing Minds in Therapy: Emotion, Attachment, Trauma and Neurobiology*. New York: W. W. Norton.

Wilkinson, R., & Pickett, K. (2009). *The Spirit Level*. London: Penguin.

Wilson, E. O. (2012). *The Social Conquest of Earth*. New York: W. W. Norton.

Winnicott, D. W. (1990). *The Maturational Processes and the Facilitating Environment*. London: Karnac.

Winnicott, D. W. (1991). *Playing and Reality*. London: Routledge.

Woolf, V. (1996). *Mrs Dalloway*. London: Penguin Popular Classics.

Wright, K. (1991). *Vision and Separation between Mother and Baby*. Northvale, NJ: Jason Aronson.

Yalom, I. (1980). *Existential Psychotherapy*. New York: Basic Books.
Yalom, I. (1989). *Love's Executioner and Other Tales of Psychotherapy*. London: Penguin.
Yeats, W. B. (1974). *Selected Poetry* (Ed., A. N. Jeffares). London: Pan.
Zhang, T. Y., & Meaney, M. (2010). Epigenetics and the environmental regulation of the genome and its function. *Annual Review of Psychology, 61*: 439–466.

Web resources

www.huffingtonpost.com, last accessed 18 March 2008
www.joannamacy.net, last accessed 16 February 2013
www.poetryfoundation.org, last accessed 19 February 2013
www.thevalve.org, last accessed 19 February 2013
www.cfwd.org.uk, last accessed 13 March 2013
www.bu.edu/wpc/Papers/MetaMann.htm

INDEX